Race,
Modernity,
Postmodernity

W. Lawrence Hogue

Race, Modernity, Postmodernity

A Look at the History and the Literatures of People of Color Since the 1960s

STATE UNIVERSITY OF NEW YORK PRESS

Production by Ruth Fisher
Marketing by Nancy Farrell

Published by
State University of New York Press, Albany

©1996 State University of New York

Printed in the United States of America

For information, address the State University of New York Press,
State University Plaza, Albany, NY 12246

Library of Congress Cataloging-in-Publication Data

Hogue, W. Lawrence (Date)
    Race, modernity, postmodernity : a look at the history and the
literatures of people of color since the 1960s / W. Lawrence Hogue.
        p.   cm.
    Includes bibliographical references and index.
    ISBN 0-7914-3095-2 (acid-free paper). — ISBN 0-7914-3096-0 (pbk.
    acid-free paper)
    1. American literature—Minority authors—History and criticism.
    2. American lite███████████████████████ and criticism.
    3. Minorities—█████████████████████century.
    4. Postmoderni████████████████s. 5. Modernism
(Literature)—United States. 6. Minorities in literature. 7. Race
in literature. I. Title
PS153.M56H64 1996
810.9' 920693—dc20   95-49336
                                                               CIP

10   9   8   7   6   5   4   3   2   1

In the spirit
of
heterogeneity, diversity, and hybridity

Contents

Preface / ix

Acknowledgments / xi

1. Race, Modernity, Postmodernity: A Look at the
   History of People of Color since the 1960s / 1

2. The Retreat from Modernity: Toni Morrison's *Song
   of Solomon* and N. Scott Momaday's *House Made of
   Dawn* / 29

3. The Limits of Modernity: Richard Rodriguez's
   Hunger of Memory and Andrea Lee's *Sarah
   Phillips* / 75

4. Problematizing the Historical Past: Maxine Hong
   Kingston's *The Woman Warrior* and David Bradley's
   The Chaneysville Incident / 111

5. The Postmodern Subject: Maxine Hong Kingston's
   Tripmaster Monkey and Richard Perry's
   Montgomery's Children / 151

Bibliography / 199

Index / 205

Preface

This book, *Race, Modernity, Postmodernity: A Look at the History and the Literatures of People of Color since the 1960s,* focuses on and celebrates the complex, diverse, heterogenous, and hybrid life of people of color in the United States. It explores how desires are repressed, ignored, and subordinated when they encounter rigid, naturalized narratives, either in the forms of literary texts, critical discourses, cultural and political discourses, or canon formations. *Race, Modernity, Postmodernity* reads eight literary texts and autobiographical narratives written by people of color—Asian American, Hispanics, African Americans, and Native Americans—against the tenets of modernity and postmodernity, rather than just against racial tradition. First, it argues that these texts are not static representations of the state of being "colored" in America, but rather they form a dialectic tradition, both against themselves and also in relation to the larger intellectual issues from the 1960s to the present. It makes an implicit case for studying the connections and shared themes in the literary production of the four major nonwhite racial groups in the United States.

Second, *Race, Modernity, Postmodernity* takes seriously the dialogue between the creative intellectual of color and the so-called "mainstream" intellectual trends of the past three decades. It makes the case that texts such as Toni Morrison's *Song of Solomon,* Richard Rodriguez's *Hunger of Memory,* Maxine Hong Kingston's *The Woman Warrior,* and N. Scott Momaday's *House Made of Dawn* can be read with reference to their treatment of the philosophical tenets and epistemological concepts of modernity and postmodernity. Assuming that people of color in the United States are not outside (Western) history and rationality, *Race, Modernity, Postmodernity* interprets these eight texts with reference, not to race or racial tradition exclusively, but to the European-American philosophical debate about the shift from modernity to postmodernity.

Race, Modernity, Postmodernity is comprised of five chapters. The first chapter, "Race, Modernity, Postmodernity: A Look at the History of People of Color since the 1960s," examines the continual and more visible integration of people of color into America's modernization process (mass culture) and the subsequent rise of a postmodern American society. It problematizes and then uses the construct called racial tradition. The second chapter, "The Retreat from Modernity: Morrison's *Song of Solomon* and Momaday's *House Made of Dawn,*" investigates how these two texts posit a position, a naturalized pre-modern, pre-industrial social space, anterior to modernity as the resolution to modernity's alienation and fragmentation, lack of social identification, and lack of historical continuity. The third chapter, "The Limits of Modernity: Andrea Lee's *Sarah Phillips* and Richard Rodriguez's *Hunger of Memory,*" explores the issue of sameness, the entrapment of people of color in the values and conventions and definitions of mainstream modern society as a move to achieve freedom, and the subsequent rejection of their racial identities and racial cultures.

Chapters four and five examine the shift from modernity to postmodernity in the literatures of people of color. In chapter four, "Problematizing History: David Bradley's *The Chaneysville Incident* and Maxine Hong Kingston's *The Woman Warrior,*" *Race, Modernity, Postmodernity* examines the blurring of the boundary between history and fiction and the crossing of the line from modern to postmodern aesthetics. The fifth and final chapter, "The Postmodern Subject: Kingston's *Tripmaster Monkey* and Richard Perry's *Montgomery's Children,*" focuses on postmodernity and the postmodern subject, and the ways American writers of color since the 1960s have engaged and textualized postmodern experiences in their respective racial and cultural groups

Houston, Texas

Acknowledgments

Parts of several chapters in *Race, Modernity, Postmodernity* have been published as individual essays in journals. I want to thank these journals for permission to reprint. "An Unresolved Modern Experience: Richard Rodriguez's *Hunger of Memory*" is reprinted with permission of the publisher of *The Americas Review* 20:1 (Houston: Arte Publico Press—University of Houston: 1992); "The Limits of Modernity: Andrea Lee's *Sarah Phillips*" is reprinted with permission of the publisher of *MELUS* 19:4; "Postmodernity Comes to Montgomery: Richard Perry's *Montgomery's Children*" is reprinted with permission of the publisher of *Obsidian II* 9:1; and "Problematizing History: David Bradley's *The Chaneysville Incident*" is reprinted with permission of the publisher of the *CLA Journal* 38:1. I also want to thank the students in my graduate seminar, "Race, Modernity, Postmodernity," during the Spring and Summer semesters of 1991. They graciously allowed me to organize the seminar around the argument of this book. A special thanks to a former graduate student, Lisa Lee, who introduced me to Anthony C. Yu's *The Journey to the West*, which was instrumental in writing the chapter on Kingston's *Tripmaster Monkey*. An enormous debt to my friend, colleague, and anthropologist, Quetzil Castañeda, whose fingerprints are all over the first chapter. He forced me to be true to Michel Foucault's concept of history by constantly exposing my attempts to use a meta-narrative to write the chapter. Another debt is due to my colleague, Elizabeth Gregory, who read and critiqued an earlier draft of this manuscript. Without the genuine and patient assistance of Ms. Donna Butler of the English Department at the University of Houston, my computer illiteracy would have done me in a long time ago. At her expense, I occasionally carry the day. Finally, a deep gratitude to Ms. Carola F. Sautter, Senior Editor, and Ms. Ruth Fisher, Production Editor, of SUNY Press, for their professionalism.

1

Race, Modernity, Postmodernity:
A Look at the History of People of Color since the 1960s

> "Postmodernism as it is generally understood
> involves a radical break, both with a dominant culture
> and aesthetic, and with a rather different moment of
> socioeconomic organization against which its
> structural novelties and innovations are measured:
> a new social and economic moment (or even system),
> which has variously been called media society, the
> 'society of the spectacle' ... , consumer society ... ,
> the 'bureaucratic society of controlled consumption'
> ... , or 'postindustrial society'".[1]

Since the 1960s, as Fredric Jameson suggests in the
above quote, there have been emergent social, economic,
political, and cultural discourses and formations on the
horizon in Western societies. The emergent forms of a
new commercial culture, the rise of computer and
information networks, the mechanization of culture, the
mediation of culture by the media, and the emergence of
the decentered, postmodern subject are producing a new
social reality. And in the United States, people of color—
Asian Americans, Native Americans, African Americans,
and Hispanics—are an integral part of these transformations, this new emergent social reality, this postmodern
American society.

Many reasons have been given for the condition of
postmodernity in the West. Fredric Jameson calls post-

modernism the "cultural logic of late capitalism" where transnational corporations globalize production, thereby causing them to become devoid of loyalty to nations of origin. According to Jameson, in the shift in global economic organization, national markets grew into world markets.[2] Jean-Francois Lyotard, in *The Postmodern Condition,* attributes the emergence of postmodernity to the breakup of master narratives such as those of the Enlightenment, Marxism, and the Spirit—narratives of the gradual emancipation of humanity from slavery and class oppression. The decline of master narratives, argues Lyotard, is due to the renewal of the spirit of capitalism's free enterprise, along with the growth of certain techniques and technologies in science.[3] Without master narratives man is left without external principles of authority.

Although there is an ongoing debate about the meaning and significance of postmodernity, there is a consensus that it constitutes conceptions of space and time that are different from the conceptions of space and time as defined by modernity and racial tradition. Postmodernity, especially in the social, political, and cultural spheres, provides a critical space to assess modernity and racial tradition and the cultural objects they produced. From postmodernity's emphasis on discontinuity, the fragmented, decentered subject, and on the rejection of those postulates that are totalizing, metaphysical, and essentialist, I examine race and racial traditions in contemporary American society. Thus, I reconstruct American history and culture since the 1960s with the aim of showing how people of color have become an integral part of a postmodern American society. Finally, it is from postmodernity's anti-foundationalism that I explain certain narratives and texts written by people of color since the 1960s, focusing on how these writers engage and textualize modern and postmodern experiences in their respective racial groups.

In the contemporary literature, a vision of racial communities as being defined by racial tradition has been distilled. A racial tradition is an ideological construction that reproduces a value system that we typify and classify from our modern context as traditional. I use this term, racial tradition, to identify the ideological construction of this vision, specifically how it follows within a master narrative that, since the rise of capitalism, has dichotomized and yet conjoined two oppositions: the rural/urban and the European/non-European.

Racial tradition, particularly as it is constituted in the United States, tends to closely resemble ethnicity. Like ethnicity, a racial tradition usually connotes a self-perceived group of people who hold in common a set of what Clifford Geertz calls "primordial affinities and attachments,"[4] or traditions and folkways not shared by the other people with whom they are in constant contact and interaction. Such traditions typically include "folk" beliefs and practices, language, and a value system—an inherited cluster of mores, ethics, and aesthetics. But these primordial affinities and attachments are neither essential nor original to racial tradition. Rather, they are artifices of the moment, which construct and invent the idea of the individual who is connected to a community through a shared past. Cosmologically, a racial tradition, as it is ideologically constructed in the United States, usually has a transcendent realm—the belief that there is another reality that transcends the reality within which everyday experience unfolds. Chantal Mouffe pinpoints the conception and ideological operation of tradition in society with the following:

> Tradition allows us to think our own insertion into historicity, the fact that we are constructed as subjects through a series of already existing discourses, and that it is through this tradition which forms us that the world is given to us and all political action made possible.[5]

It is here, in this objectified and homogenized conception of tradition, that racial cultural nationalists in the United States fall into a trap of taking the rhetorical ideological construct of continuity (and unity and wholeness) as being an essential relation of continuity. In other words, continuity is a historical artifice constructed by oppressed and marginalized racial individuals through political struggle, resistance to hegemonic forms, contestations, and economic marginalization. Furthermore, this vision of racial tradition is constructed on the basis of appropriation, objectification, homogenization, and reification of heterogeneous cultures from Mexico, Central and South America, Africa, and Asia.

The underlying assumption of this ideologically racially constructed tradition is the belief that racial communities have been isolated, that they are autonomous, homogeneous, integrated, and essentially authentic. The popular and accepted belief is that these communities are pre-modern, that they have not been affected by modern American society or the modernization process. But these racial communities, whether they are in the rural margins or pushed into urban pockets in the United States, are not pre-modern or pre-industrial communities. They are fundamentally modern. Even during legal and *de facto* segregation, people of color belong to capitalism and the modernization process. The Marxist and anthropological debates on world system models have shown that these marginalized and repressed racial communities—or these zones of internal colonialism—have been structured by the modernization process as the underbelly of modernity and that the people of these communities internalized some of the definitions, cognitive styles, and values of an emerging, commercial American culture.[6] In other words, within the topography of modernity, both as economic and cultural movement, these communities are not isolated but are integrated as variously designated sites of refuge, exploitation, underdevelopment, and future labor resources.

From this perspective it is obvious that there has been a conscious effort by some members of these communities to define/maintain these communities as zones of tradition that are constructed as pre-modern, pre-industrial, pre-commercial, and non-capitalist. This effort is in direct response to the *de facto* intrusion of capitalism and modernity, as well as to the pervasive racial oppression. To argue this is to argue precisely against the idea that the members of these communities are passive, agency-less actors whose society, cultural forms, and psychologies are determined by an imperialist or intruding capitalism. They are not. Within Marxist social science, these marginal racial communities are understood as cultures of resistance.[7] Their resistance and agency hinge on constituting their cultures as "outside the modern," specifically as being pre-modern. Thus, they fall within the modernist meta-narrative that denies "coevalness" to the rural and/or non-European other. There are several discourses within which this meta-narrative unfolds: for example, the romanticist movement within literature, the anthropological imagination of the primitive, and the sociological theorization of Gemeinshaft and Gesellschaft. All date to the birth of capitalism.

Given this broader socio-historical context, I use the concept of racial tradition to refer to a form of modernity which is nonetheless constructed and conceived in opposition to modernity. This racial modernity has been critical of the constitution of the classical metropolitan tradition of modernity as its mirror that reflects off this internal other. It exists as the subversive other constantly reminding the classical tradition of its limitations and exclusions. This idea pushes us to understand modernity as a tradition. Thus, I define the classical or traditional modernity as the common-sense, unmarked meaning of "modernity." Of course, the marked sense of modernity is indicated by the label "high modernism."

Thus, racial tradition, modernity, and postmodernity involve three distinct conceptions of space and time—so distinct, in fact, that racial tradition, in the political context of the United States, is effectively contradictory to modernity and postmodernity. First, racial tradition and modernity connote two different conceptions of space and time. Whereas racial tradition connotes wholeness, homogeneity, historical continuity, and a sense of common ancestry or place of origin, classical modernity connotes the loss of metaphysical meaning, rampant individualism, nihilism, hedonism, alienation, fragmentation, the lack of social identification, and the lack of historical continuity. Whereas racial traditions consider the past as a model, or a guiding example, modernity's hallmark is the impulse to experiment, to break with the past. And while the construction of racial tradition links community and culture to the land, modernity links community and culture to the city and technology.

Whereas racial tradition connotes collectivity and modernity implies the loss of metaphysical meaning, alienation, and frag-mentation, postmodernity engages reflexity and fragmented authority, questions concepts of subjective consciousness and historical continuity or any totalizing and homogenizing system. Postmodernity interrogates the notion of consensus. It critiques and dispenses with not only positivism and Marxism, but human-ism as well, since it calls into question Enlightenment notions of the modern subject. Whereas modernity defines the subject as a unity, postmodernity constructs the subject as decentered, as possessing various subjective positions or a network of desires. Postmodernity is characterized by late capitalism's dissolution of bourgeois hegemony and the development of a heterogeneous mass culture. This aspect of late capitalism is associated with the shift to a so-called "information society," which has been defined as the "explosion of electronic media, the shift from print literacy to images, and the penetration of the commodity form throughout all cultural production."[8]

In political terms, the erosion of what Andreas Huyssen calls the "triple dogma modernism/modernity/avantgardism," or high modernism, and the supercession of that dogma by a new dogma, of postmodernity, is contextually related to the emergence of the problematic of otherness. This otherness includes the different experiences of women and racial and sexual minorities into the sociopolitical sphere in the United States.[9]

Yet, despite the adversity, incongruency, and antagonism that exist among them, the social formations of racial tradition (i.e., communities imagined as pre-industrial and pre-modern), modernity, and postmodernity are very much a part of the present experiences of people of color in the United States. But, as we have seen, these three modernities (post-, the classical, and the racial) have distinct conceptions of space and time. How, then, can a racial tradition, which I have identified as being modernist, be part of the birth of the postmodern? How did racial groups who view themselves as part of a collective tradition become an integral part of individualistic postmodern America?

Before the 1960s, the four major non-white racial groups— Asian Americans, African Americans, Hispanics, and Native Americans—in the United States were understood to practice racial cultures that were unquestionably modelled on the ideological construction of a racial tradition. In this construction, culture was a realm of value where individuals within each racial group were socialized into an unfragmented racial tradition. Institutional racism and racial loyalty reinforced these racial traditions and put into operation forms of control that sought the homogenization of the racial individual to the group. However, differences and heterogeneity existed within these communities, although they were subordinated, repressed, and overlooked. In the industrial and technological revolution that had been trans-forming the United States since the 1880s, people of color, as I have stated earlier, were not only affected by, but were a profoundly integral part of, this economic, social, and psychological revolution, i.e., the process of modernization, as its margin and supplement. They were excluded from mainstream institutions and practices and, therefore, were forced to reinvent institutions and practices in their marginalized communities that were imitations of those of the mainstream society. In short, prior to the 1960s, people of color were the underbelly and anchorage of modernity.

Although people of color have been in the United States since its inception, they have been marginalized in a variety of ways. There has been a considerable attempt to fully exclude people of color from full and equal participation in and integration into America's economic, social, political, and educational institutions. Nonetheless, as I stated earlier, full exclusion is structurally impossible, for these racial communities have been forced into the position of being a labor commodity to be exploited. Thus, they serve as what Jacques Derrida calls "supplement."[10] (For Derrida, "supplement" refers to writing as a contradictory action which both replaces and adds to the putative "reality" it represents. I would like to apply the term to traditional racial communities who add to the "reality" of the modernization process.) Through their labor, racial communities make the modernization process possible in the United States. African Americans have been in the United States for more than three hundred years. Yet, most African Americans—through legal slavery and *de facto* segregation—were banned from the fruits, while directly participating in the United States' economic and social transformation. For two hundred years, slavery legally prevented African Americans from reaping the educational, social, political and economic rewards provided by the mainstream American society, despite the fact that African Americans served as a pool of cheap labor to be exploited by capitalists as they laid the foundation for the United States' economic emergence. And as slaves they were commodities; thus, in what sense can one speak of capitalist penetration into African American communities in the twentieth century? After Reconstruction, a host of Jim Crow laws were enacted that were designed to further deny African Americans access to the rewards provided by mainstream America.

Similar kinds of marginalizations and exclusions kept Asian Americans—people of Japanese, Chinese, Filipino, Korean, Cambodian, Vietnamese, and Indian descent—from receiving the educational, social, and financial compensations of being full and equal participants in mainstream American institutions. It was not until 1952 that immigrants from all Asian groups were considered eligible for United States citizenship.[11] Asian Americans encountered this exclusion of citizenship and all of the subsequent rights despite the fact that 250,000 Chinese arrived in California between 1849 and the early 1880s, and that large immigrant populations of Japanese and Filipinos would arrive during the first half of the twentieth century. They would form a critical labor pool for agriculture and the building of the railroad system, which allowed for the western expansion of the imperial United States.

Like African Americans and Asian Americans, Hispanics were marginalized, excluded, and kept from full and equal participation in America's technological revolution until the 1960s. They too were denied the fruits while they participated directly in the economic development within the United States. Hispanics—who include immigrants and the colonized from Mexico, Puerto Rico, Cuba, and Central and South America—have been in the United States for as long as five hundred years and for as recently as five seconds. Today, they may number eighteen million or twenty million or twenty-three million.[12]

Like the aforementioned groups of people of color, Hispanics were segregated socially, culturally, economically, and educationally. The Treaty of Guadalupe Hidalgo, which brought the northern reaches of Mexico under the United States' legal jurisdiction, explicitly guaranteed that the Mexicans who elected to stay in the United States would enjoy "all the rights of citizens of the [United States] according to the principles of the Constitution." But by the end of the nineteenth century, Mexicans had been largely dispossessed of their property and relegated culturally and socially to a lower-class status. Prior to the 1960s, and still today, they existed as sites of economic exploitation. Their political and economic status was insecure and their work was often seasonal in nature. They were forced into a dual-wage system where they received low wages, frequently below those received by white Americans for the same type and amount of work.[13] Or, as in the case of Puerto Ricans-Americans, they became an underdeveloped and cheap labor pool of domestics. In parts of Texas prior to the 1960s, Mexican Americans were segregated in movie houses, refused service in food shops, and denied access to public facilities such as housing, employment, and education. In the Northeast, particularly in places such as New York City and Hartford, Connecticut, Puerto Ricans encountered similar *de facto* segregation in housing and employment.

Finally, the category "Native American" is an artifice of the colonial collision. It is composed of multiple socio-cultural groups who share a colonial history as Indians. They, too, were marginalized in and excluded from full and equal participation in mainstream American institutions and practices. First, there was the military conquest of the Native Americans and their subsequent removal to reservations. But, almost from their first interactions, Native Americans sought education from the United States government. In more than one-quarter of the approximately four-hundred treaties entered into by the United States government between 1778 and 1871, education was one of the specific services Native Americans requested in exchange for their lands.[14] But in the formalized education provided by the United States, Native American students were forced to embrace Western ideas and culture, whose price was the repression and denial of their own cultures. Many students were forced into a cultural no-man's land where they remained torn between two worlds. Most students simply dropped out of the system. This uniform curriculum for all Native American schools in which Native American cultural heritage, language, and traditions were ignored and deprecated continued well into the twentieth century. It was only with the establishment in 1968 of the twenty-two tribally controlled community colleges and the two tribally controlled four-year colleges, along with the establishment of Native American Studies Programs and Departments by predominantly white American universities, that Native American students received an education that stressed indigenous values and included Native American history.

But the lack of necessary skills—due to inadequate education and, more importantly, racism in employment and housing outside/beyond the reservation—denied most Native Americans the opportunities to participate fully and equally in, and therefore receive the educational, social, and financial compensations of, America's mainstream institutions and its technological revolution. Native Americans encountered these denials despite the fact that they also served as a resource for cheap labor and economic exploitation in the United States' modernization process. They were segregated socially and physically from the general white American population as early as the 1850s. In 1849 and 1850, the Commissioner of Indian Affairs, Orlando Brown, devised a plan to concentrate the various Native American tribes of the plains in designated regions. Treaties were made that limited the Native American movement in the west. By 1950, most Native Americans had been effectively segregated on reservations.[15]

In delineating the legal and *de facto* social, educational, and economic barriers that marginalized people of color from central participation in and integration into America's modernization process and that prevented them from sharing equally in the fruits of its harvest, I am not arguing that people of color *were not affected* by urbanization and advancements in technology—by this technologically transformed, urban American society—before the 1960s. More importantly, and contrary to popular beliefs, I am arguing that until the 1950s and 1960s, due to legal and *de facto* segregation, the majority of Native Americans, African Americans, Hispanics, and Asian Americans lived in segregated, marginalized communities, such as the urban enclaves that became known as East L.A., Harlem, Chinatown, Japantown, etc. Within these areas of dense residential settlement, all of the different economic and social classes coexisted. They elaborated distinct institutions, catering to their special needs and tastes. They maintained ideologically constructed notions of racial communities that possessed a value system that typifies the traditional and that were represented by certain qualities such as homogeneity, wholeness, and historical continuity. Differences, struggles, conflicts, contestations did exist within these racial communities and were tolerated in varying degrees. But racism, racial loyalty, and forced segregation assisted in the subordination and repression of these differences within these communities.

A number of events and trends occurred in the United States in the 1950s and 1960s that have caused a serious threat to, or transformation of, these marginalized, racial communities and their ideologically constructed non-commercial, transcendental cultures. These events and trends propelled members of these communities into classical modernity and into a postmodern America. First, by the 1960s, the majority of people of color lived in America's large metropolitan areas. By the 1980s, at least seventy to eighty percent of African Americans lived in cities. Since 1960, over 200,000 Native Americans have left their reservations and moved to metropolitan centers throughout the United States. According to a Department of Interior study in 1986, only twenty-five percent of Native Americans still live on reservations.[16] Although the initial Mexican immigrants were farm laborers, they have immigrated increasingly to the cities of the Southwest. In 1977, an estimated eighty to eighty-five percent of the Mexican American population lived in cities. Cuban Americans comprise the majority population in Miami, Florida. Dominicans joined with Puerto Ricans to become a dominant Hispanic presence in New York City and Chicago. Central Americans flocked into and around the District of Columbia. Asian Americans are also highly urbanized, with ninety-three percent living in metropolitan areas. Among those living in metropolitan areas, about half live in central cities and half in suburbs.[17] In short, the population of the major American cities is comprised of people of color. This means that people of color are using their numbers to change the political, cultural, educational, and economic landscape of America's metropolitan areas.

The movement of people of color into the urban areas coincides with the proliferation and extension of mass culture and the mediation of culture by the media, which increases the visibility of already existing heterogeneity in these marginalized, racial communities. As it occurs in the rest of the United States, social identity is reworked by mass media, which in turn is responding to the sociological changes that are occuring in society.

The coexistence of African Americans, Hispanics, and Asian Americans in the same communities or in close proximity to each other in the urban areas means a certain amount of political, social, and economic tension. Hispanics tend to clash with African Americans over political power and political representation as they attempt to carve out their own political turf, since these areas were once dominated by African Americans. African Americans tend to clash with Asian Americans over economic issues, since Asian Americans have become the new entrepreneurs in traditional African American communities. In political terms, this emergence of different peoples of color into the urban sociopolitical sphere in the United States contributes to its political postmodernity and indicates a rupture of the once black-white polarized race relations in the United States.

A second event in the 1960s that reoriented the marginalization of people of color, and undermined the black-white polarization, from the mainstream American institutions and practices was a change in racial attitudes in the United States. The end of World War II marked the close of one of the most racist periods in United States history. The period between World War II and the 1960s is considered one of the most economically prosperous in the United States. In the 1950s and 1960s, middle class people of color had grown in numbers in relation to the economic prosperity in the rest of the society. Their perception of their expanding economic growth failed to comprise a corresponding elevation in their social status and political power. Thus, they began the successful challenge to the legal, educational, economic, social, and political apparatuses and institutions that had denied them full equality. With pressure from Civil Rights groups[18] and the liberal sector of the white American population, states began to pass and enforce anti-discrimination statutes. Under pressure from these Civil Rights groups, California abolished legal school segregation in 1947. Arizona granted Native Americans the right to vote in 1948, and in 1952, Asian immigrants became eligible for citizenship.[19] In 1948, the California Supreme Court ruled that anti-miscegenation laws were unconstitutional because they violated the right of equal protection.[20] In addition, with pressure, the federal government began the elimination of discriminatory practices.

The enforcement of Civil Rights laws made the political process and political self-representation a reality for people of color. These laws banned discrimination in housing and employment. They provided more economic and educational opportunities for people of color. They made available to people of color certain exclusively white social, economic, educational, and cultural traditions and institutions. In short, these Civil Rights laws legally made accessible to people of color the institutions and practices of mainstream American society.

First, opportunities became available to people of color in education. In the late 1960s, America's colleges and universities began to enroll larger numbers of students of color. The grandchildren and great-grandchildren of slaves and immigrants used education for social and economic mobility. The number of African Americans enrolled full time at American colleges and universities nearly doubled between 1970 and 1980.[21] Black college student enrollment jumped from fewer than 350,000 students to more than a million. At the nation's law schools, where, prior to the 1970s, people of color were seldom found, African Americans are now about five percent of the total population.[22] Hispanics comprise a comparable, if not higher, percentage of the total law school student population.

The number of students attending college increased for other people of color. By the 1970s, Japanese Americans sent ninety percent of their children to college. In fact, according to the Japanese American Research Project (1978) and the Report on *The Economic Status of Americans of Asian Descent,* (published by the U.S. Commission on Civil Rights in 1988), Japanese Americans have the highest median education level among both whites and non-whites in the United States, followed by Chinese Americans, then Anglo Americans. Despite the fact that Asian Americans in 1990 comprise only 5.5 percent of the U.S. population, they represent eleven percent of the students at Harvard, ten percent at Princeton, sixteen percent at Stanford, twenty-one percent at MIT, and twenty-five percent at the University of California at Berkeley.[23] Also, with the establishment of tribal colleges and an increase in Native American students on the campuses of American colleges and universities, the 1970s and 1980s produced a generation of college-educated Native Americans who moved into positions of leadership in both their respective tribes and the Bureau of Indian Affairs.

As a result of the enactment of Civil Rights laws and the rate of economic growth in the period after World War II, a second avenue of opportunity became available to people of color in the workplace, in politics, and in housing. The corporate and business worlds, including media institutions, were forced to become more sensitive to the historical exclusion of people of color. The Small Business Association and federal set-aside programs aimed at increasing the number of people of color in business. The economic growth among people of color, and their presence in America's once exclusively white institutions and practices, had a profound effect. These institutions and practices had to accommodate and adjust to the people of color's presence.

A third event in the 1960s that undermined the marginalization and exclusion of people of color from the mainstream institutions and practices was a change in industrial culture. The change entails the emergent forms of a new commercial culture. It is associated with the shift to a so-called "information society," conceived as a larger transformation that includes the explosion of electronic media, the shift from print literacy to images. Although commodity forms generate and satisfy needs and desires, modern and postmodern individuals are not just passive agents. Rather, they are part of new sociological and cultural changes that also affect the media and commodity production.

This integration and increased visibility of working-class and middle-class people of color into America's modernization process and emergent form of commercial culture mean that a larger percentage of people of color, who have weakened ties to their ideologically constructed racial traditions, are susceptible to such modern experiences as alienation, fragmentation, hedonism, narcissism, nihilism, the lack of historical continuity, and the lack of social identification. In this sense, they have become a part of America's classical modernity, as the negative. This integration also means that racial individuals increasingly also experience the de-centering of the subject and the disconnectedness from anything human—that is, human as it is defined by the Enlightenment's concept of the unified subject, historical continuity, and profoundity—that characterizes postmodern life. Working-class and middle-class racial individuals, like their white counterparts, take on new "class" identities generated by high modernism and problematize the values of their ideologically constructed racial tradition that has become increasingly inadequate to fully explain their lived experiences.

The explicit integration of middle-class and working-class people of color into the modernization process where mass culture or a new commerical culture dominates can help us to explain the devastation of these marginalized, racial communities and the undermining of their ideologically constructed cultures. Given their various "new" accesses to mainstream institutions and practices, many people of color have had greater opportunities to participate in the continual reinscription of marginalized, racial cultures into commodity form. This reinscription has included the popular television mini-series "Roots" and "The Civil War," series such as "The Bill Cosby Show," "The Jeffersons," commercials about "real," "authentic" non-normative Hispanics and African Americans buying and selling American products, the popular novels of Louise Erdrich, Victor Villasenor, Alice Walker, Toni Morrison, N. Scott Momaday, Amy Tan, and Maxine Hong Kingston, which appropriate the cultural past into normative literary conventions, and the crossover rhythm and blues of Whitney Houston, Diana Ross, and Lionel Richie.

But the integration of people of color into America's classical modernity is a complicated event. I do not want to simply argue that people of color become insulated middle-class individuals in the same way as many of their white counterparts. Many people of color bring styles, approaches, sensibilities, racial pride, psychological scars and complexes, and other concerns to their middle classness which have been informed by historical racial oppression. They bring appropriated cultural forms and languages not only from their marginalized racial communities but also from Asia, South, Central and North America, and Africa. Many middle-class people of color continue to support, what Cornel West calls the "emergent ... political class ... primarily to ensure upward social mobility" of their racial groups.[24]

In addition, because many middle-class people of color are one generation removed from, or still have familial links with, impoverished, marginalized traditional racial communities, and because most still experience racial discrimination, they tend to be, or are forced to be, more sensitive to and aware of the pain, suffering, and injustice of those Americans who continue to be economically and socially marginalized.

The opening up of America's mainstream institutions and practices, and the educational, economical, and social integration of people of color into the modernization process in the United States have increased the number of educated, middle-class people of color. The elimination of the legal barriers has stimulated an exodus of the colored middle class from marginalized spaces in the rural and urban areas. This is a pregnant moment, because it entails the racial pluralization of institutions and practices and thus the creation of an image of America as a *newly* heterogeneous society. This has to do with the proliferation of people of color into designated public spaces such as the media, the workplace, and educational institutions where persons of multiracial identities can interact and intermix.

A more complicated process occurs with regard to residential spaces, which in various ways contributed to what has been identified as the postmodern condition. As is well known, the suburbanization of the cities was propelled by the taking over of inner city white residential areas by middle-class blacks who were leaving their marginalized communities. As middle-class blacks moved out of traditional, marginalized racial communities and into once all-white residential areas (or into newly developed middle class black communities), whites moved to white suburban communities. In contrast, with middle-class Hispanics and Asian Americans, there was more of an infiltration by them into previously exclusively white residential areas, urban and suburban.

With this spatial and cultural break, in the case of middle-class African Americans, or dispersion, in the case of middle-class Asian Americans and Hispanics, the mythical vision of the racial community as an integral cultural whole became untenable: the importance of class, identities, alliances, and interests disrupted the modernist ideological construction of race or racial tradition as isolated cultures and homogenous communities.

Simultaneous with the integration of working-class and middle-class people of color into America's modernization process and mass culture, marginalized, racial communities are further fragmented and eroded by the emergence of the subculture of the non-middle class, particularly among Hispanics and African American youths. As William Julius Wilson argues, "the socioeconomic status of the most disadvantaged members of America's people of color has deteriorated rapidly since 1970."[25] An increasing maldistribution of wealth, the exodus of the middle class from marginalized, racial communities to predominantly white and suburban communities or to newly designed middle-class racial communities, the shift in the U.S. economy from goods-producing to service-producing industries, the international flow of wage labor migrants, the increasing polarization of the labor market into low-wage and high-wage sectors, the relocation of manufacturing industries out of the central cities, and the heavy burden of racism have increased and made visible the working poor and the urban and reservation non-middle class of Hispanics, African Americans, Native Americans, and, to a lesser degree, Asian Americans. (These economic and technological changes have also produced and made visible a large white lower middle class and working poor population, a population that would be used in the revolt against gains acquired by people of color since the 1960s.)

These post-1960s spatially demarcated marginalized communities, both rural and urban, continue to be heterogeneous, and they have developed new features and characteristics. They are the homes of Catholics, Protestants, and Muslims. They are comprised of cultural nationalists and other political activists. The unemployed, the welfare dependent, the working poor, and the unsanctioned working rich also live in these communities. African American, Asian American, and Hispanics gangs live in these communities. These marginalized communities have become sites of high unemployment. Drug use and sales have become rampant or highly visible, and life in prison has become an integral part of the way of life. Traditional family structures, in many instances, have been superseded by female-headed families, particularly among African Americans and Hispanics. In addition, there is a pervasive immersion in America's new commercial culture, and traditional notions of moral authority have been undermined or problematized, particularly as they are defined by racial tradition. In the absence of master narratives, or with racial traditions diminished, mini-narratives, new forms of sensibilities, and new conceptions of the subject become visible, which are in contrast to the modalities of the racial traditions. (Although some of these sensibilities are pathological, or are the result of some individuals' feeling alienated from a normative American society, I do not want to define these communities entirely as pathological or abnormal. To do so is to assume that there is some universal norm by which to measure all sensibilities.) However, in the case of traditional Chinese and Japanese communities, many have been revitalized by the recent Asian immigrants from Vietnam, Hong Kong, and Korea.

Finally, it is the integration or incorporation of people of color and their subjective and political experiences into the various mainstream social, political, educational, and artistic institutions in the United States that problematizes the concept of the United States as a white male, middle-class-centered society. Critics have called this incorporation political postmodernity, which operates to a complex conjuction of conditions. And as I have discussed earlier, it involves the everyday effects of the news media and communicative technology as well as the great redistribution of power and population that have accompanied the new structures of commodity production.

The emergence of various forms and experiences of "otherness" in the cultural sphere contest, or lessen, the importance of high modernism, which Stanley Aronowitz defines as involving a "reliance on formal democratic processes, growth politics based on an unalloyed support for industrialism, and, of course, sexual and power hierarchies."[26] As "other," people of color, along with gays and women, in their emphasis on assimilating differently, in their emphasis on exhuming repressed and excluded histories, in their emphasis on exploring forms of gender- and race-based subjectivity in aesthetic production and experiences, and in their refusal to be limited to standard canonization, add a whole new dimension to the critique of a white, middle-class, male-centered society and of high modernism and help to issue forth a postmodernism that allows alternative forms of culture to emerge. Thus, the emergence of "otherness" challenges the importance of a white male, middle-class-centered society. This new field of differences articulates a new arrangement of power.

Of course, the undermining and contesting of standard canonizations have caused certain sectors of the white American population to resist this emerging heterogeneity in the educational and cultural spheres and to attempt to restore to hegemony a codified version of high modernism that is mostly white, male, and upper middle class. Several cultural and political organizations and groups resist and attack America's emerging heterogeneity. Some that come immediately to mind are: former chairwoman Lynne Cheney's and the Reagan-Bush National Endowment for the Humanities' talk of promoting classical works and traditional values of family and religion; Allan Bloom's advocating a return to the classical works in *The Closing of the American Mind;* the move by angry white men and the Republican revolt of 1994 against civil rights gains and tolerances such as Affirmative Action programs, federal set-aside programs, and the concept of multiculturalism or cultural diversity, which gave people of color some access to mainstream institutions, usually under the guise of an attack on political correctness. Of course, this resistance/reaction by certain sectors of the white American population will not disenfranchise women and people of color. It will not return America to a pre-1950s society, where only white males occupy mainstream social, economic, political, and educational apparatuses and institutions. The revolt/reaction will not reverse the proliferation of people of color into designated public spaces where persons of different racial identities can interact and intermix. Despite the revolt, American will not return completely to a white male, upper middle-class-centered society. For several reasons, the revolt/reaction has to be interpreted as a last stand, as a refusal to accept emergent power arrangements.

History, an increased population of people of color, and mass culture are on the side of this heterogeneity. In many of the largest urban counties in the United States, and in a few non-metropolitan counties, no single ethnic or racial group is a majority. These counties are examples of the trend toward greater diversity. A high diversity rate implies new political alliances and new cultural hybrids. As a consequence of higher diversity, enormous sociological changes have occurred in American public schools, colleges, and universities over the last twenty years. The ethnic profile of both students and faculty has undergone a dramatic transformation.[27] In the public schools and on college and university campuses across the country, especially in populous states such as California, Texas, New York, and Illinois where students of color comprise from thirty-five to fifty-five percent of the student population, students of color have refused to allow a European-oriented curriculum to be forced upon them. They have demanded and are demanding a curriculum that reflects their histories and experiences.

Of course, the fact that there has been the emergence of various forms of otherness in the social, educational, and cultural spheres, which contest the notion that America is ruled by a middle-class, white-male-centered narrative, does not mean that dominant patriarchial and racial and class narratives have disappeared. As I have mentioned earlier, the ruling social order through the media and mass culture permits heterogeneity while at the same time colonizing that otherness and appropriating it for its own purposes.

In addition, the fact that people of color, gays, and women, as "other," help to usher in a postmodern eclecticism in American life does not necessarily mean that women, gays, and people of color are postmodern, or that their artistic and cultural works are disruptive and are culturally postmodern. As I will show later, people of color can be politically conservative, liberal, and radical and their artistic productions can be realistic, existential, modern, as well as postmodern. Fredric Jameson, Andreas Huyssen, and other postmodern critics tend to see people of color as being only a part of political postmodernity, or as part of what Hutcheon calls the ex-centric who are different, marginal, and, therefore, able to disrupt the center.

However, these postmodern critics never perceive a double bind that stems from a paradox of the de/centeredness of the postmodern. On the one hand, there are members of these ex-centric groups who embody the image of sameness and therefore do not merely reinforce but also reinscribe the vision of the center in the United States. On the other hand, the highly visible racial individual who pursues an essentialized contestation of the image of the same in the United States also re-centers that which has been decentered in postmodern America. Precisely, here is the paradox. In the transformation of racial communities into a postmodern, mass-cultured American society, "there is no longer," argues Howard Winant, "any single articulating principle or axial process with which to interpret the racial dimensions of all extant political/cultural projects. In this absence of a comprehensive challenge to the racial order as a whole, racial categories, meanings, and identities, [and the notion of a centered, mainstreamed America] have become 'decentered,'"[28] except through our persistent and nostalgic reconstitution of a center that does not exist.

Because of the disintegration of traditional racial communities where most people experienced or knew common, hegemonic racial or ethnic cultures, and because of the variety of experiences across social, educational, and economic traditions that have subsequently emerged within these once-tight groups, racial groups today do not constitute monolithic entities. They can no longer be perceived as exotic, inscrutable others, or their members as noble savages without complex consciousnesses, who are incomprehensible. Racial groups can no longer be perceived as mysterious others whom white people view as belonging to different species. The modernization process and mass culture have made it possible for all Americans to share similar cognitive styles, images, social practices, and lived experiences.

Theorists of postmodernity have labelled this phenomenon I have outlined as a blurring of categories such as race, gender and class. But it would be more appropriate to understand this postmodern condition as a reworking, and thus recategorization, of social practices, identities, symbols, and experiences that have previously been assigned to marginalized or hegemonic cultural communities. While people of color incorporate cultural forms from each other and from the once-dominant white society, more whites seek out the knowledge, styles, and attitudes of their non-white counterparts. Other examples include crossover music by white and black artists, the surge of popularity among white males for militant black rap groups such as Public Enemy, the transracial exchange of taste in clothing, language, and hair styles, and the eclectic approach Americans are developing toward food. Certainly, this crossing of cultural boundaries and traditions can be interpreted as a way of not dealing with troubling racial issues. In many instances, this is true. But it can also be interpreted as a desire to come to terms with one's racial limitations and to develop what Timothy Simone calls a "capacity to be daring, provocative and generous."[29]

This means that postmodernity problematizes traditional racial categories, meanings, and identities. It exposes race as being something that is not essential, but a construct. Of course, this is not to minimize the importance of race in our society, for it still plays a big role in how individuals are perceived, defined, and treated. But now race becomes one of many factors that comprise a racial individual's social identity. In problematizing racial categories, meanings, and identities, postmodernity does not allow racial individuals who do not comply with, or live within the boundaries of, these traditional, essential categories and meanings to be defined as abnormal, deviant, pathological, etc. They are just different.

In addition, the supposed elimination of differentials stemming from postmodernity, mass culture, the production process, and transracial cultural exchange does not mean that people of color have achieved full equality in the United States. Inequalities still exist behind the screen of consumer goods. Hispanics, African Americans, and Native Americans are still underrepresented in professional and graduate schools. They are still discriminated against in housing and employment. They still experience police brutality because of their skin color. Despite their high median income and their astounding success in medicine and engineering, Asian Americans, along with other racial minorities, still feel that they have been barred from the boardrooms of corporate America. Few people of color are wielding power as executives and administrators in the top ranks of corporate America. Also, differentials in access to consumption remain. Because people of color constitute a larger percentage of America's poor, they have less money to purchase America's consumer goods.

Finally, there are still those naturalized representations of events and situations relating to race that, as Michael Omi argues, have racist premises, which are generated and reaffirmed by the various mainstream institutions and practices, such as the police, the media, and the literature.[30] Most Americans still believe that most African American and Hispanic males are drug addicts and convicts, that most of the people on welfare are African Americans and Hispanics. Most Americans still believe that African Americans and Hispanics are lazy and are the source of violence. Most Americans still think that Native Americans are lazy drunks who do not want to work, and that African Americans and Hispanics are less intelligent than white Americans. They think that Asian Americans are whiz-kid scholars and hardworking greengrocers, totally ignoring the fact that there are Asian Americans who are homeless. Cultural politics must continue to address both these naturalized representations that have racist premises and the new sources of inequality in postmodern America.

The integration of people of color into America's social, educational, political, and economic institutions, practices, and traditions, on the one hand, and the continued existence of economic and social inequalities and certain naturalized racist premises (which are generated or quietly tolerated by those same institutions and practices), on the other hand, create another paradox for many people of color.

The Civil Rights movement and its antecedents must be understood in structural terms, as a struggle to de-racialize the middle class. In other words, the struggle for the middle-class person of color is to be accepted, to "pass," as middle-class instead of being excluded as racial other. Yet the struggle has abided by an assumption of race imposed by the hegemonic community, and is internalized by proponents of racial traditions. That is (i.e., in order to struggle for legitimate acceptance as middle class), the racial other must re-proclaim his racial identity in order to advocate for his Englightment-derived rights. Thus, there is a contradiction in seeking one's rights as an essential yet non-racial human and having to re-racialize oneself to attain those rights.

It is this paradox that, on the one hand, makes us think, that the traditional narratives of race or racial traditions are no longer valid or useful and, on the other hand, makes narratives of racial tradition so vibrant. This paradox causes some people of color to live not by the rules and traditions (for example classical modernity) within which they have been socialized but by certain essentialized racial and cultural narratives that are incongruent with the reality of their own lived experiences but are imposed upon them by hegemonic mainstream and minority practices. Here we are talking about second- or third-generation middle-class people of color who are the product of a modern or postmodern America, but whose only defense against racism and inequalities is to return to the racial collective, to an "outdated" racial or cultural narrative, which represses their non-racial or other class identities.

The paradox also causes some people of color to attempt to reject their race completely. Here we are talking about first- and second-generation middle-class people of color who have internalized uncritically the cognitive styles and values of the mainstream society and therefore repress their racial self or beginnings because that self and those beginnings are not sanctioned by the mainstream society. In both instances, in the uncritical acceptance of the mainstream society's values and definitions and in the adoption of essentialized, collective narratives, the modern racial individual is alienated from, and is forced to repress, his own complex, subjective lived experiences. In a postmodern America, where diverse individual experiences make grand narratives problematic and where the autonomy of the individual reigns supreme, what has to be examined is the power differential between the ruling social order, which possesses the power to colonize and appropriate images and cultural practices, and lesser empowered (racial) social groups, which do not possess these powers in the same measure, and how this power differential causes individuals to look at and define their lives through traditionally defined group and/or national experiences, as opposed to identifying themselves as autonomous beings. By focusing on the ways the power dynamics (which always abide by an assumption of race) in the media and other agencies of production and transmission in postmodern American society work to create and recreate racial formation, we can begin to explain/understand some of the dynamics of racial formation in the United States, the tension between identifying oneself as a member of a collective racial body and identifying oneself as an autonomous or independent being.

The following chapters will examine the literatures of Asian Americans, Native Americans, Hispanics, and African Americans. They will interpret the literatures against the tenets and perspectives of modernism and postmodernism, rather than against racial and cultural paradigms exclusively. The objective is not to ignore race, but to ascertain how writers of color since the 1960s have textualized and resolved modern and postmodern experiences and dilemmas and conflicts, brought on by the integration of people of color into the modernization process since the 1960s, within their respective racial groups. Particular attention is given to the role race and racism play in this new social formation and to the kinds of cultural, social, and literary narratives and models these writers have used to bring equilibrium or resolution to social subjects (characters) whose modern and postmodern lived experiences alienate them from traditional racial identities.

Second, these chapters will examine how minority and main-stream and feminist critics and reviewers have received the modern and postmodern experiences in texts by people of color since the 1960s. Literary texts have no value or worth outside of that which is imputed by their readers. We can determine how a culture values a given book by examining how it has been received and assessed by that culture's official, representative readers: its reviewers, critics, and scholars.

In *Literary Theory: An Introduction,* Terry Eagleton argues that literary books are not judged and assessed by an innocent, universal criterion. They do not possess intrinsic values that transcend the matrices of history. Rather, he argues, literary theory, which determines the worth of literary books, is "indissociably bound up with political beliefs and ideological values."[31] Literary theory is less an object of intellectual inquiry in its own right than a "perspective in which to view the history [and literary texts or cultural objects] of our time."[32]

This means that literature that deals with human meaning, values, language, feeling, and experience will be inevitably defined and interpreted by critical practices that have culture-specific "broader, deeper beliefs about the nature of human individuals and societies, problems of power and sexuality, interpretations of past history, versions of the present and hopes for the future."[33] In short, literary theory helps, willingly or not, to sustain and reinforce certain assumptions about life, human nature, and society. It presupposes a certain use of literature. There is no literature that is "really" great independent of the ways in which that literature is viewed within specific forms of social and institutional life.

Finally, these chapters will examine how the various feminist, cultural-nationalist, and mainstream critics and reviewers use literature to reinforce certain assumptions about life, human nature, and society, how they impute values to these texts to serve their own ideological needs.

NOTES

1. Fredric Jameson, "Foreward," in Jean Francois Lyotard, *The Postmodern Condition: A Report on Knowledge* (Minneapolis: University of Minnesota Press, 1984), p. vii.

2. Fredric Jameson, *Postmodernism, or The Cultural Logic of Late Capitalism* (Durham, N.C.: Duke University Press, 1991), p. xxi.

3. Jean Francois Lyotard, *The Postmodern Condition: A Report on Knowledge* (Minneapolis: University of Minnesota Press, 1984), p. 37.

4. Clifford Geertz, *The Interpretation of Cultures* (New York: Basic Books, Inc., 1973), pp. 259–260.

5. Chantal Mouffe, "Radical Democracy: Modern or Postmodern?", translated by Paul Holdengraber, in *Universal Abandon? The Politics of Postmodernism,* edited by Andrew Ross (Minneapolis: University of Minnesota Press, 1988), p. 39.

6. For a more detailed explanation, see Eric Wolf, *Europe and the People without History* and Peter Worsley, *The Three Worlds: Culture and World Development.*

7. For additional readings into the concept of cultures of resistance, read James C. Scott, *Weapons of the Weak: Everyday Forms of Peasant Resistance,* and Michael Hechter, *Internal Colonialism: The Celtic Fringe in British National Development, 1536–1966.*

8. Ian Angus and Sut Jhally, eds., *Cultural Politics in Contemporary America* (New York and London: Routledge, 1989), p. 5.

9. Andreas Huyssen, *After the Great Divide: Modernism, Mass Culture, Postmodernism* (Bloomington: Indiana University Press, 1986), p. 219.

10. Jacques Derrida, *Of Grammatology,* translated by Gayatri Chakrovorty Spivak (Baltimore: John Hopkins University Press, 1967), p. 281.

11. *The Economic Status of Americans of Asian Descent: An Exploratory Investigation,* by Harreit Orcutt Dulcep, U.S. Commission on Civil Rights, 1988, p. 6.

12. Thomas Weyr, *Hispanics. U.S.A.: Breaking The Melting Pot* (New York: Harper & Row, 1988), p. 1.

13. Estrada, Garcia, Macias, and Mal Donaldo, "Chicanos in the United States: A History of Exploitation and Resistance," *Daedalus* 110 (1981): pp. 105, 109.

14. Leonard Dinnerstein, et al. eds., *Natives and Strangers: Ethnic Groups and the Building of America* (New York and London: Oxford University Press, 1979), pp. 254, 255.

15. Leonard Dinnerstein, et al., eds., *Natives and Strangers,* p. 256.

16. Leonard Dinnerstein, et al., eds., *Natives and Strangers,* p. 258.

17. William O'Hare, "A New Look at Asian Americans," *American Demographics* 12 (October 1990): p. 30.

18. Here I am talking about Civil Rights groups (such as the NAACP, B'nai B'rith's Anti-Defamation League, the National Urban League, the Japanese American Citizen League [JACL], national Native American legal groups), and advocacy organizations (such as the Native American Rights Fund, the National Indian Youth Council, the Association of American Indian Affairs, the League of United Latin American Citizens [LULAC], the Mexican American Political Association).

19. Robert A. Wilson and Bill Hosokawa, *East to America: A History of the Japanese in the United States* (New York: William Morrow & Co., 1980), p. 247.

20. Ronald Takaki, *Strangers from a Different Shore: A History of Asian Americans* (New York: Viking Penguin, 1989), p. 406.

21. William Julius Wilson, *The Truly Disadvantaged: The Inner City, the Underclass and Public Policy* (Chicago: University of Chicago Press, 1987), p. 109.

22. David Lauter and Lee May, "A Saga of Triumph, A Return to Poverty: Black Middle Class Has Grown but Poor Multiply," the *Los Angeles Times* (Orange County Edition), April 2, 1988, Part 1, p. 16.

23. Ronald Takaki, *Strangers from a Different Shore*, p. 4.

24. Cornel West, *Race Matters* (Boston: Beacon Press, 1993), p. 52.

25. William Julius Wilson, *The Truly Disadvantaged*, p. 109.

26. Stanley Aronowitz, "Postmodernism and Politics," in *Universal Abandon? The Politics of Postmodernism*, edited by Andrew Ross (Minneapolis: University of Minnesota Press, 1988), p. 48.

27. James P. Allen and Eugene Turner, "Where Diversity Works: America's Most Diverse Counties Are Leading the Way for the Rest of Society," *American Demographics* 12 (August 1990): p. 36.

28. Howard Winant, "Postmodern Racial Politics: Difference and Inequality," *Socialist Review* 20 (January-March 1990), p. 124.

29. Timothy M. Simone, *About Face: Race in Postmodern America* (New York: Autonomedia, 1989), p. 219.

30. Michael Omi, "In Living Color: Race and American Culture," in *Cultural Politics in Contemporary America*, edited by Ian Angus and Sut Jhally, p. 113.

31. Terry Eagleton, *Literary Theory: An Introduction* (Minneapolis: University of Minnesota Press, 1983), p. 194.

32. *Ibid.*, p. 195.

33. *Ibid.*, p. 195.

2

The Retreat from Modernity:
Toni Morrison's *Song of Solomon* and
N. Scott Momaday's *House Made of Dawn*

The most potent form of ideological response by contemporary American writers of color to modernity and the modernization process is cultural nationalism: the belief that a return to the values and mores of one's cultural heritage can resolve the problems of modernity. The aim of the writers who respond thus is to rescue the dignity and autonomy of their respective cultural lives and arts from a degraded mass culture, which is characterized by commercialism, alienation and fragmentation, narcissism and hedonism, spiritual emptiness, rampant individualism, the lack of historical continuity, and the lack of social identification. Rather than allow their art and lives to become contaminated by modernity's mass culture, which has its own built-in stereotypes about people of color, writers of color such as Toni Cade Bambara in *The Salt Eaters,* Paule Marshall in *Praisesong For the Widow,* Leslie Silko in *Ceremony,* Guy Garcia in *Skin Deep,* N. Scott Momaday in *House Made of Dawn,* Frank Chin in *Donald Duk,* Toni Morrison in *Song of Solomon* and others withdraw to what Jurgen Habermas, in "Modernity—An Incomplete Project," calls a "position *anterior* to modernity."[1]

These writers want to wipe out mass culture and replace it with a culture, or an established, hegemonic racial tradition of standards and values, that is essential in nature and, therefore, is self-grounding. Their normative view of society and culture is one where all parts miraculously interpenetrate and require no rational justification. Thus, their strategy is to write a moral fiction that reclaims for literature and their culture and their people the values of wholeness, transcendence, and historical continuity. One of the chief functions of a cultural tradition, explains Suzi Gablik in *Has Modernism Failed?* is the creation of exemplary models for a whole society.[2]

This chapter focuses on Toni Morrison's *Song of Solomon* (1977) and N. Scott Momaday's *House Made of Dawn* (1968), whose alienated and fragmented protagonists reject modernity and modernist culture and find wholeness and historical continuity in ideologically, culturally, and racially constructed traditions that are represented by certain qualities as homogeneity, wholeness, and historical continuity. In most instances, these racial traditions are represented as being pre-modern, pre-industrial, and non-capitalist.

Toni Morrison began writing at a time, the 1970s, when African American literature was marked by a prevalent, modern style of perception and feeling. Existentialism, secularism, rationalism, and individualism pervade the fiction of the major African American writers, such as Richard Wright, Ralph Ellison, James Baldwin, and Charles Wright, who wrote a genuine modern literature. Reading Ellison's *Invisible Man*, Wright's *Native Son*, Baldwin's *Another Country*, and Wright's *The Messenger*, one receives an overwhelming sense of fragmentation, ephemerality, and chaotic change. Their fiction is a literature that promises adventure, joy, growth, and transformation of the self and the world. Their fiction does not retreat to the cultural values and norms of the racial past; it is concerned with the plight of the individual in the modern world. And as modern literature, it threatens "to destroy everything we have, everything we know, everything we are."[3]

Toni Morrison, in *Sula* and *Song of Solomon*, revolts against this prevalent style, this official order in contemporary African American letters. Morrison is not concerned ultimately with modern individuals' search for unique individual experiences on the stage of modern history. She is concerned with the collective, with the "elaborately socialized world of black people" that existed before African Americans were integrated into the American modernization process.[4] Morrison is concerned with reintroducing the reading public, including African Americans, to an African American racial tradition, the collective African American cultural and historical past—a past that has been ignored, repressed, or rejected in the modern fiction of Wright, Ellison, and Baldwin. Finally, she is concerned with offering that cultural past or racial tradition as a solution to the alienation and fragmentation of contemporary Americans, particularly contemporary African Americans. Morrison states: "Ralph Ellison and Richard Wright—all of whose books I admire enormously—I didn't feel were telling *me* something. I thought they were saying something about *it* or *us* that revealed something about *us* to *you*, to others, to white people, to men. Just in terms of the style, I missed something in the fiction."[5]

Morrison's *Song of Solomon* is a response to modernity. It is antagonistic to the power of money and of rationalized conceptions of space and time over daily life. Therefore, it moves against the tight constraints of a purely monetary expression of value and the systematized organization of space and time as they are embodied in Macon Dead Sr. Through Pilate and Milkman, *Song of Solomon* aims to liberate the materializations of money, space, and time under conditions of capitalism and return them to their "original," [pre-modern] agrarian glory. Therefore, through textual strategies, it exhausts, or presents as totally unredeemable, any positive attributes of modern life—thereby manipulating the tendency of the reader to accept the free and spirited Pilate, who is the embodiment of the pre-modern cultural past and of what has been lost in modern industrial society, as the alternative to the lack of social identification, the crass materialism, the secularism, the alienation and fragmentation, the stifling rationalism, and the rampant individualism of modern, mass culture.

At the center of *Song of Solomon* is the sojourn of a young protagonist, Milkman Dead, who, at the age of thirty, is alienated and still lacks social identification. Approaching his thirtieth birthday, Milkman, a modern subject who needs a temporal unification between the past and the future in the present, realizes that he is fragmented, that he lacks wholeness, that he does not know who he is. Looking in the mirror, he becomes cognizant of the fact that his face lacks "coherence, a coming together of the features into a total self."[6] Until this moment in his life, Milkman has lived a careless, uninformed, and haphazard life. He is selfish, self-centered, and spoiled. "His life was pointless, aimless, and it was true that he didn't concern himself an awful lot about other people. There was nothing he wanted bad enough to risk anything for, [to] inconvenience himself for." (p. 107)

He has contempt for everyone. He strikes his father for slapping his mother, without knowing the history of his parents' relationship. He sends his cousin and girlfriend, Hagar, a Christmas present and a farewell letter at the same time. He tries to break up Corinthians's one love affair because he thinks that her boyfriend, Porter, is not good enough for her, and he steals from his aunt Pilate. Finally, he is a prisoner of his father's upper-middle-class household, which is completely objectified and commodified.

After recognizing his alienation and fragmentation and his lack of social identification, Milkman thinks constantly of escape and adventure: he wants to fly away. He has modern aspirations. "To be modern," argues Marshall Berman, "is to find ourselves in an environment that promises adventure, power, joy, growth, [and] transformation."[7] But, like the peacock perched on the rooftop of the defunct Buick, Milkman cannot fly away because he cannot "give up the shit that weighs [him] down." For Milkman, to fly like a bird—something he has stopped believing he could do since he was four years old—is to become completely modern: to escape commitment, family, and history, to give up his material possessions, and to become totally free and adventurous.

What Milkman as a modern protoganist desires is what Paul de Man in his seminal essay on literary modernity calls moments of "genuine humanity—moments at which all anteriority vanishes." De Man sees the radical rejection of history as "necessary to the fulfillment of our human destiny and as a condition for action." Milkman is prepared to reject the past; but he has not found a "human destiny"[8]: "He just wanted to beat a path away from his parents' past, which was also their present and which was threatening to become his present as well ... [but] he could not visualize a life that much different from the one he had." (pp. 180–181) At this stage in his awakening, he, like his father, sees money as the vehicle that will allow him to be free, to fly, to escape the past and present of his family.

In devising her strategies to resolve Milkman's modern dilemma, to find his "human destiny," Morrison in *Song of Solomon* provides Milkman with two options to negotiate in generating a balanced identity: he has the upper-middle-class, materially, emotionally, and spiritually stifling lifestyle of his father, Macon Dead, Sr., and the empty, rootless urban black bourgeoisie; and he has the free, spontaneous, and emotionally and spiritually filled lifestyle of his aunt, Pilate, and his cultural past.

Milkman grows up in Macon Dead, Sr.'s house. Macon Dead, Sr., is the epitome of the modern entrepreneur who surrenders himself to the urban-industrial imperatives with fanatical conviction. Macon Dead, Sr., grew up with a father, another Macon Dead, who was able to balance human warmth and compassion with industriousness. He showed care and love for his two children at the same time that he, like Faulkner's Sutpen in *Absalom, Absalom!,* built an empire: "[Macon Dead] had come out of nowhere, as ignorant as a hammer and broke as a convict, with nothing but free papers, a Bible, and a pretty black-haired wife, and in one year he'd leased ten acres, the next ten more. Sixteen years later he had one of the best farms in Montour County." (p. 237)

By the time Macon Dead, Sr., is seventeen, he is "pressing forward in his drive for wealth." Therefore, when he leaves Shalimar and settles down in the industrial, urban north, he has already begun what Berger, Berger, and Kellner, in their discussion of modernization and consciousness, call a "process of accommodation." He begins to understand at least some of the presuppositions that govern "his work and everyday living situation."[9] He internalizes the cognitive styles and normative themes such as rationality, impersonality, and machinelike functionality that are intrinsic to a modern technological society. Macon Dead, Sr., to use the words of Suzi Gablik, adopts the "bureaucratic, managerial type of culture characterized by mass consumption and economic self-seeking."[10]

To achieve social status, Macon Dead, Sr., acquires and accumulates property. His keys, a sign of his importance, represent the houses he owns. His house and car are his "way of satisfying himself that he was indeed a successful man." (p. 31) To acquire social respectability, he marries the daughter of the only black doctor in town. He is the inevitable: he, like Jerome Avey in Paule Marshall's *Praisesong for the Widow,* gives his body and soul to the scientific and industrial revolution. His motto for freedom becomes, as he lectures Milkman, one of owning things: "Let me tell you right now the one important thing you'll ever need to know: Own things. And let the things you own own other things. Then you'll own yourself and other people too." (p. 55)

But Macon Dead, Sr.'s quest for freedom, his accumulation of wealth is turned into a system of oppression. At the personal level, he pays enormously, for he brings this atomizing and calculating business style into other areas of his life. He becomes "a hard man, with a manner so cool it discouraged casual or spontaneous conversation." (p. 15) In becoming successful materially and financially, he represses his animal instincts and impulses because human things are incompatible with the moral basis of a rational conduct of life. The consequence is that he becomes sexually, spiritually, and emotionally dead, as his name signifies.

In addition to the human price he inflicts upon himself, Macon Dead, Sr.'s freedom is achieved at the expense of treating others in objective and instrumental terms. He puts Guitar's grandmother, Mrs. Bains—whom he does not see as a person—out on the streets when she cannot pay her rent because she has to feed her children. "Macon Dead remembered—not the woman, but the circumstances at number three. His tenant's grandmother or aunt or something had moved in there and the rent was long overdue." (p. 21) When Macon Dead, Sr., is informed by Freddie, "the town crier," that Porter, a tenant, is about to kill himself with a shotgun a day before rent is due, Macon Dead, Sr., goes to the site, not to save Porter's life, but to procure his rent. "Put that thing [shotgun] down and throw me my goddam money! ... Float those dollars down here, nigger, then blow yourself up!" (p. 25) He refuses to send Milkman to college because he believes that "college was time spent in idleness, far away from the business of life, which was learning to own things." (p. 69)

More devastating, however, is the havoc Macon Dead, Sr.'s quest for freedom wreaks on the rest of his family. He lives in a house that is "quiet ... but is not peaceful." His wife, Ruth, who has been crippled and devastated by the stifling and cold middle-class style of her father, Dr. Foster, is desolated by him. She begins "her days stunned into stillness by her husband's contempt and [ends] them wholly animated by it." (pp. 10–11) Ruth becomes a prisoner in Macon Dead, Sr.'s house: "Like a lighthouse keeper drawn to his window to gaze once again at the sea, or a prisoner automatically searching out the sun as he steps into the yard of his hour of exercise, Ruth looked for the water mark several times during the day. ... Like the keeper of the lighthouse and the prisoner, she regarded it as a mooring, a checkpoint, some stabler visual object that assured her that the world was still there, that this was life and not a dream." (p. 11)

Unable to function healthily in her husband's house, Ruth becomes twisted emotionally. She sees her son, Milkman, not as a "separate real person" but as the symbol of "passion," as "the last occasion she had been made love to." This passion, or the absence thereof, causes Ruth to nurse Milkman until he is four years old because it makes her "daily life bearable." Furthermore, Ruth's bankrupt and oppressive marriage prompts her to lie naked on her father's dead body and to visit his grave frequently because he was the only person in her life that she felt cared about her.

In addition to the validation that breastfeeding her son gives her, Ruth also comes alive when she is threatened by death. Having developed a jealousy of death for taking her father from her, she becomes quite animated when Hagar threatens Milkman's life, and when Hagar dies. In the former instance, Ruth, "with the same determined tread that took her to the graveyard [of her father] six or seven times a year," pays Hagar a visit. In the latter, when Hagar dies and there is not enough money for a "decent funeral," Ruth walks "down to Sonny's Shop and stare[s] at Macon without blinking." He comes up with the money.

Finally, Macon Dead, Sr.'s calculating, impersonal, and rational style has an equally ruinous effect on his two daughters. Because of their father, Corinthians and Magdalena called Lena grow up to become pathetic cripples: "Under the frozen heat of his glance they tripped over doorsills and dropped the salt cellar into the yolks of their poached eggs. The way he mangled their grace, wit, and self-esteem was the single excitement of their days." (p. 10) They lived at home through their thirties, spending their time making velvet roses. Unable to define their worth within his business design, Macon Dead, Sr., stifles their growth, personal identity, and voice. His "disappointment in his daughters sifted down on them like ash, dulling their buttery complexions and choking the lilt out of what should have been girlish voices." (p. 10)

As pathetic cripples, Corinthians and Magdalena called Lena never develop healthy, functional existences in the world. Despite the fact that Corinthians attended Bryn Mawr, spent a junior year studying in France, and spoke good French, she is unable to find employment, maturity, and independence: "Bryn Mawr had done what a four-year dose of liberal education was designed to do: unfit her for eighty percent of the useful work in the world. First, by training her for leisure time, enrichments, and domestic mindlessness. Second by a clear implication that she was too good for such work." (p. 190) Corinthians is unable to find a husband because she lacks drive and initiative. "Those men [black male professionals] wanted wives who could manage, who were not so well accustomed to middle class life that they had no ambition, no hunger, no hustle in them." (p. 189) Therefore, at the age of forty-two, Corinthians realizes that her mother's dream of marrying her daughters off to doctors will not materialize, and that she no longer has the option to become a teacher or a librarian. Hence, unbeknownst to her parents, she hires herself out as a maid. She also begins an affair with Henry Porter, one of her father's tenants and a member of the Seven Days—an organization whose objective it is to kill a random white person every time, and on the same day of the week, a white person kills a black.

Magdalena called Lena's life is even more pathetic than Corinthians's. As Wilfred Samuels and Clenora Hudson-Weems point out in *Toni Morrison,* "Corinthians's educational pursuits and her brief employment as a maid indicate her desire for personal freedom."[11] On the other hand, Magdalena called Lena's drives and desires are totally repressed. She receives neither educational pursuit nor brief employment. She does not attend college because she was afraid of what her father would do to her mother. She never establishes any contact with the outside world. Her outburst against Milkman is the only indication of her unhappiness. Thus, she spends her life making roses, cleaning up after her brother, Milkman, and living in total fear of her father.

The portrait that Morrison in *Song of Solomon* paints of the Dead family specifically and of the black middle class generally is one of pathos, perversion, and repression. No member of this family, or of this class in the text, has any redeeming qualities and values to offer Milkman as he searches for social identification and a meaningful, fulfilled life. In *A Theory of Literary*

Production, Pierre Macherey argues that the literary "work cannot speak of the more or less complex opposition which structures it ... the book is not self-sufficient; it is necessarily accompanied by a *certain absence,* without which it would not exist. A knowledge of the book must include a consideration of this absence ... for in order to say anything, there are other things *which must not be said.*"[12] The present is constituted as a result of the absent. Thus, Morrison, in *Song of Solomon,* uses several strategies that allow her to present a given set of experiences and repress or subordinate others. First, *Song of Solomon's* strategy of rendering middle-class life as perverted, grotesque, atomizing, emotionally, spiritually, and sexually dead functions to deny it as a possible alternative for Milkman and the reader. But to make middle-class life appear plausible, *Song of Solomon* has to signify certain "real" or historical pegs that are associated with the class. It also has to be silent about, or subordinate, the attractive or positive images of this class. For example, although Corinthians attends college, travels to Europe, and is considered "elegant," the text is completely silent on the richness of these experiences.

In addition, *Song of Solomon* alludes to, but represses, the *actual* experiences of middle- and upper-middle-class life. The reader is told that the Dead family visits Honoré, where wealthy blacks own beach homes. The reader is informed of the Dead family's vacations and weekend visits to other cities. *Song of Solomon* also alludes to the teas attended by the Dead family and other upper-middle-class blacks. These are all expected historical pegs or features that are associated with upper-middle- class life. But *Song of Solomon* never shows the reader descriptions of these upper-middle-class experiences. It never shows this class operating within its own context or logic. Of course, it cannot, for the presence of these experiences will not only counter its grotesque and perverted portrait of upper-middle- class blacks, but will also provide Milkman and the reader with possible vibrant and viable experiences within upper-middle- class, modern black life.

Furthermore, in not giving the reader any knowledgeable insights into, or in being completely silent on, the lives of the other black doctors and dentists who live in the Dead family's neighborhood and who are not perverted or grotesque, *Song of Solomon* manipulates the tendency of the reader into believing that the black upper-middle-class as a whole is heartless, cold, and sterile. In addition, *Song of Solomon* uses comments from other characters to reinforce this particular image or stereotype of Macon Dead, Sr., and other upper-middle-class blacks, especially entrepreneurially minded blacks. When Macon Dead, Sr., threatens to evict Mrs. Bains for non-payment of rent, Mrs. Bains retorts: "A nigger in business is a terrible thing to see. A terrible, terrible thing to see." (p. 22) Similarly, *Song of Solomon* defines all of Pilate's experiences with the black moneyed class as negative. "All her encounters with Negroes who had established themselves in businesses or trades in those small midwestern towns had been unpleasant." (p. 145)

Second, *Song of Solomon's* strategy of rendering the Seven Days, the only political organization in the text, as an inhuman organization denies any viable modern political alternative to Milkman's and the reader's fragmentation and alienation and their possible search for constructive, modern political change. The Seven Days is organized as a response by blacks to the murder of blacks by whites. It believes there "ain't no law for no colored man except the one sends him to the chair." It has seven members for the seven days of the week. The organization believes that all white people are responsible for black murders; therefore, it can kill white people randomly, as whites kill blacks. When Milkman asks Guitar why the organization doesn't go after only those white individuals who kill blacks, Guitar responds: "It doesn't matter who did it. Each and every one of them could do it. So you just get any one of them. There are no innocent white people, because everyone of them is a potential nigger-killer, if not an actual one." (p. 156) Therefore, the Seven Days kills random white people every time that a white person kills a black. For every "Negro child, Negro woman, or Negro man ... killed by whites and nothing is done about it by *their* law and *their* courts, this society selects a similar victim at random, and they execute him or her in a similar manner if they can." (p. 155)

But the Seven Days rejects those values and conventions that *Song of Solomon* will eventually offer as a solution to Milkman's alienation and fragmentation, to his quest for a meaningful life. Because of secrecy and the fear of betrayal, members of the Seven Days are required to isolate themselves from family, friends, and society. They must reject ties to the past and channel their energy completely into the brotherhood of the Seven Days. In short, the

Seven Days is a brotherhood based not on life but on death. Thus, in presenting the Seven Days as the only option for political action, *Song of Solomon* is completely silent on those modern civil rights organizations that take an enlightened and humanistic approach to black murders and racism, that might provide Milkman with a modern political alternative for political change and social identification.

Finally, in addition to denying Milkman and the reader modern economic (as manifested in Macon Dead, Sr.) and political (as manifested in the Seven Days) options to resolve their alienation and fragmentation, to find a meaningful life in the modern world, *Song of Solomon* dismisses liberal education (as manifested in Corinthians) as an option and is completely silent on any other educational options. But, in showing the upper-middle-class blacks as lacking any redeeming value, in showing the Seven Days as being devoid of any humanistic virtues, and in dismissing liberal education in a single stroke, *Song of Solomon* enhances Pilate, and the cultural values of the pre-modern past that she represents, as the *only* viable option for Milkman and the reader.

Who is Pilate? How does she differ from Macon Dead, Sr.? And what truth does she represent? Discussing modernization in *The Condition of Postmodernity,* David Harvey argues that each distinctive mode of production or social formation constructs differently social time and social space.[13] In *Song of Solomon,* Macon Dead, Sr., and Pilate belong to two different conceptions of time and space. He is constructed as modern and she is construct- ed as pre-modern. Macon Dead, Sr.'s conception of time and space, which is defined through the organization of social practice fundamental to maximization of profit, and which is symbolized by the clock, contrasts enormously with the natural rhythms of Pilate's agrarian life. Unlike her brother, Pilate is free, sponta- neous, and spritually and emotionally alive. She is uncluttered by the materialism and the rationalism of middle-class life. Her house, which sits back from an unpaved road, lacks most modern essentials: it has no furniture, no electricity or gas, no indoor bathroom, and no telephone. It has no street address. Pilate and her daughter, Reba, and her granddaughter, Hagar, use candles and kerosene lamps for light. They keep warm and cook with wood and coal. They pump their "kitchen water into a dry sink through a pipeline from a well and live pretty much as though progress was a word that meant walking a little further down the road." (p. 27) Unlike Macon Dead, Sr., who has adjusted to the temporal structure of modern technology, Pilate follows no routine, punches no clock, and tells time by the sun. She makes her living by selling an illegal substance, wine.

But despite the lack of modern technology, or because of its absence, Pilate's house is full of life, spirit, and spontaneity. Individual desires and wants are able to exercise themselves freely in her house without being subjected to the external concerns of middle-class life. There is singing in her house, usually without music. Pilate's, Reba's, and Hagar's eating habits are instinctive; they eat when and what they want, and "no meal was ever planned or balanced. ... They ate what they had come across or had a craving for." (p. 29)

Whereas Macon Dead, Sr.'s, modern, industrial conception of social space is divorced from religious or cosmological significations, Pilate's social space is conceptualized as a mysterious cosmology populated by some external authority. Her cosmology is not modern or rational; it is pre-modern and non-rational. She confers regularly with her dead father, and she believes that people die only when they want to: "Don't nobody have to die if they don't want to." (p. 141) Whereas Macon Dead, Sr., takes on his father's pioneering and entrepreneurial skills, Pilate takes from her father his ability to care and love, to live in harmony with the earth.

Morrison in *Song of Solomon* introduces, through Pilate, the artist in her role as shaman—a mystical, priestly, and political figure in pre-modern cultures, who, after coming close to death or an accident or a severe illness (Pilate's transformation comes as a result of isolation for not having a navel), becomes a visionary and a healer. The shaman's function is to balance and center society, integrating many planes of life's experiences and defining the culture's relationship to the cosmos. When the domains of the human and the transcendent fall out of balance, as they have in the upper-middle-class black world of the Dead family, as well as in the urban milieu of the Seven Days, it is the shaman's responsibility to restore the lost harmony and to reestablish equilibrium. As Bonnie J. Barthold points out: "Pilate becomes ... a spiritual 'pilot,' who needs not ask what truth is because, without knowing it, she embodies it."[14]

Pilate, as the master shaman, functions to restore the lost harmony in Milkman—and in other modern African Americans who believe that the transcendental aspirations of mankind can be translated into purely secular equivalents and who believe that culture must be wholly entrusted to the mindscape of scientific rationality—and to reestablish equilibrium by reconnecting Milkman to his extended family, history, and culture. First, Pilate is responsible for Milkman's life. She provides Ruth with the love potion that seduces Macon Dead, Sr., and leads to Milkman's conception. After Milkman's birth, Pilate is more concerned or "interested in this first nephew of hers than she was in her own daughter, and even that daughter's daughter." (p. 19) Second, she freely acquaints Milkman with his family's history. She tells him about his father's warm and compassionate early years in Virginia and about his grandfather's murder. Third and finally, it is Pilate's lost or misplaced gold that initiates Milkman on a journey that will change his entire life. But, initially, Milkman is too much his father's son to understand the voice of the shaman. He is too busy exploiting women and living an aimless, hedonistic life to think about his cultural past or about fulfilling his own existential needs.

It is Milkman's desire for money and Pilate's gold that lead him first to Danville, Pennsylvania, where Reverend Cooper makes him aware of his people, his "links." Stories about his family that he had only "half listened to before suddenly became real and meaningful." After listening to Reverend Cooper, he now understands what Macon Dead, Sr., means by having "worked right alongside [his] father." It did not mean that his father was "boasting of his manliness," but that he "loved his father; had an intimate relationship with him; that his father loved him, trusted him, and found him worthy of working 'right alongside' him." (p. 236)

In Shalimar, Virginia, Milkman uncovers the last pieces of his puzzled past—the part of his cultural heritage that exists unchanged in the present. In *The Dynamics of Modernization*, Cyril Black describes a pre-modern, pre-industrial society as one that is static. Its members never expect to change their occupation. In this agrarian society, the sense of achievement inspired by a desire to get ahead or to gain new privileges is consequently limited. The relatively static life of most members protects them from the need to adapt themselves to people and situations not encountered in childhood, and few have any conception of the larger world. An agrarian or pre-industrial society is socially stable, with patterns of behavior tending to remain constant from generation to generation.[15] In addition, the rather rigid social structure of pre-industrial societies tends to inhibit individualism.

The Shalimar that Milkman returns to is a pre-industrial, patriarchal traditional society. But it is also a town where the men rely on "women and children" for their food. It is a trusting town where people do not lock their doors. It is cut off from public transportation, and there seems to be very little communication with and influence from the outside modern, industrial world. In Shalimar women carry nothing in their hands, and they are unencumbered by the conventions of modern society. They "sat on porches, and walked in the road swaying their hips under cotton dresses, bare-legged, their unstraightened hair braided or pulled straight back into a ball." (p. 266) The people of Shalimar are familiar with the same song—a song they all know because they share the same heritage and the same language.

Because they are too familiar with the fixed norms and values that govern their small, insulated world, they recognize Milkman immediately as an outsider. His materialistic attitude, along with his exploitive attitude toward women, informs the people of Shalimar that he is not one of them: "They looked with hatred at the city Negro who could buy a car as if it were a bottle of whiskey because the one he had had broken. ... They had seen him watching their women and rubbing his fly. ... They had also seen him lock his car as soon as he got out of it in a place where there couldn't be more than two keys twenty-five miles around. ... They looked at his skin and saw it was as black as theirs, but they knew he had the heart of the white men who came to pick them up in the trucks when they needed anonymous, faceless laborers." (p. 269)

In Shalimar, Milkman undergoes a transformation that reconnects him to this earthy past. This transformation is accomplished through a series of tests. First, he is tested by the young men when he finds himself "involved in a knife-and-broken bottle fight," which he survives. Second, through a hunt, he is tested by the older men who want to know if he can survive *without* his material possessions and *with* his bare essentials: "There was nothing here to help him—not his money, his car, his father's reputation, his suit, or his shoes. ... Except for his broken watch, and his wallet with about two hundred dollars, all he had started out with on the journey was gone. ... His watch and his two hundred dollars would be of no help out here, where all a man had was what he was born with, or had learned to use." (p. 280)

On the hunt, Milkman is confronted with his alienation not only from the life rhythms of the earth, but also from the concomitant basic survival skills. It is these basic survival skills, made inept by his materialistic possessions and by his comfortable, insulated upper-middle-class life, that Guitar has in mind when he accuses Milkman of being a "man that can't live there [in Montgomery, Alabama]. If things ever got tough," he warns Milkman, "you'd melt." (p. 104) What Guitar has missed about the South is the woods, the hunting, and the harmonious existence with the earth. Milkman awakens to man's historical relationship with the earth: " ... and he found himself exhilarated by simply walking the earth. Walking it like he belonged on it; like his legs were stalks, tree trunks, a part of his body that extended down down down into the rock and soil, and were comfortable there—on the earth and on the place where he walked." (p. 284) On the hunt, Milkman becomes aware that he has lost ties with the earth, that he has forgotten how to communicate with the earth's other creatures—a form of communication that pre-dates modern, industrial society.

But in his transformation, Milkman reconnects with more than the earth. He also reconnects to a cultural past. He learns from Susan Byrd, a distant cousin, that his grandmother, Sing Dead, who was Native American, left with his grandfather, Jake, "on a wagon headed for Massachusetts." Milkman also discovers Solomon's Leap, Ryan Gulch, and the "song of Solomon," which is a song that embodies his own history and heritage—a song that Pilate has been singing all her life. Milkman's discovery of the song symbolically represents his discovery of his membership in a family, a community, and a history: "He was curious about these people. He didn't feel close to them, but he did feel connected, as though there was some cord or pulse or information they shared. Back home he had never felt that way, as though he belonged to anyplace or anybody." (p. 296) This connection with the people of Shalimar begins the resolution to his alienation and fragmentation, his lack of social identification and his lack of historical continuity, as well as the end to his hedonistic, exploitative, and materialistic ways. It begins the coming together of his "incoherent face."

In the transformation, Milkman identifies himself through a constructed, African history and thereby transcends his alienation. As transcendent subject, he opts for signification practice within a linear history, which represses the heterogeneous historical possibilities offered by Ruth, Macon Dead, Sr., Guitar and others. In fact, Milkman's history reflects a social order grounded in phallocentrism, his own egocentrism, and Western logocentrism.

The change in Milkman begins to manifest itself immediately. He becomes a more sensitive and compassionate individual. He begins to see the people of Shalimar not in objective and instrumental terms, but as people. He begins to treat women differently. *Song of Solomon's* description of Milkman's and "natural" Sweet's brief time together lovingly shows an egalitarian spirit Milkman has acquired by alternating "he did" and "she did." Discovering in the people of Shalimar a sense of belonging, he becomes a part of a whole. In addition, he begins to understand his mother's "hopeless, helplessness." Finally, he develops compassion for his father's mission in life.

Yet Morrison in *Song of Solomon* undermines Milkman's newfound historical and cultural heritage by critiqueing it. Although Milkman views the "song of Solomon" as a song that embodies his own culture and heritage, the song does not glorify his great-grandfather Solomon's flight. It speaks of a voice that bemoans his loss, a voice that does not wish to be abandoned. "O Solomon don't leave me here/Cotton balls to choke me." (p. 307) Yet Milkman chooses from Susan Byrd's information that which allows him to construct a phallocentric history. He ignores the song's voice. In addition, through Sweet, *Song of Solomon* further exposes Milkman's cultural heritage, his history's phallocentrism. As Milkman brags to Sweet about Solomon's glorious flight, Sweet is not impressed: "'Oh him,' she laughed. 'You belong to that tribe of niggers?'" And as Milkman proceeds to celebrate his newfound cultural heritage, Sweet asks the question that shores up the darker side of Solomon's flight. "'Who'd he leave behind?'" (p. 332) The implication is that others pay for Solomon's flight to freedom. Again, we discern how Milkman's history is grounded in phallocentrism. But Morrison exposes the problem with phallocentrism. On the one hand, it is repressive for the Other—women (Ruth, Hagar, etc.), black, and oral. But, on the other hand, it demonstrates that the phallocentric signifying practice is unhealthy (physically, emotionally, and sexually) for those who are in some ways empowered by it: Macon, Guitar, and Dr. Foster.

That Milkman is no longer a subject in crisis could make him a modern-hero-who-finds-the-grail. Even with this perspective, he cannot fulfill the entire role. What has he to take back to the community? A personal narrative that has no significance outside himself. He could return to the community, but his material position would be no different. He would simply feel better about it. In not positing Milkman as either hero or anti-hero, Morrison undermines the whole concept of the modern heroic quest motif.

Yet this critique of Milkman's newfound phallocentric historical and cultural heritage, along with the undermining of the concept of the modern heroic quest motif, means that *Song of Solomon,* unlike most modernist texts, presents no narrative or signifying practice as a transcendental signified. The text appears decentered. It appears not to present a governing structure. Yet by the end of the text, the critiqued phallocentric cultural narrative, which has been reconstituted by Milkman and *Song of Solomon,* is the only narrative or resolution that *Song of Solomon* offers the reader for his alienation and fragmentation, his lack of historical continuity, and his lack of society identification. And from its ending, Morrison in *Song of Solomon* assumes, without any irony, that this cultural narrative is liberating for Milkman. "For now he knew what Shalimar knew: If you surrendered to the air, you could *ride* it." (p. 341) Thus Morrison in *Song of Solomon* presents a deconstructive style which undermines any notion of a transcendental signified or absolute moral narrative. But this deconstructive style counters Morrison's modernist tendency for, and expectation of, closure. This means that the text imposes ultimately a transcendental signified, a tradition or an essentialized narrative on its heterogeneous elements and themes.

In this deconstructive, essentialized narrative offered by *Song of Solomon,* the reader sees how, in his search for Pilate's gold, Milkman finds a tradition that is represented by certain qualities such as wholeness and historical continuity. But in his rediscovery of his past, which has a different conception of the subject, he cannot remain a modern individual, someone who has to reject history and the past to achieve his freedom. In a static, pre-industrial social formation that is governed by fixed norms and traditions, individuality has no place in the vocabulary of human ideals. (This term, individuality, is a part of the invention of modern society.) In the static, pre-industrial social formation, the individual becomes a representation of the social. There is nothing that is specifically individual. This means that the individual's unique wants and desires are repressed. Also, in the rediscovery of his past, Milkman's modernist flight—his desire to escape family, commitment, and history, to become totally free and adventurous—at the beginning of *Song of Solomon* is transformed at the conclusion of the novel so that it represents a flight into the pre-modern.

Therefore, *Song of Solomon,* in resolving Milkman's modern condition—his alienation and fragmentation, his crass materialism and hedonism, his lack of historical continuity, and his lack of social identification—sacrifices his individuality, his selfhood, and returns him to the values and conventions of a racial tradition that is represented as being pre-modern, where the freedom of human action is more limited and social roles are strictly prescribed. In short, *Song of Solomon* resolves Milkman's modern dilemma by seeking to restrain individualism through the reimposition of traditional forms of authority.

But what is *Song of Solomon's* retreat if not a resurrection of the lost racial traditions set against modernity? "Narrative," writes Jean-Francois Lyotard in *The Postmodern Condition,* "is the quintessential form of customary knowledge. ... The consensus that permits such knowledge to be circumscribed and makes it possible to distinguish one who knows from one who doesn't is what constitutes the culture of a people."[16] Seeing that modern African American life lacks this unified narrative, Morrison in *Song of Solomon* imposes a narrative. *Song of Solomon* reads into the American and African American historical past a very strong contemporary sensitivity to and nostalgia for wholeness and historical continuity.

But, in putting this contemporary nostalgia for wholeness and historical continuity, this appropriated unified narrative of the historical past to work, *Song of Solomon* shows how this narrative, or these cultural forms and values, from the past cannot be imposed effectively on the heterogeneous, modern present. Both

Macon Dead, Sr., and Guitar knew, lived, and practiced these agrarian values before moving to the industrial, urban North. Both knew the cultural past. As I have discussed earlier, Macon Dead, Sr., grew up in the culture, and with the values, of Shalimar. According to Pilate and Circe, Macon Dead, Sr., was a "natural" when he was young. He knew and lived of the land. He worked alongside his father in the fields. He was also gentle and compassionate with his sister when she was young. "For a dozen years she [Pilate] had been like his own child." He knew family and he belonged to a culture and a community.

Likewise, Guitar was also a "natural." Before coming North, he had acquired the skills to survive with his bare essentials. He knew the rhythm of the earth. "Everybody said I was a natural. I could hear anything, smell anything, and see like a cat. ... And I was never scared—not of the dark or shadows or funny sounds, and I was never afraid to kill anything." (p. 85) Guitar does not like sugar, a manufactured sweet, only natural sweets. He also knows the song that embodies the cultural heritage. When he and Milkman visit Pilate and she sings "O' Sugarman," he shows a "slow smile of recognition."

This means that both Macon Dead, Sr., and Guitar practiced the values and knew the history and culture that Milkman discovers in Shalimar. Yet neither is able to survive in, or make sense of, the urban North with these agrarian values and this transcendent cultural narrative. Shalimar and the urban North have two different conceptions of social time and social space; they have two different cognitive styles. With his father's murder by whites who want his land as a catalyst, Macon Dead, Sr., realizes this difference. He decides that freedom means owning things. Therefore, he internalizes the normative themes of rationality, of impersonality, and of bureaucratic culture that had been imposed upon him. Identification with the bureaucratic culture of the urban North, writes Herbert Marcuse in *One-Dimensional Man*, is not illusion but reality. Macon Dead, Sr.'s urban reality constitutes a more progressive stage of alienation. His reality has become "entirely objective." He is "swallowed up by his alienated existence." His alienated existence makes obsolete his cultural past and the agrarian values of the South. According to Marcuse, in modern, technological society, "there is only one dimension, and it is everywhere and in all forms."[17]

As for Guitar, the condition of the urban North—the economic exploitation, the racism, the poverty, the impersonality, and the bureaucratic culture—have forced him to abandon his natural skills, the conceptions of social time and social space of the agrarian South, and to adapt to the conceptions of time and space of his present environment. In joining the Seven Days, Guitar does not go astray because somebody did not tell him about his history and culture. *He knew them.* He does not go astray solely because of the way the whites treat his father. Rather, he goes astray because the demands of modern life and self-preservation force him to live in a perpetual present and in a perpetual change that obliterates traditions of the kind which the agrarian social formation of Shalimar "was able in one way or another to preserve." To reject the modern ways of Macon Dead, Sr., and Guitar, as *Song of Solomon* does, is to sever the cultural from the social and the economic, and then blame modern culture for the ills of modernity and the modernization process.

Furthermore, it is only a matter of time before Shalimar, the living embodiment of these traditional agrarian values and unified cultural narrative, is overtaken by the modernization process. Shalimar is an economically depressed town. Solomon's General Store, which is the heart and soul of the town, is where men who have no land of their own wait for the work that seldom comes. Shalimar, *Song of Solomon's* holdout against the modernization process that threatens to crush traditional values, is a dying town. Actually, the end is on the way: "Visitors to Shalimar must be rare, and new blood that settled here nonexistent." (p. 266)

If Shalimar provides Milkman with the knowledge to resolve his "incoherent face," to find social identification, historical continuity, and wholeness, what is his future? In Shalimar, Milkman's newfound knowledge leads him back to Pilate. There is "something he felt now—here in Shalimar, and earlier in Danville—that reminded him of how he used to feel in Pilate's house." (p. 296) If Pilate is the "woman who had as much to do with his future as she had his past," if she is the exemplar by which Milkman is to live his future life, then how does she survive modernity? First, Pilate is marginal in her brother's hegemonic, modern, industrial world. She exists "barely within the boundaries of the elaborately socialized world of black people." She belongs to what Peter L. Berger calls a "cognitive minority" within the black community. A "cognitive minority" is a group formed around a body of deviant "knowledge," a group of people whose view of the world differs significantly from the one generally taken for granted in their society.[18]

But to survive the challenge to her knowledge, or to cope with doubt, a member of a cognitive minority can keep her truths to herself—thus depriving them of all social support—or she can try to gain converts; or she can seek for some kind of compromise. Pilate vacillates between keeping her truths to herself and gaining converts. Milkman is her only convert; she fails to even convert her daughter Reba and her granddaughter Hagar—if she ever tries. But, although she has the social skills to get Milkman and Guitar out of jail, Pilate—who in the return to Shalimar with Milkman "blended into the population like a stick of butter in a churn"—is not competitively skillful at modern society's conceptions of time and space. The text presents no evidence that she possesses the rigor or knows the rationality required to compete successfully in modern society. (Of course, this is not to say that she cannot and will not survive modernity.) Therefore, she does not stand a chance of holding out against the imperatives of a complex, modern industrial society. Discussing Pilate's inability to reproduce herself in modern, industrial society, Susan Willis states: "Pilate demonstrates the insufficiency of the agrarian social mode to provide for its members once they are transplanted to urban consumer society. Her strength and resourcefulness cannot be passed on to her daughter [Reba] and granddaughter [Hagar] because each is more distant from the rural society in which Pilate worked and grew up."[19] Yet Willis does not take her argument to its logical conclusion. Milkman is an urban contemporary of Reba and Hagar. If Pilate cannot pass on her agrarian values to her daughter and granddaughter, then she cannot pass them on to Milkman. Therefore, Milkman will not be able to practice Pilate's agrarian values in the urban, industrial North, just as Macon Dead, Sr., and Guitar are not able to practice these values in the industrial north. The adoption of these agrarian values moves him to the margin of modern, industrial society. With them, he cannot be an active, central player in modern society.

In *Song of Solomon,* the retreatism and rebellion of Pilate and Milkman are as unsatisfactory as the submission and conformity of Macon Dead, Sr. Resistance remains essentially a negative unless it leads the modern individual beyond a mere posture of defiance. Only a personal modern individual who is able to resist the tyranny of the modern, industrial world by standing in ethical personal relationship with it will stand a chance of holding out against the imperatives of modernity. To stand a chance of holding out against these imperatives, Milkman and Pilate will have to proceed in conjunction with, and not retreat from, the urban industrial system. They will have to use the system's institutions as channels for positive change instead of for self-seeking as does Macon Dead, Sr. Only in this way can they strive to rescue themselves from the system, even while they are enmeshed in it. In this way they will be stewards, and not victims, of their modern circumstances.

Morrison's *Song of Solomon* is rebelling against the stifling rationalism, the hedonism, the alienation and fragmentation, the lack of social identification, and the lack of historical continuity that characterize much of contemporary African American life. It wants to move against the tight constraints of a purely monetary expression of value and the systematized organization of space and time. Finally, it wants to reconnect man with his non-rational components—the animal instincts, wants, and desires. But Morrison in *Song of Solomon* does not realize the sentiment of traditional agrarian values and a unified, pre-modern and pre-industrial cultural narrative within a novel dealing with modern African American life. It does not test the viability of these agrarian values and this pre-modern, and pre-industrial cultural narrative in a contemporary constellation; it does not provide a contemporary context for the rational to accommodate the non-rational.

As with Morrison's *Song of Solomon*, N. Scott Momaday's *House Made of Dawn* (1968) also presents a modern protagonist, Abel, who, after a stint in the U.S. Army, finds himself alienated not only from the white society, but also from the traditional Pueblo culture that nurtured him. Like *Song of Solomon, House Made of Dawn* resolves Abel's modern condition—his alienation and fragmentation, his lack of social identification, and his lack of historical continuity—by retreating to an essentialized and romanticized traditional Pueblo cultural past. Also, like Morrison in *Song of Solomon,* Momaday in *House Made of Dawn* wants to save and preserve the dignity of Native American life and culture from the impurities of modern American culture and Western civilization. He wants to offer the values of a modern, ideologically constructed tradition that is represented as the pre-modern, traditional past as a solution to the alienation and fragmentation of contemporary Native Americans. But, unlike Morrison's Milkman, Momaday's Abel is truly tragic because his cultural past—his only hope for survival, wholeness, continuity—has vanished; and Momaday in *House Made of Dawn* is unable to visualize, or is completely silent on, a healthy, modern Native American in the secularized and technological present.

Through textual strategies, Momaday in *House Made of Dawn* achieves several goals. First, he shows how the intrusion of the modernization process and Catholicism effect the decline of traditional Native American cultures. Second, in his unattractive and dismal portraits of urban Native Americans such as Ben Benally and Tosamah, Momaday in *House Made of Dawn* suggests that the possibility of life for Native Americans in the urban, technological present is almost nil. Thus, the present in the text—here represented by traditional Pueblo Culture—is constituted as a result of certain subordinations and absent representations. *House Made of Dawn "is not self*-sufficient; it is necessarily accompanied by a *certain absence,* without which it would not exist." As a modernist text, which must posit a transcendental signified/resolution, it must establish a hierarchy where it privileges certain experiences, subordinates some, and represses others.

The modern dilemma of *House Made of Dawn* is manifested in Abel, a young Pueblo, who is a modern fragmented and alienated individual in search of home and freedom. He has been torn from the reservation at Walatowa and his harmonious relationship with his grandfather, Francisco, who is the embodiment of the traditional Pueblo culture, and from the traditional Pueblo culture itself, to serve in the United States Armed Services. Serving in the Armed Services is Abel's first encounter with secularized, technological modern American society whose conceptions of social time and social space and whose cognitive style contrast enormously with conceptions of time and space and the communicative infrastructure of the Pueblo's everyday life.

The experiences and encounters in the modern American society and in the Armed Services are disorienting and devastating. They tear him away from home. The Army takes him away "from everything he knew and had always known."[20] Before leaving the reservation, Abel had never been in a motorcar before; he had never "sat by a window in the bus and felt the jar of the engine and the first hard motion of the wheels." (p. 25) A recurrent image of the war is one of dead bodies and of a massive machine about to kill him. "He didn't know where he was, and he was alone. No, there were men about him, the bodies of men; he could barely see them strewn among the pits, their limbs sprawling away into the litter of leaves. ... He didn't know where he was, could not remember having been there and gone to sleep. For hours, days perhaps, the whir and explosion of fire had been the only mooring of his mind to sleep. ... The machine concentrated calm, strange and terrific, and it was coming. ... The sound of the machine brimmed at the ridge, held, and ran over, not intricate now, but whole and deafening. His mouth fell upon the cold, wet leaves, and he began to shake violently. ... He was shaking violently, and the machine bore down upon him, came close, and passed him by." (pp. 26–27)

The disoriented experiences in the Army have disrupted and severed his relationship with Pueblo culture, making him a modern alienated and fragmented individual. Returning drunk to the reservation after being released from the Army, Abel is able to remember "everything in advance of his going" to war. "It was the recent past, the intervention of days and years without meaning, of awful calm and collision, time always immediate and confused, that he could not put together in his mind." (p. 25) The war experiences have also severed communication with and memory of his grandfather, Francisco, with whom he is unable to enter into a dialogue: "Earlier Abel had returned to his grandfather's house, but the old man was not there. Nothing had yet passed between them, no word, no sign of recognition." (p. 31) Abel has become inarticulate in the language of his cultural past: "He had tried in the days that followed to speak to his grandfather, but he could not say the things he wanted, he had tried to pray, to sing, to enter into the old rhythm of the tongue, but he was no longer attuned to it." (p. 57)

On the morning after his return to Walatowa, Abel continues his attempt to reconnect with Pueblo culture. He climbs the hill outside the village. In the growing light of the day, he looks out over the land. First, he tries to reestablish contact with the land and the culture of his tribe by searching for a sign in his environment: "He stood for a long time, the land still yielding to the light. He stood without thinking, nor did he move; only his eyes roved after something ... something." (pp. 27–28) Abel is trying to feel his way back, argues Matthias Schubnell, to the center which has been lost to him.[21] Seeing his grandfather and some of the other Indians working in the fields, Abel acquires for a moment the old familiar sense of unity with the land—a union which is the cornerstone of traditional Pueblo culture. "The breeze was very faint, and it bore a scent of earth and grain; and for a moment everything was all right with him. He was at home." (p. 32) But even as Able recognizes that he has not lost entirely the ties to his Pueblo culture, he soon finds himself unable to participate fully in the ceremonial life of the Pueblo people.

At the Jemez celebration, which is held five days after his return to the reservation, Abel's participation in the game of the Chicken Pull proves a failure. "When it came Abel's turn, he made a poor showing, full of caution and gesture." (p. 43) When the albino as the victorious rider turns against Abel and starts beating him with the rooster in accordance with the rules of the game, Abel is unable to cope with the situation. "Abel was not used to the game, and the white man [the albino] was too strong and quick for him." (p. 44) His war experiences have estranged Abel from the old rites and traditions of the Pueblo people.

Although Abel, in his youth on the reservation, had some feelings of isolation, he has not always been alienated from Pueblo culture. He was born into his position as an outsider: "He did not know who his father was. His father was a Navajo, they said, or a Sia, or an Isleta, an outsider anyway, which made him and his mother and Vidal somehow foreign and strange." (p. 15) The lack of family ties, argues Matthias Schubnell, prevents Abel's full integration into the Pueblo community.[22]

But, when he is growing up on the reservation at Walatowa, Abel also internalizes and lives comfortably within a traditional Pueblo culture, which has a mythical-thought cognitive style, and a language where, to make sense out of existence and human and natural phenomena, meaning evolves from a homology between natural and human conditions. Describing this traditional Native American conception of social space and social time, Ben narrates: "You grow up out there, ... someplace like Kayenta or Lukachukai. You grow up in the night, and there are a lot of funny things going on, things you don't know how to talk about. A baby dies, or a good horse. You get sick, or the corn dries up for no good reason. Then you remember something that happened the week before, something that wasn't right. You heard an owl, maybe, or you saw a funny kind of whirlwind; somebody looked at you sideways and a moment too long. And then you *know*. You just know. Maybe your aunt or your grandmother was a witch." (p. 137) Flashbacks from his childhood show an Abel who has a warm relationship with his grandfather and the land. They also show an Abel who is indoctrinated into the rites of traditional Pueblo culture. He knew the "motion of the sun and the seasons." He rises early to be near the "stream at daybreak" to kill his first doe. When he is five years old, he climbs upon the horse behind his brother, Vidal, and they go "out with their grandfather and the others. ... It was a warm spring morning, and he and Vidal ran ahead of the planters over the cool, dark furrows of earth and threw stones at the birds in the gray cottonwoods and elms." (p. 14)

But after the Army, Abel is unable even to identify the source of his alienation and fragmentation. "He tried to think where the trouble had begun, what the trouble was. There was trouble; he could admit that to himself, but he had no real insight into his own situation. Maybe, certainly, *that* was the trouble; but he had no way of knowing. ... Then suddenly he was overcome with a desperate loneliness, and he wanted to cry out." (p. 97) But, events never allow Abel to locate the source of his troubles. The killing of the albino costs Abel six years in prison. In prison, his alienation and fragmentation are further symbolized by his view of the prison wall: "The walls of his cell were white, or perhaps they were gray or green; he could not remember. After a while he could not imagine anything beyond the walls except the yard outside, the lavatory and the dining hall—or even the walls really. They were abstractions beyond the reach of his understanding, not in themselves confinement but symbols of confinement. The essential character of the walls consisted not in their substance but in the appearance, the bare one-dimensional surface that was white, perhaps, or gray or green." (p. 97) The fact that he cannot remember the color of his cell is indicative of his general anesthetized state. "He had lost his place. He had been long ago at the center, had known where he was, had lost his way, had wandered to the end of the earth, was even now reeling on the edge of the void." (p. 96)

And just as Abel remains, until the end of the novel, alienated from the traditional Pueblo culture, he also remains, throughout the novel, entirely divorced from the conceptions of social time and social space of the modern, industrial American society. After his return to Walatowa after the Army, he has a brief affair with Angela Grace St. John, a white American who is visiting Walatowa from Los Angeles, an affair in which he hardly communicates. Seven years later, when she visits him in a Los Angeles hospital, he remains silent. Ben narrates: " … he didn't ever say anything about [their meeting] afterward. I couldn't tell what he was thinking. He had turned his head away … . " (p. 170) He never learns Angela's language. And although he has lived with whites in the Army, Abel does not seem to understand or be familiar with the way whites "kid around" with Indians, calling them "chief and talking about firewater and everything." (p. 138)

Perhaps the most dramatic example of Abel's alienation from modern, industrial society is shown during his trial for the murder of the albino. At the trial, Abel remains silent while the white society and its sense of justice—and in total ignorance of his concept of language, justice and culture—condemn him in a language and a culture that he cannot understand. "[Abel] sat like a rock in his chair, and after a while no one expected or even wanted him to speak. That was good, for he should not have known what more to say. Word by word by word these men were disposing of him in language, *their* language, and they were making a bad job of it. … He had killed the white man. It was not a complicated thing, after all; it was very simple. It was the most natural thing in the world. Surely they could see that, these men who meant to dispose of him in words. They must know that he would kill the white man again, if he had the chance, that there could be no hesitation whatsoever. For he would know what the white man was, and he would kill him if he could. A man kills such an enemy if he can." (p. 95)

What the white society does not understand is that within Pueblo culture, evil must be confronted. Trying to explain this different cosmology, this different definition of reality, Father Olguin states at Abel's trial: " … that in [Abel's] own mind it was not a man he killed. It was something else. ... We are dealing with a psychology about which we know very little. ... There is no way to be objective or precise about such a thing [as witchcraft]. ... I believe that this man was moved to do what he did by an act of imagination so compelling as to be inconceivable to us." (p. 94) At one of his extraordinary sermons, John Big Bluff Tosamah describes succinctly the different communicative infrastructures of Native Americans and white Americans. "And [whites] can't help you because you don't know how to talk to them. They have a lot of *words,* and you know they mean something, but you don't know what, and your own words are no good because they're not the same; they're different, and they're the only words you've got." (p. 144)

Abel's final chance to find a home, a social identification, and self-actualization in the industrial American society occurs in Los Angeles. When he is released from prison, he moves to Los Angeles. But in Los Angeles, he is never able to adjust to the urban temporality, or to understand, what Berger, Berger, and Kellner in *The Homeless Mind* call some of the presuppositions that govern his work and everyday living situations.[23] First, he cannot understand the sea; it is not of his world. Second, Abel finds it difficult to find a social niche. The Relocation Center brings him to Ben Benally's place of employment, but he has no place to live. Ben takes him home and he becomes comfortable with Ben because the two share "those old ways, the stories and the sings, Beautyway and Night Chant." (p. 133) Third, other people such as his parole officer and the welfare workers will not leave him alone. Unable to hold down a job, Abel begins to drink excessively. His final blow comes when he is beaten brutally by the policeman Martinez. Afterward, he becomes a zombie, dead in mind and body, and "he want[s] to die."

As a consequence, and with Ben's assistance, Abel returns to the reservation of Walatowa and to an uncertain future. When Ben takes Abel to the bus station for his return trip home, he notices how he has been physically injured: "He looked pretty bad. His hands were still bandaged, and he couldn't use them very well. It took us a long time to get there. He couldn't walk very fast." (pp. 127–128) Abel is returning home to die. The most important quality he needs for survival on the reservation is a healthy body, which he does not have. During the first two days after his arrival home, he continues to drink heavily. It takes Francisco's sickness and eventual death to transform his life, to reconnect him with Pueblo culture and history, to bring him transcendence, wholeness, historical continuity, and social identification.

Francisco's death is preceded by several flashbacks to his youth. Within them, we see many of the fixed norms and values and conventions that comprise Pueblo culture. We see the ritual killing of a bear as part of a rite of passage into the Kiva society; we see how grandfathers instruct their grandsons in the knowledge of the land and earth: "They must learn the whole contour of the black mesa. They must know it as they know the shape of their hands, always and by heart. ... They must know the long journey of the sun on the black mesa, how it rode in the seasons and the years, and they must live according to the sun appearing, for only then could they reckon where they were, where all things were, in time." (p. 177) In one of the last flashbacks, Francisco tells Abel about the dawn runner who endures pain and fear to procure a "voice in the clan." As Lawrence J. Evers points out, through Francisco's memory Abel is re-taught his ordered relation to place and how it is expressed in the race of the dead.[24]

Francisco dies on the night of February 27, and after Abel has prepared the body for traditional burial, he takes it to Father Olguin for a Christian burial. Then, Abel runs, and in the run, he is reconnected with the rituals, rites, and values of his culture. He endures the pain and finds his own "voice in the clan": "All of his being was concentrated in the sheer motion of running on, and he was past caring about the pain. Pure exhaustion laid hold of his mind, and he could see at last without having to think. He could see the canyon and the mountains and the sky. He could see the rain and the river and the fields beyond. He could see the dark hills at dawn. He was running, and under his breath he began to sing. There was no sound, and he had no voice; he had only the words of the song." (p. 191) In this final run, Abel reconciles himself with the culture where an appreciation and knowledge of the land and nature are essential. Finally, Abel, like Milkman, finds spiritual redemption, wholeness, and historical continuity through a return to his own people, his own center, at Walatowa.

But, although the reconciliation with the knowledge of the land, nature, and culture allows Abel to achieve self-actualization, the song of his newfound culture has "no sound, and he had no voice, he had only the words of a song." The words—the rituals and ceremonies—of the culture are available to Abel, but the condition for the possibility of their existence has disappeared. Given its fictive portrayal in *House Made of Dawn,* traditional Pueblo culture has not only declined but has almost become extinct.

House Made of Dawn shows a Pueblo culture that has declined with the rise of modern American society. First, the Catholic church made its inroad onto the reservation at Walatowa with the clear intention of converting the people from traditional Pueblo religion, which is an integral part, if not the core, of their culture, to Catholicism. Father Olguin, who is symbolically and literally diseased and blinded in one eye, has no respect for, and is incapable of comprehending, Pueblo culture and ceremonies. When Francisco dies, Abel performs the traditional Pueblo burial rites before he informs Father Olguin of the death. Father Olguin's reaction is a sad commentary on the narrow sectarianism of a faith that refuses to tolerate rituals and beliefs that are different from its own. Father Olguin complains to Abel about the hour, arguing that the burial could wait until morning. It is only when Abel rushes away that the Father agrees to help: "I understand! Oh God! I understand—I understand!" (p. 190) But Father Olguin does not understand. During the seven-year period (1945–1952) that he has been at Walatowa, his missionary zeal—"the once-hectic fire of his spirit"—was for the conversion of the Pueblo. That zeal dissipates with his realization that he cannot successfully convert the Pueblo to Catholicism. In a letter to his brother, Father Nicolas, one of Father Olguin's predecessors and someone whose letters allow Father Olguin to get a "glimpse of his own ghost," describes Francisco thusly: "He is one of them & goes often in the kiva & puts on their horns & hides & does worship that Serpent which even is the One our most ancient enemy." (p. 50)

Although the Catholic church does not successfully convert the Pueblo people, its presence on the reservation at Walatowa undermines the communicative infrastructure and the fixed norms and values of traditional everyday life. The Pueblo acquired "from their conquerors only the luxury of example. They have assumed the names and gestures of their enemies." There

was once a time, *House Made of Dawn* seems to argue, when
Pueblo men worked the land, when the gods and the weather
were good, and when things were bountiful. Now the ringing of
the Angelus starts their day and the Pueblo youth attend
Catholic schools and serve the Catholic priest at mass, instead of
praying in "Tanoan to the old deities of the earth and sky." The
priests on the reservation have established the practice of giving
the dead Christian burials.

Second, the United States' modernization process also contributes to the decline and disintegration of traditional Pueblo
culture. Its norms and values have penetrated the everyday life of
the Pueblo people. The once-sacred rituals have become empty
and commercialized. They have been transformed into a carnival
of Saints' parades that lack any spiritual meaning. Commenting
on the transformation of the once sacred Pecos bull procession,
the text states: "[the Pecos bull] was a sad and unlikely thing, a
crude and makeshift totem of revelry and delight. There was no
holiness to it, none of the centaur's sacred mien and motion, but
only the look of evil. ... But it was a hard thing to be the bull, for
there was a primitive agony to it, and it was a kind of victim, an
object of ridicule and hatred; and harder now that the men of the
town had relaxed their hold upon the ancient ways, had grown
soft and dubious." (p. 75) Angela Grace St. John, an outsider at
the carnival, can also recognize that something is wrong in the
rituals. Seeing the white man, the albino, in the parade at the
feast of Santiago, Angela was "thrilled to see [the horse] handled
so, as if the white man were its will and all its shivering force
were drawn to his bow. A perfect commotion, full of symmetry
and sound. And yet there was something out of place, some flaw
in proportion or design, some unnatural thing." (p. 43)

Although there is some resistance, the decline seems
inevitable. Francisco's generation, who "have never changed their
essential way of life," is probably the last generation to comfortably resist the modernization process, Catholicism, and Western
civilization. But, even Francisco, the embodiment of the old
Pueblo ways, is mysteriously diseased. First, his father is one of
the priests. This means that he is not pure Pueblo. Second,
perhaps, literally and figuratively, his stiffened, disease-riddled
leg symbolizes cultural decay: "The crippled old man in leggings
and white ceremonial trousers shuffled out into the late after-

noon. He dried his eyes on his sleeve and whimpered one last time in his throat. He was grown too old, he thought. He could not understand what had happened. But even his sorrow was feeble now; it had withered, like his leg, over the years, and only once in a while, when something unusual happened to remind him of it, did it take on the edge and point of pain." (p. 71)

The disintegration and decline of traditional Pueblo culture, as it is represented in *House Made of Dawn,* is having a devastating effect on Abel's modern generation. The ravages of alcohol and drugs, high unemployment, and inadequate education have produced a Pueblo underclass of youth that has its own modern culture of alienation, fragmentation, lack of historical continuity, lack of social identification, hedonism, narcissism, suicide, and spiritual sterility. This modern culture on the Walatowa reservation, which is in total contrast to the modalities of traditional Pueblo culture, has helped to extinguish the fire in many of those who remember the old ways. Describing young Navajos in a bar, *House Made of Dawn* tells us: "The rain diminished, and with nightfall the aftermath of the storm moved slowly out upon the plain. The last of the wagons had gone away from the junction, and only three or four young Navajos remained at Paco's. One of them had passed out and lay in his vomit on the floor of the room. The others were silent now, and sullen. They hung upon the bar and wheezed, helpless even to take up the dregs of the wine that remained. The Precious ring of sweet red wine lay at the bottom of a green quart bottle, and the dark convexity of the glass rose and shone out of it like the fire of an emerald. The green bottle lay out in the yellow glow of the lamp, just there on the counter and within their reach." (p. 76)

It is this generation and this cultural malaise that Abel returns to after serving in the Armed Services. It is also in the midst of this cultural malaise that Abel finds his cultural past. But with the death of Francisco and the disappearance of the conditions for the existence of traditional Pueblo culture, Abel's new-found cultural past can only exist as myth. It can exist in the tale that Angela Grace St. John tells her son, Peter, whom she is carrying during her stay at Walatowa. Angela, who came to Walatowa with her flesh and spirit separated, does not think of her body as beautiful. "She could think of nothing more vile and obscene than the raw flesh and blood of her body." (p. 36) Her association with the Pueblo culture and her affair with Abel make her life richer, because Abel, at least from what we can surmise from the story she tells her son, and the people of Walatowa teach her to appreciate her body and to achieve a reconciliation of flesh and spirit. When she returns to Los Angeles, Angela sustains her life with a self-fulfilling myth. It is a story of a young Indian brave who "was born of a bear and a maiden ... he was noble and wise. He had many adventures, and he became a great leader and saved his people." (p. 169) And, just as it does in Angela's tale, the traditional Pueblo culture can exist as an appropriated myth in *House Made of Dawn*.

In finding wholeness, historical continuity, and transcendence in the vanishing pre-modern and pre-industrial cultural past, Abel resolves his modern dilemma. In the artistic realm, *House Made of Dawn*, like *Song of Solomon*, saves Abel and the life and culture of the Pueblo people from being contaminated by modern culture and the modernization process. Like Morrison in *Song of Solomon*, Momaday in *House Made of Dawn* creates an enormous *impasse*, or blockage, by making an ideologically constructed traditional Pueblo cultural past that is represented as pre-modern, pre-industrial, and vanishing serve as the *only* viable and healthy alternative to the alienation, fragmentation, and lack of social identification of Abel's generation. In response to the question, "why are you not an existentialist, for example, a 'modern' man looking at the world as separate from the person?", Momaday says: "On the basis of my experience, trusting my own perceptions, I don't see any validity in the separation of man and the landscape. Oh, I know that the notion of alienation is very widespread, in a sense very popular. But I think it's an unfortunate point of view and a false one, where the relationship between man and the earth is concerned. Certainly it is one of the great afflictions of our time, this conviction of alienation, separation, isolation. And it is certainly an affliction in the Indian world. But there it has the least chance of taking hold, I believe, for there it is opposed by very strong forces. The whole world view of the Indian is predicated upon the principle of harmony in the universe. You can't tinker much with that; it has the look of an absolute."[25] By making an ideology out of the norms and values of the Pueblo's cultural past and then having those norms and values inform its production, Momaday entraps *House Made of Dawn* in what Terry Eagleton calls a "representational epistemology," which "mistakes the disintegration of certain traditional ideologies of the subject for the subject's final disappearance."[26]

It is Momaday's ideological construction of the Native American individual as being whole and connected to history, culture, and the land, or his "absolute" notion that the Native American is "predicated upon the principle of harmony in the universe" that causes *House Made of Dawn* to reject and subordinate the modern, urban experiences of Ben Benally and the postmodern experiences of Tosamah as viable options for Abel and the reader. The sterility and tawdriness of Ben Benally's apartment as well as the meaningless monotony of the work that Ben and Abel do at the packing factory are indicative of modern America as an unsatisfactory existence. In moving from the reservation to Los Angeles, Ben settles down and begins what Berger, Berger, and Kellner in *The Homeless Mind* call the "process of accommodation."[27] He rejects or represses the past and internalizes the cognitive structures and the temporality that are intrinsic to a modern economy. He comes to understand some of the rules that govern his work and everyday living situations. He convinces himself that the life he feels compelled to live is, in fact, better and ultimately more fulfilling than the life he knew on the reservation. Freedom for Ben, as with *Song of Solomon's* Macon Dead, Sr., lies in attaining the American Dream. Ben rationalizes: "Once you find your way around and get used to everything, you wonder how you ever got along out there where you came from. There is nothing there, you know, just the land, and the land is empty and dead. [In the city] you never have to be alone. You go downtown and there are a lot of people all around, and you're having a good time. You see how it is with them, how they get along and have money and nice things, radios and cars and clothes and big houses. And yet you want those things; you'd be crazy not to want them. And you can have them, too; they're so *easy* to have. You go down to these stores, and they're full of bright new things and you can buy just about anything you want. The people are real friendly most of the time, and they're always ready to help you out." (p. 164)

Yet *House Made of Dawn* exposes and undermines the veracity and possibility of Ben's American dream by showing the failure rather than the success of the dream. It shows the failure in the way it portrays Ben's existence. He lives in the dingy squalor of a single room with only one curtainless window. The floor leaks, the pipes knock, and the atmosphere is alternately stuffy and cold. For employment, Ben works long hours in a packing factory as a menial laborer, which does not provide him with enough money to have "nice things, [such as] radios and cars and clothes and big house[s]." Despite his claim that people are friendly, he does not have many friends. In fact, Abel is the only person with whom he can share his native religion. The facts of his lonely life and the hopes that he harbors are ironically counterpointed. As with Macon Dead, Sr., Ben's pursuit of the American Dream hides the reality of his life from him. He deadens his mind and violates his soul trying desperately to convince himself that the material values of modern, technological America are worth dedicating his life to.

House Made of Dawn undermines further Ben's life as a viable option for Abel and the reader when it shows, through flashbacks, how Ben's memories of growing up on the reservation are full of precise, beautiful, and evocative details that belie his remark that the land is empty and dead and that there is nothing where he comes from. The land recalled in the flashbacks is rich with vitality and meaning and the life is full of compassion and love: "And it was getting late and you rode home in the sunset and the whole land was cold and white. And that night your grandfather hammered the strips of silver and told you stories in the firelight. And you were little and right there in the center of everything, the sacred mountains, the snow-covered mountains and the hills, the gullies and the flats, the sundown and the night, every-thing—where you were little, where you were and had to be." (p. 143) Such exposition only highlights the sadness of Ben Benally's life in which fiction is substituted for fact, hope for truth, and words for things. To survive the city, Ben feels he must escape the reality of his existence. He feels that he must "take it easy and get drunk once in a while and just forget about who you are." (p. 144) Freedom for Ben means self-delusion.

John Big Bluff Tosamah's life, like Ben Benally's, does not reproduce the convention of either the ideologically constructed Native American subject or the enlightened Western modern subject forged through a certain temporal unification of the past and future with the present. Therefore, Tosamah also does not provide a viable *modus vivendi* for Abel or the modern reader. Tosamah, the Priest of the Sun, is in a peculiarly privileged position in *House Made of Dawn*. He has the capacity to bring spritual gifts to his people, to be a savior of sorts. He is given the role of Kiowa tribe historian. It is in one of his sermons that he narrates the Kiowa's migration to Rainy Mountain, of their adoption of the sacred sun dance doll, Tai-me, of their birth as a tribe from a hollowed-out log, and of their decline.

John Big Bluff Tosamah is constructed as a postmodern subject. Discussing schizophrenia or decenteredness as a basic feature of postmodernism, Frederic Jameson defines schizophrenia as "the breakdown of the relationship between signifiers ... since the schizophrenic does not know language articulation in that way [does not have the experience of temporality], he or she does not have an experience of temporal continuity either, but is condemned to live in a perpetual present to which the various moments of his or her past have little connection and for which there is no conceivable future on the horizon. In other words, schizophrenic experience is an experience of isolated, disconnected, discontinuous material signifiers which fail to link up into a coherent sequence. The schizophrenic thus does not know personal identity in our sense, since our feeling of identity depends on our sense of the persistence of the 'I' and the 'me' over time."[28]

On the other hand, "the schizophrenic will clearly have a far more intense experience of any given present of the world than we do, since our present is always part of some larger set of projects which force us selectively to focus our perceptions."[29] Certainly, in borrowing from Lyotard and other postmodern scholars, Jameson describes succintly the experience of postmodernity and the postmodern subject. But in calling the postmodern subject schizophrenic, rather than just a subject who is constructed differently, who takes various subjective positions, he naturalizes the notion of the modern subject who needs a temporal unification between the past and future and then uses it, through contrast, to define the postmodern subject as an aberrant. Because I accept and find useful his description of the postmodern subject, I will use it to discuss Tosamah. But I will disengage with his negative use of the term schizophrenia.

First, Tosamah is an "isolated, disconnected, discontinuous material" signifier, who fails to "link up into a coherent sequence." He can change personas: "Just then a remarkable thing happened. The Priest of the Sun seemed stricken; he let go of his audience and withdrew into himself, into some strange potential of himself. His voice, which had been low and resonant, suddenly became harsh and flat; his shoulders sagged and his stomach protruded, as if he had held his breath to the limit of endurance; for a moment there was a look of amazement, then utter carelessness in his face." (pp. 85–86) Unlike Ben, Tosamah, who was not raised on a reservation, is vitally disconnected from the wellspring of traditional Native American culture: the acceptance of mystery, the love of the land, and the importance of rituals. Ben speaks the truth when he remarks that Tosamah cannot comprehend "the act of imagination" that causes Abel to kill the albino. Instead of focusing on the inner self, as a modernist such as Abel or Ben would do, Tosamah does not respect any frontier, or any external metaphysical narrative. He acts according to his wants and desires. His life becomes a series of performances. He does not surrender to either the American Dream or the values of Kiowa's traditional culture.

Second, Tosamah's identity is not a single entity. He is a decentered subject; he is a series of selves that are superimposed upon each other and that exist in the same space. He is a savior and a historian. He is also a ringleader of a group of Native Americans in Los Angeles. He is a Priest. There does not seem to be a conflict among or contradiction between his many selves. His success has been achieved by using various language games to craftily manipulate his fellow Indians, adopting the white society's dislike of the Native American and asserting both his belief in the old Indian rituals and his place in the mainstream society. For example, on the one hand, he tells his congregation how the white man conceives and manipulates language: "Now, brothers and sisters, Old John was a white man, and the white man has his ways. ... He talks about the Word. He talks through it and around it. He builds upon it with syllables, with prefixes and suffixes, and hyphens and accents. He adds and divides and multiplies the Word. And in all of this he subtracts the Truth." (p. 87)

But on the other hand, Tosamah uses language in the same way that he accuses the white man of using it, and to much the same purpose. By manipulating a variety of verbal styles in the Gospel According to John, Tosamah keeps members of his congregation off balance, dazzling them as much as enlightening them. He combines biblical oratory, street talk, exposition, and the simple direct narrative style: "'In the beginning was the Word.' I have taken as my text this evening the almighty Word itself. Now get this: 'There was a man sent from God, whose name was John. The same came for a witness, to bear witness of the Light, that all men through him might believe.' ... In the beginning was the Word. ... ' Now what do you suppose old John *meant* by that? That cat was a preacher." (p. 86) Tosamah relates to his audience on several levels simultaneously to establish at once his oneness with, and difference from, them. He is perceived as a fellow Indian sharing a similar culture and values, as a ghetto brother sharing the hardship of the street, and as a teacher in both the shamanistic and professional senses.[30]

Tosamah's various performances show how he does not belong to an ancestral narrative. In fact, he turns the ancestral narrative into just another performance. For the Kiowa, there is a magical correspondence and congruity between words and things. Words are Truth. Tosamah, in telling the history of the Kiowa people, recalls that for his grandmother, Aho, "words were medicine; they were magic and invisible. ... They were beyond price; they could neither be bought nor sold." (p. 89) And although he tells the cultural history of his Kiowa forefathers, it too becomes a part of his performance. His tale is too abstract and too intellectual, too divorced from traditional Kiowa's traditions. But *House Made of Dawn,* in denying Tosamah as a viable option for Abel, undermines Tosamah's various performances. It defines him in the negative, or as an aberration. In the Priest of the Sun's first sermon, the text describes Tosamah's rhetorical delivery pejoratively when he has scarcely begun: "Conviction, caricature, callousness: the remainder of his sermon was a going back and forth among these." (p. 86)

Because Momaday's traditional, pre-modern, ideological construction of the Native American individual, or his "absolute" concept that the Native American is "predicated upon the principle of harmony in the universe" informs *House Made of Dawn,* the modern and postmodern experiences of Ben Benally and Tosamah must be perceived as aberrant and, therefore, cannot be viable alternatives for Abel and the reader. This ideological construction of the subject, along with an essentialist concept of culture, does not give priority to the question of its own legitimation. The concept "certifies itself in the pragmatics of its own transmission without having recourse to argumentation and proof."[31]

It is this "representational epistemology" informing *House Made of Dawn* that causes it to be silent on or to repress—the present can only be constituted through absences—those modern Native Americans who have made a healthy and practical transformation—and therefore achieved freedom or positionality—in a modern American society. James Welch, in *The Death of Jim Loney,* presents such a character in Jim Loney's sister, Kate, who is "extraordinary" because she survives the decline and disintegration of traditional Native American culture. Kate makes the transition by abandoning the past, acquiring an American education, internalizing the cognitive style and values of modern America, and moving to Washington, D.C., to work for the Bureau of Indian Affairs. Kate has the "ability to live in the present"; she decides that it is "only the present" that matters. Likewise, Louise Erdrich, in *Love Medicine,* and Gerald Vizenor, in *The Heirs of Columbus,* present such characters. Erdrich's Albertine Johnson and Nector Kashpaw and Vizenor's crossbloods are modern and postmodern Native American characters who exist healthily in modern American society. Even Sitko Ghost Horse in Jamake Highwater's *Kill Hole* negotiates a hybrid space that allows him to exist healthily in modern society.

House Made of Dawn is also silent on those modern Native Americans who have eschewed traditional rites and rituals about the land and nature and adopted certain modern American economic practices on the reservation. Again, James Welch, who is less romantic about the Native American cultural past than N. Scott Momaday, in *Winter in the Blood* produces such a character in the nameless protagonist's mother, Teresa, who rejects the past and adopts certain economic practices from the capitalist society to use the land for commercial purposes.

But *House Made of Dawn* has to exclude or repress these options because it, like *Song of Solomon,* is locked in an essentialist notion of culture and a definition of the subject that are pre-modern, and it constitutes this essentialist notion of culture through certain absences. It refuses to accept or validate modernist and postmodernist tendencies. To acknowledge the modern and postmodern options of Ben Benally, Tosamah, Kate, and Teresa, *House Made of Dawn* would have, to use the words of Terry Eagleton, "to relinquish [its] epistemological paranoia and embrace the brute objectivity of random subjectivity."[32] It would have to admit that some Native Americans live healthily in a postmodern America without the assistance of traditional Native American narratives.

The retreat of *Song of Solomon's* Milkman and *House Made of Dawn's* Abel to ideologically and racially constructed traditions, which are defined by qualities of wholeness and historical continuity that are *anterior* to modernity, as a way of resolving their alienation and fragmentation, their lack of social identification, places them squarely in the canon of Western literature and more specifically within the confines of American literature. Both texts fall within a modern master narrative, the romanticist movement, that, since the rise of capitalism, has dichotomized and yet conjoined two oppositions: the rural/urban and the European/non-European. Both texts choose the rural over the urban. Also, Abel and Milkman successfully follow the traditional mythical pattern of initiation of heroes like Oedipus, Theseus, and Prometheus.[33] Both *Song of Solomon* and *House Made of Dawn* can be classified as *bildungsromans* insofar as their narratives follow the growth and the development of their protagonists' personal identities.[34] Morrison in *Song of Solomon* and Momaday in *House Made of Dawn* are in the tradition of Hemingway, Whitman, and Faulkner in seeing nature as the source of energy and as the place where everything is alive, related, and meaningful. Finally, in their reaction against the continuing development of science, technology, and materialism, Morrison in *Song of Solomon* and Momaday in *House Made of Dawn* are in the tradition of such American Transcendentalists as Emerson and Thoreau, who would say of the world around them that they would have none of its "dirty institutions."[35]

Finally, Morrison in *Song of Solomon* and Momaday in *House Made of Dawn* sell essentialized pre-modern and pre-industrial African American and Pueblo history and culture. Both texts have a use-value that stems from the meaning they generate. Discussing how she views African Americans and African American culture, Toni Morrison states: "My own use of enchantment simply comes because that's the way the world was for me and for black people that I knew. In addition to the very shrewd, down-to-earth, efficient way in which they did things and survived things, there was this other knowledge or perception, always discredited but nevertheless there, which informed their sensibilities and clarified their activities. It formed a kind of cosmology that was perceptive as well as enchanting, and so it seemed impossible for *me* to write about black people and eliminate that simply because it was unbelievable."[36] Enchantment informs or colors the production of African American life and culture in *Song of Solomon.* What we get in Pilate and the town of Shalimar is what Martha Bayles calls "Morrison's romanticization of magic." In *Song of Solomon* the harsh realities of racial and economic oppression and the pain of joblessness are transformed into "painless enchantment."[37] Instead of a representation of these harsh realities, the reader gets Pilate, who does not seem inconvenienced or put out by the lack of modern appliances; who knows how to boil the perfect egg. The reader gets Milkman, who discovers a legendary great grandfather, Solomon, who could fly. The reader does not get a glimpse of how these women of Shalimar struggle to survive amidst economic poverty, but rather an image of "enchanted" women who are free, who are unencumbered by the weight of the modernization process.

Perhaps the most visible image of the women of Shalimar is not one of women who struggle to make ends meet despite the fact that their husbands are unemployed, but one of women who walk down the streets and do not carry anything in their hands. In *Song of Solomon,* this idea of African Americans who once existed in an enchanted state represses any human and social oppression. It subordinates the inevitable tension and conflict that come within and between pre-modern, organized society and nature.

Likewise, *House Made of Dawn* romanticizes Pueblo culture. To view Pueblo culture as one that is organic—where man exists harmoniously as an integral part of nature—is to ignore the inevitable tensions, conflicts, and contradictions that come in all social formations. It is to repress in the end Abel's initial alienation in Pueblo culture because he is an outsider and the possible conflict that could have occurred because Francisco's father is white. *Song of Solomon* and *House Made of Dawn* have a use-value that stems from the meaning they generate. Both ultimately generate safe and romantic meanings of culture and history in the American historical past that are very American.

Both commodify, package, and sell African American and Pueblo cultures for public consumption.

If *Song of Solomon* and *House Made of Dawn* have been deemed "great" literature by American, African American, and Native American scholars and critics, is it because they generate or affirm certain "ideological values" and "political beliefs" sanctioned within both American and minority social, literary, and institutional lives? A close scrutiny of the critical articles on the two texts indicates that what the critics and scholars like and focus on in their discussions of the two texts are pre-modern and pre-industrial themes and ideological values such as racial essentialism, wholeness within the subject, unified community, and historical continuity, which are consistent with and part of a set of broader political beliefs and definitions of human nature and society that have been naturalized and are held by many Americans.

For example, *Song of Solomon* is heralded as a "great" novel by most mainstream American and African American critics because it generates essentialist, traditionalist, and cultural-nationalist values. As I stated earlier, mainstream American critics privilege *Song of Solomon,* and therefore include it in the canon of Western literature, because its protagonist, Milkman, can be interpreted as following the traditional mythical pattern of initiation of heroes like Oedipus, Theseus, and Prometheus, which is the hallmark of Western white male literature. This reading of *Song of Solomon* within the traditional mythical pattern of initiation is best exemplified by David Cowart's article on *Song of Solomon,* which emancipates "[Morrison] from her own literary ghetto" into the canon of Western literature by showing how she reproduces the same themes in *Song of Solomon* as does Faulkner in *Go Down, Moses* and Joyce in *A Portrait of the Artist as a Young Man.* Like *Song of Solomon,* "Joyce's great novel ... concerns the formation of its protagonist's character, and it, too, develops the theme of the family romance. Stephen Dedalus, like Morrison's hero, finds himself at odds with his immediate family and looks to a remote figure of legend and myth as his authentic parent."[38]

But most African American critics appropriate *Song of Solomon* into their own racially constructed African American traditions and their own essentialist ways of defining African American reality. Unlike mainstream white critics, they see and identify in *Song of Solomon* an entirely new set of themes and motifs that generate or affirm their particular political beliefs and ideological values. For instance, Barbara Christian argues that "the relationship between her [Morrison's] characters' belief systems and their view of Nature, is basic to her works and is one of the principal reasons why her novels emanate a feeling of timelessness even as they are so pointedly concerned with the specificity of her characters' communities."[39] Norris Clark holds that *Song of Solomon* "incorporates many of the aesthetic nuances which not only adequately reflect the black American experience—historically, culturally, psychologically and socially—but also reach toward mythic and epic proportions."[40] And Harry Reed sees *Song of Solomon* as a "major contribution to nationalist thought."[41]

Song of Solomon and *House Made of Dawn* are considered valuable or great by literary critics and scholars who essentialize and universalize certain racially constructed traditions that are represented by qualities such as wholeness in subject, unity in community, historical continuity, and oneness with nature because these texts present and transform modernity—the rejection of history, rampant individualism, hedonism, and the impulse to experiment—back into an ideologically contrived permanent, timeless cultural tradition of wholeness and historical continuity. Perhaps it is their reproduction of certain literary themes and narrative strategies that explain the enormous success of both *Song of Solomon* and *House Made of Dawn,* that explain how they garnered the National Book Critics Award and the Pulitzer Prize respectively.

NOTES

1. Jurgen Habermas, "Modernity—An Incomplete Project," in *The Anti-Aesthetic: Essays on Postmodern Culture,* edited by Hal Foster (Port Townsend, Wash.: Bay Press, 1983), p. 14.

2. Suzi Gablik, *Has Modernism Failed?* (New York: Thames and Hudson, Inc., 1984), pp. 83–84.

3. Marshall Berman, *All That Is Solid Melts into Air: The Experience of Modernity* (New York: Penguin Books, 1982), p. 15.

4. Colette Dowling, "The Song of Toni Morrison," *New York Times Magazine* (May 20, 1979); p. 58.

5. Charles Ruas, *Conversations with American Writers* (New York: Knopf, 1985), p. 218.

6. Toni Morrison, *Song of Solomon* (New York: Signet, 1978). pp. 69–70. All further references will be to this edition and will be given in the text.

7. Marshall Berman, *All That Is Solid Melts into Air,* p. 15.

8. Paul de Man, "Literary History and Literary Modernity," in *Blindness and Insight* (Minneapolis: University of Minnesota Press, 1983), p. 141.

9. Peter Berger, Brigitte Berger, and Hansfried Kellner, *The Homeless Mind: Modernization and Consciousness* (New York: Vintage Books, 1974), p. 122.

10. Suzi Gablik, *Has Modernism Failed?,* p. 16.

11. Wilfred Samuels and Clenora Hudson-Weems, *Toni Morrison* (Boston: Twayne Publishers, 1990), p. 74.

12. Pierre Macherey, *A Theory of Literary Production* (London: Routledge, 1978), pp. 84, 85.

13. David Harvey, *The Condition of Postmodernity: An Enquiry into the Origins of Cultural Change* (Cambridge: Basil Blackwell, 1989), p. 201.

14. Bonnie J. Barthold, *Black Time: Fiction of Africa, the Caribbean, and the United States* (New Haven: Yale University Press, 1981), p. 179.

15. Cyril Black, *The Dynamics of Modernization* (New York: Harper & Row Publishers, 1966), p. 26.

16. Jean-Francois Lyotard, *The Postmodern Condition: A Report on Knowledge (Minneapolis:* University of Minnesota Press, 1985), pp. 18–19.

17. Herbert Marcuse, *One-Dimensional Man: Studies in the Ideology of Advanced Industrial Society* (Boston: Beacon Press, 1964), p. 11.

18. Peter L. Berger, *Modern Society and the Rediscovery of the Supernatural* (Garden City, N. Y.: Doubleday, 1969), p. 7.

19. Susan Willis, "Eruptions of Funk: Historicizing Toni Morrison," in *Black Literature and Literary Theory,* edited by Henry Louis Gates, Jr. (New York: Methuen, 1984), pp. 279–280.

20. N. Scott Momaday, *House Made of Dawn* (New York: Perennial Library, 1977), p. 25. All further references will be to this edition and will be given in the text.

21. Matthias Schubnell, *N. Scott Momaday: The Cultural and Literary Background* (Norman: University of Oklahoma Press, 1986), p. 113.

22. Matthias Schubnell, *N. Scott Momaday: The Cultural and Literary Background,* p. 105.

23. Berger, Berger, and Kellner, *The Homeless Mind,* p. 122.

24. Lawrence J. Evers, "Words and Place: A Reading of *House Made of Dawn,*" in *Critical Essays on American Literature,* edited by Andrew Wiget (Boston: G.H. Hall and Co., 1985), pp. 185–86.

25. Joseph Bruchac, "N. Scott Momaday: An Interview," *The American Poetry Review,* vol. 13, no. 4 (July/August 1984): pp. 14–15.

26. Terry Eagleton, "Capitalism, Modernism and Postmodernism," in *Against the Grain: Selected Essays* (London: Verso, 1986), p. 144.

27. Berger, Berger, and Kellner, *The Homeless Mind,* p. 122.

28. Fredric Jameson, "Postmodernism and Consumer Society," in *The Anti-Aesthetic: Essays on Postmodern culture,* edited by Hal Foster (Port Townsend, Wash.: Bay Press, 1983), p. 119.

29. *Ibid.,* p. 119.

30. Bernard A. Hirsch, "Self-Hatred and Spiritual Corruption in *House Made of Dawn,*" *Western American Literature* 17 (February 1983), p. 310.

31. Jean Francois Lyotard, *The Postmodern Condition: A Report on Knowledge,* p. 27.

32. Terry Eagleton, "Capitalism, Modernism, and Postmodernism," in *Against the Grain,* p. 144.

33. James W. Coleman, "Beyond the Reach of Love and Caring: Black Life in Toni Morrison's *Song of Solomon,*" *Obsidian II: Black Literature in Review* I (Winter 1986): pp. 151–152.

34. Chiara Spallino, "*Song of Solomon:* An Adventure in Structure," *Callaloo* 8 (Fall 1985): pp. 510–511.

35. James Barbour and Thomas Quirk, "Introduction," in *Romanticism: Critical Essays in American Literature,* edited by James Barbour and Thomas Quirk (New York: Garland Publishing Inc., 1986), p. 17.

36. Christina Davis, "Interview with Toni Morrison," *Presence Africaine* 145 (1988): p. 144.

37. Martha Bayles, "Special Effects, Special Pleading," *New Criterion* 6 (January 1988): pp. 37, 38.

38. David Cowart, "Faulkner and Joyce in Morrison's *Song of Solomon,*" *American Literature* 62 (March 1990): pp. 87, 92.

39. Barbara Christian, "Community and Nature: The Novels of Toni Morrison," *The Journal of Ethnic Studies* 7 (Winter 1980): p. 65.

40. Norris Clark, "Flying Black: Toni Morrison's *The Bluest Eye, Sula* and *Song of Solomon,*" *Minority Voices* 4 (Fall 1980): p. 51.

41. Harry Reed, "Toni Morrison, *Song of Solomon* and Black Cultural Nationalism," *The Centennial Review* 32 (Winter 1988): p. 52. For other such ideological readings, see also Joyce Wegs, "Toni Morrison's *Song of Solomon:* A Blues Song," *Essays in Literature* 9 (Fall 1982); Ralph Story, "An Excursion into the Black World: The 'Seven Days,'" *Black American Literature Forum* 23 (Spring 1989); Harue Minakawa, "The Motif of Sweetness in Toni Morrison's *Song of Solomon,*" *Kyushu American Literature* 26 (1985); Allison A. Bulsterbaum, "'Sugarman Gone Home': Folksong in Toni Morrison's *Song of Solomon,*" *Arkansas Philogical Association* 10 (1984); Philip M. Royster, "Milkman's Flying: The Scapegoat Transcended in Toni Morrison's *Song of Solomon,*" *CLA Journal* 24 (June 1982).

3

The Limits of Modernity:
Richard Rodriguez's *Hunger of Memory* and Andrea Lee's *Sarah Phillips*

Two of the most common features of literary modernism are the radical rejection of history and the hostility between high art and mass culture. First, for a modern individual to experience the raw, unmediated present, he is required to reject the frozen structures of understanding inherited from the past. The rejection of history constitutes a revelation of time itself, for there is an epochal shift in the very meaning and modality of temporality, a qualitative break in our ideological style of living history.[1] In the modern project, there is what Irving Howe calls a "bitter impatience with the whole apparatus of cognition and the limiting assumption of rationality."[2] A writer imbued with the modernist spirit will be predisposed toward experiment, if only because he or she needs to make visibly dramatic his or her break from tradition. His or her theme will tend to emphasize temporality, the process of becoming, rather than being in space and time. An individual infused with the modern impulse wants emancipation from all traditional social roles and traditional modes of servitude because they keep the self stifled and imprisoned.

Second, literary modernism or modern art aspires to save the dignity and autonomy of art and life from the culture of everyday life, from the vulgarities and contaminations of mass culture, and from the constraints of traditional culture, which denies individuality. This means that modernism has been obliged to withdraw from what an ever-expanding commercial taste has managed to appropriate and then market as "high art." Literary modernism promises a new life, and the "new" becomes the chief emblem of positive value.

A second way that writers of color in America since the 1960s resolve the modern imperative in their respective racial groups is to break with the prevalent styles of perception of the past with the hope of creating a new and more authentic style. Unlike Morrison's *Song of Solomon* and Momaday's *House Made of Dawn,* which break with the prevalent styles of modernists and retreat to an ideologically and racially constructed tradition of the pre-modern historical past, *Hunger of Memory* (1982) by Richard Rodriguez, *Sarah Phillips* (1984) by Andrea Lee, *The Joy Luck Club* (1989) by Amy Tan, *Typical American* (1991) by Gish Jen, and *The House on Mango Street* (1984) and *Woman Hollering Creek and other Stories* (1991) by Sandra Cisneros reject the values and conventions of the historical past and promise new life. They embrace modernity because they "had to pass through it [modernity] before the lost unity of life and art could be reconstructed on a higher plane."[3] The protagonists and heroines in these texts want to achieve some historically unmediated encounter with the real that will compliment their own subjective experiences.

Both the autobiographical narrator in *Hunger of Memory* and the heroine, Sarah Phillips, in *Sarah Phillips*—who together are my focus in this chapter—along with other characters, such as Dale in David Henry Hwang's *FOB,* who rejects his Chinese-ness, Ralph and Theresa in Gish Jen's *Typical American,* who reject their Chinese past, Teresa in James Welch's *Winter in the Blood,* who represses her Native American past, Kate in James Welch's *The Death of Jim Loney,* who also rejects the Native American past, Robert in David Henry Hwang's *Family Devotion,* who rejects his ethnic identity, and Ricardo in Arturo Islas's *Migrant Souls,* who rejects his Mexican heritage "to live according to the myths of North America," have existential crisis moments. These are moments when these heroines and protagonists can assume ultimate responsibility for their acts of free will without external moral principles of authority to tell them what is right or wrong. These are moments when, according to Paul de Man, a radical rejection of history becomes necessary to the fulfillment not only of their freedom, their "human destiny," but also as the "condition for action." Their break with country, community, family, or the racial past is the radical impulse that stands behind their "genuine humanity."[4]

But, although both repress the past, neither the autobiographical narrator in *Hunger of Memory* nor Sarah Phillips in *Sarah Phillips* is able to arrive at a new style, to have a successful unmediated encounter with the real. Unlike Charles Wright's protagonist in *The Messenger* (1963), who achieves an authentic life as a way of coping with modernity, both Sarah and the autobiographical narrator lose their modernist impulse, reach an impasse, and become symbols of alienation and dehumanization. Finally, both the autobiographical narrator in *Hunger of Memory* and Sarah Phillips atrophy and become entrapped in upper-middle-class conventions and values, or imitations of them, thereby repressing their racial selves and their subjective individuality. It will take a postmodern vision by these two writers that recognizes, accepts, and incorporates America's diverse cultural forms and lifestyles, which engage mass culture to accommodate their characters' subjective individualities.

Rodriguez in *Hunger of Memory* reverberates against the prevalent style of Chicano cultural nationalists who make an ideology of working-class Mexican American culture and then proceed to define Mexican American social reality and all Mexican American experiences against that ideology. In *Hunger of Memory*, Rodriguez revolts against bilingual education, Affirmative Action, and Chicano cultural nationalists because they assume a definition of Chicano or Mexican American culture that excludes his subjective lived experience. Rodriguez in *Hunger of Memory* also reverberates against the dominant society's institutions, which ignore his subjective experience as a scholarship boy and define or label him as a minority student.

The style or narrative technique that the narrator Richard Rodriguez uses to define his modern subjective experience is Richard Hoggart's concept of the scholarship boy: "I found, in his description of the scholarship boy, myself. For the first time I realized that there were other students like me, and so I was able to frame the meaning of my academic success, its consequent price—the loss."[5] The scholarship boy chooses to move from the intimacy and security of his working-class culture and join the middle class by pursuing an education. He moves between his home and the classroom, which are at cultural extremes. Within the family, the scholarship boy has the intense pleasure of intimacy; he has his family's consolation in dealing with feelings of public alienation. At school, he is instructed to trust reason, the intellect. From his parents, he learns to trust spontaneity and instinctive ways of knowing; he is taught to express and trust his feelings. In the classroom, his teachers emphasize the value of reasoning and reflection.

According to Richard Hoggart in *The Uses of Literacy,* the scholarship boy comes from the working class, whose members are for the most part destined to academic failure. Most working-class students, he believes, are barely, if ever, changed by the learning experiences of the classroom. It is only the exception who succeeds and becomes a scholarship boy or girl. First, the working-class student—with the intense gregariousness of the working-class child—has difficulty adjusting to the required discipline of the classroom. Unlike middle-class students, the working-class student goes home and sees in his parents a way of life that is not only different from, but actually starkly opposed to, that of the classroom. It is only with "extraordinary determination and the great assistance of others—at home and at school"—that a working class student can succeed. (p. 47)

Richard Rodriguez the narrator interprets his life, or imposes a structure on his life, by using Hoggart's concept of the scholarship boy. As he reconstructs his life in *Hunger of Memory,* he moves from the intimacy and security of his family's working-class Mexican American culture to the American middle class through education. He moves between his home and the classroom, which belong to two different conceptions of time and space. Richard spends the first six years of his life in a close-knit, working-class family where Spanish is spoken exclusively. Because he sees only Mexican Americans speaking Spanish, he perceives it as a private language that connotes "closeness" and "intimacy." To Richard the narrator, the family's Spanish voice insists: *"You belong here. We are family members. Related. Special to one another."* (p. 18) Richard's home is one where "the only regular guests were [his] relations."

The family's culture and language insulate and marginalize Richard and his family from the language and the cognitive style of the rest of the community, including Anglos and the general English-speaking American public. Anything outside this insulated Spanish home and culture is considered the "other." Until Richard is seven years old, he does not know the names of other children who live on his street. To survive in the English-speaking American public, Richard's parents spoke a "hesitant, accented, not always grammatical English. And they would have to strain—their tense bodies—to catch the sense of what was rapidly said by *los gringos*." (p. 13)

Entering elementary school, which is one of the carriers of modern, secularized consciousness, Richard encounters his first crisis. He comes into contact with individuals—teachers and students—who are agents of modern consciousness. His "class-mates were white, many the children of doctors and lawyers and business executives." In these contacts, Richard becomes conscious of another conception of time and space. And with these contacts, his transformation from a working-class Mexican American student to a middle-class American or scholarship boy begins. The nuns ask his parents not to speak Spanish to him at home, and Richard forgets or represses his Spanish. The conse-quence is an alienation from the communicative infrastructure of everyday working-class Mexican American life. Thus, he learns classroom English and acquires a public identity: "One day in school I raised my hand to volunteer an answer. I spoke out in a loud voice. And I did not think it remarkable when the entire class understood. That day, I moved very far from the disadvan-taged child I had been only days earlier. The belief, the calming assurance that I belonged in public, had at last taken hold." (p. 22) In internalizing the language and cognitive style of the general English-speaking American public, Richard the narrator is able to see himself as an American citizen with a normative public identity. This new public identity will give him, he believes, the freedom to seek the rights and opportunities for full public individuality.

Of course, Richard's conscious decision to repress his working-class Mexican American past and to become the exception and succeed as a scholarship boy costs him enormously. It cuts him off from his parents. First, there is less communication with his parents. Then, as Richard and his siblings learn more English and receive more education in American schools, they share fewer words with their parents. Eventually, Richard develops a psychological block and represses his Spanish entirely because it is a painful reminder of how much he has actually changed. Second, there is the loss of closeness and intimacy that had once existed at home: "We remained a loving family, but one greatly changed. No longer so close; no longer bound tight by the pleasing and troubling knowledge of our public separateness." (p. 23)

But Richard the narrator is not able to repress completely Spanish or his family's working-class Mexican American culture. When he hears Spanish spoken in public, he is reminded of his repressed past: "Sometimes in public, hearing a stranger, I'd hark back to my past. A Mexican farmworker approached me downtown to ask directions to somewhere. ... And his voice summoned deep longing. Another time, standing beside my mother in the visiting room of a Carmelite convent ... I heard several Spanish-speaking nuns ... assure us that yes, yes, we were remembered, all our family was remembered in their prayers." (pp. 25–26) The Spanish voices he hears in public recalls "the golden age of [his] youth." Later, there are other moments when he feels guilty or fails to repress successfully Spanish and his working-class Mexican heritage. "I evaded nostalgia. Tried hard to forget. But one does not forget by trying to forget. One only remembers." (p. 50) But to become a successful scholarship boy, he cannot give in; he must continue to repress this past.

It is only after Richard the narrator reaches a certain level of success—after he has completed the graduate work toward his Ph.D. in Renaissance Literature and is researching his dissertation—that he can gesture nostalgically toward the past. He grows nostalgic because his success as a scholarship boy, as a scholar, becomes precarious. Although he has successfully abandoned his past, he does not feel that he has successfully entered the "community of academics." Until the moment that he has this relevation in the British Museum, Richard's distance from the past has been measured by how successfully he has become a scholarship boy: "The boy who first entered a classroom barely able to speak English, twenty years later concluded his studies in the stately quiet of the reading room in the British Museum." (p. 43)

But, at the zenith of his success as a scholarship boy, Richard the narrator encounters another crisis. He feels alienated from the public identity he has adopted: "I found myself in the British Museum, at first content, reading English Renaissance literature.

But then came the crisis: the domed silence; the dusty pages of books all around me; the days accumulating in lists of obsequious footnotes; the wandering doubts about the value of scholarship. My year in Britain came to an end and I rushed to 'come home.' Then quickly discovered that I could not. Could not cast off the culture I had assumed." (p. 160) This means that Richard has not been successfully assimilated into his American public identity, or has not become Hoggart's acclimated scholarship boy. He has not become the successful middle-class American male that he claims to have become.

Despite the fact that Richard the narrator informs the reader constantly that success and gain for the working-class Mexican American come only through education, he never shows the success or the gain—certainly not at the personal level. Early in his life, Richard discerns the need to reject Spanish and working-class Mexican American culture because they would doom him to failure. Only through education and a public identity does he have the opportunity to succeed, to become successful. But what does success mean for Richard? Existential freedom? A form of personal speech? One's own unique style? Careerism? Celebrity?

According to *Hunger of Memory,* being a scholarship boy does not mean existential freedom, a form of personal speech or one's own unique style. The scholarship boy is not original. "The scholarship boy is a very bad student. He is the great mimic; a collector of thoughts, not a thinker; the very last person in class who ever feels obliged to have an opinion of his own." (p. 67) Because Richard is preoccupied with being a scholarship boy—that is, imitating, rather than assessing critically, the classical education offered him—he represses his own desires, his own alienated modern experiences, his own individual style—the very things that are the true sources of creativity and originality. In short, the convention of the scholarship boy does not "fit" Rodriguez's modern experience—basically that of being torn between two cultures—for no social role in modern times can be a perfect fit.

Additionally, Richard the narrator's concept of education, which he labels a success, appears vacuous. It does not provide for intellectual growth or personal development. He reads books not because they will offer him growth personally and intellectually, but because they represent to him the image of the educated person. "What *did* I see in my books? I had the idea that they were crucial for academic success, though I couldn't have said exactly how or why. In the sixth grade I simply concluded that what gave a book its value was some major idea or theme it contained. If that core essence could be mined and memorized, I would become learned like my teachers." (p. 62)

For Richard, books and the concept of the scholarship boy are not vehicles he can use to find a language or style to articulate his own experiences of alienation and fragmentation. They do not become the tools he can use to refashion consciousness, or to remake the self, or to develop a "new" life. Instead, they exist as objects that allow him to escape his existence as an existential being who is caught between two American cultures. They become ornaments to validate his adopted image of the middle-class American male. "When I read William Saroyan's *The Human Comedy,* I was immediately pleased by the narrator's warmth and the charm of his story. ... Another summer I [was] determined to read all of the novels of Dickens. Reading his fat novels, I loved the feeling I got—after the first hundred pages—of being at home in a fictional world where I knew the names of characters and cared about what was going to happen to them. And it bothered me that I was forced away at the conclusion, when the fiction closed tight, like a fortune teller's fist—the futures of all the major characters really resolved." (p. 63)

In this response to Dickens's novels, Richard gives a sanitized reading of them. He omits or excludes the social criticism that is so much a part of Dickens's fiction. He excludes any discussion of the horror of poverty and urbanization that is evident in Dickens's "fat novels." He represses Dickens's criticism of an economic system that makes slave laborers out of children. Lastly, he ignores the harsh realities of urban life that Dickens describes in minute detail. Wouldn't some of these unpleasant features of human exploitation in Dickens be likely to remind Richard of the plight of his parents and other working-class Mexican Americans whose work consists of a "dark succession of warehouse, cannery, and factory jobs."?

Entrapped in a suit that does not fit, or in the image of Hoggart's concept of the scholarship boy, Richard's portrait of himself lacks any sense of perception or vision. Because, as a scholarship boy, he is forced to be "hollow within," he takes on the perspective or point of view of the teacher in his presence or of the book he is currently reading: "I lacked a point of view when I read. Rather, I read in order to acquire a point of view." (p. 64) And although the adult Richard the narrator criticizes this method of learning, Richard, the author, shows nothing from his adult life to indicate that he is no longer "hollow within," that he has a larger scheme or perspective to view his life.

There is only one instance in *Hunger of Memory* where Richard the narrator speculates on the significance of being a scholarship boy. When he returns home to live with his parents after spending a year at the British Museum, he surmises that being a scholarship boy allows him to think abstractly and conceptually about himself and his parents. "The ability to consider experience so abstractly allowed me to shape into desire what would otherwise have remained indefinite, meaningless longing in the British Museum. If, because of my schooling, I had grown culturally separated from my parents, my education finally had given me ways of speaking and caring about that fact." (p. 72) But there is no evidence in the text to indicate that his thinking "abstractly and conceptually" is a sign of intellectual or personal growth.

More importantly, although Richard the narrator claims to be a successful scholarship boy and a middle-class American male who has assimilated into the dominant American public identity and becomes nostalgic while researching and writing his Ph.D. dissertation in Renaissance literature at the British Museum, a close scrutiny of the portrait of his life as it is reconstructed in *Hunger of Memory* proves otherwise. *Hunger of Memory* shows unconsciously a Richard Rodriguez who has always been marginal to the experiences of the middle-class, white, American male because he is a person of color. The problem is that the convention of the scholarship boy that he imposes on his life forbids him to talk about his private self, his subjective modern experience. Discussing Richard's marginalization from his Mexican American working-class background, Ramon Saldivar argues that Richard "feels himself capable of functioning only as an isolated and private individual, deprived of any organic connection with his ethnic group, his social class, and finally even his own family. He is a solitary man, and he does not feel himself part of the social whole. Privacy and isolation are his essential features, even when he functions in the public arena."[6]

Thus, as Saldivar makes clear, it is the "isolated and private" Richard who is marginalized from both working-class Mexican American culture and middle-class white America. White Americans single him out for ridicule because of his dark skin: "In public I occasionally heard racial slurs. Complete strangers would yell out at me. ... A boy pedaled by and announced matter-of-factly, 'I pee on dirty Mexicans.'" (p. 117)

Furthermore, unlike most middle-class, white, Americans who have no identities outside of their class, Richard is fully aware that his origin does not derive from middle-class America, but from a racial group that is discriminated against because of its skin color. Growing up, he listens to his parents talk about the mistreatment of Mexicans in California border towns. He hears the stories of his relatives being refused admittance to an all-white swimming pool because they are brown. Also, Richard's interest in the "progress of the southern black Civil Rights movement" shows a profound personal identification with the dispossessed, the downtrodden.

Also, more importantly, nowhere in his education, or in his movement in the dominant American society, has he been perceived as a middle-class American. Throughout elementary and secondary school, Richard is perceived a being different from the middle-class American norm. During elementary school, when he walks home with his white classmates, Richard encounters daily racial remarks. "Such remarks would be said so casually that I wouldn't quickly realize that they were being addressed to me. When I did, I would be paralyzed with embarrassment, unable to return the insult." (p. 117) In high school, he is withdrawn and marginal. He does not fit in socially; he avoids school dances and other activities.

Even in college, he is perceived differently. At Stanford University, he is aware that he is different from the "golden children of Western America's upper middle class." (p. 130) Unlike them, he notices and feels connection with the Mexican American janitors and gardeners working on campus. On a visit to the home of one of his upper-middle-class white friends, he becomes conscious of, and identifies with, the black maid. As a college student at Stanford and later at Columbia and Berkeley, he is reminded that he is not just another middle-class American male. At Berkeley, he recognizes that his white classmates do not perceive him as being one of them: "To many persons around him, he appears too much the academic. There may be some things about him that recall his beginnings—his shabby clothes; his persistent poverty; or his dark skin (in those cases when it symbolizes his parents' disadvantaged condition). ... " (p. 65) The Hispanic students at Berkeley also remind Richard that he is different, that he is not just a middle-class American male. When they need someone to teach a minority literature course at a barrio community center on Saturdays, they ask Richard and he refuses.

Finally, Richard's experience as a scholarship boy and his internalization of the cognitive style and the values of high art and canonical Western literature ("I have taken Caliban's advice. I have stolen their books. I will have some run of this isle." [p. 3]) alienate him from other Mexican American students. Richard feels uncomfortable with Mexican American students who call themselves Chicano—"a term lower-class Mexican Americans had long used to name themselves"—who embrace working-class Mexican American culture, who talk loudly in Spanish on campus, and who graduate "to work among lower-class Hispanics at barrio clinics or legal aid centers." They belong to the working-class Mexican American culture that he has rejected. Richard sees those Mexican American students who come to Berkeley through an Affirmative Action program as constituting an experience that is different from his. To him, they are minority students who, unlike him, are alienated from public life. He is a scholarship boy who has used education to become a middle-class American. They have come to the university in a group; he has come to the university alone. They are still tied to their parents' working-class culture; he has rejected his parents culturally.

But, as the above discussion shows, experientially, Richard the narrator is not a middle-class American male. His alienation from his own working-class background and from middle-class white Americans constitutes his subjective modern experience, which goes unresolved in *Hunger of Memory*. Richard never attempts to define his own existence, to create a new life outside these two social groupings. Instead, he imposes Hoggart's concept of the scholarship boy on his existential existence and it fails, thereby forcing him into an impasse. The impasse comes when Richard goes on the job market, where he is treated not as a successful scholarship boy who has made the transformation from the working class to the middle class, but as a minority who is an excellent candidate for an Affirmative Action position.

Thus, he enters another crisis. Realizing that he has not been able to assert successfully his adopted public identity as a "non-white reader of Spenser and Milton and Austen," Richard the narrator rejects all minority jobs offered. "I wanted to teach; I wanted to read; I wanted this life [academic life]. But I had to protest. How? Disqualify myself from the profession as long as Affirmative Action continued? Romantic exile? But I had to. Yes. I found the horizon again. It was calm." (p. 171) He also rejects Affirmative Action—the government program that aims at making higher education accessible to the poor, or to "socially disadvantaged" minorities—because it offers reforms solely in racial, rather than class terms: "No one seemed troubled by the fact that those who were in the best position to benefit from such reforms were those blacks [and other minorities such as himself] least victimized by racism or any other social oppression—those culturally, if not always economically, of the middle class." (p. 145) And with this crisis he reaches another impasse. Is the problematics of his subjective modern experience ever resolved? Does he ever find a voice and a narrative to capture successfully his modern experience?

Hunger of Memory's uncritical acceptance of the ideology of the scholarship boy, and of the middle-class American male as the norm and the *only* option for success for working-class Mexican Americans in the United States, denies the options and possibilities presented by the emergence of various forms of "otherness" in the American cultural sphere—"otherness" that would give Richard the critical space to critique canonical Western literature, the middle-class American male convention, and the concept of the scholarship boy. "It was especially the art, writing, film-making and criticism of women and minority artists," argues Andreas Huyssen in *After the Great Divide,* "with their recuperation of buried and mutilated traditions, their emphasis on exploring forms of gender- and race-based subjectivity in aesthetic productions and experiences, and their refusal to be limited to standard and canonization, which added a whole dimension to the critique of high modernism and to the emergence of alternative forms of culture."[7] This pluralizing rhetoric of postmodernism has something to do with the sociologically significant emergence of women, people of color, and gays in the cultural sphere—an emergence that rejects the abstract category of single otherness and undermines the legitimacy and sanctity of a canon or tradition that defines the middle-class American male as the norm. In the culturally diverse postmodern American society echoed in Huyssen's comments, the concepts of the scholarship boy and of the middle-class American convention become not the *only* American forms of culture, but two among many forms of American culture.

A Richard Rodriguez who had the vision to recognize, accept, and incorporate America's diverse cultural forms and lifestyles would have enormous freedom. First, he would no longer be "annoyed ... to hear [Chicano] students on campus loudly talking in Spanish," for Spanish would be considered one of America's many languages. Second, he would accept the urban black teenagers whose voices he cannot "inch past" because they have the sounds of the outsider, because they would be recognized as not outsiders but a part of America's rich, diverse population. They represent one of America's many diverse public identities. Third, with a vision that incorporates America's diverse cultural forms, Richard could embrace bilingual education and black English because their "feelings of public separateness" and their "brazen intimacy" would be viewed as other cultural forms along with those of the Italian Americans, Jewish Americans, and Greek Americans who also contribute to America's diverse population.

More importantly, a healthy postmodern American vision that incorporated all of America's diverse cultural forms and public identities would allow Richard the narrator to accept his own existential condition as a being who is caught between two American cultural forms. He could become proud of his brown body; he could engage his guilt for not being macho, admit his "sexual anxieties" and his "physical insecurity." (p. 130) He could embrace not only his educational achievements or the concept of the scholarship boy, but also his working-class Mexican American culture and the Spanish language. All could coexist. Lastly, with a vision that incorporated all of America's diverse cultural forms, he could devise a definition of his own life that was in harmony with his own lived experiences.

But rather than seek existential freedom, a new life in the plurality of American cultures, Richard the narrator supersedes the inadequate model of the scholarship boy with another model, that of the American upper-middle-class celebrity, a model which has its own features of fame, fortune, and the good life. It is a commodified and reified status, disconnected from history and social reality, that attempts to transcend race and class. It is only as a celebrity that Richard achieves his Americanization. "In the past months I have found myself in New York. In Los Angeles. Working. With Money. Among people with money. And at leisure—a weekend guest in Connecticut; at a cocktail party in Bel Air." (p. 3) His Americanization is reinforced on those occasions when he has been travelling abroad for several weeks and returns to hear "the high sound of [middle-class] American voices." He listens to those voices with pleasure, "for [their sound] is now the sound of [his] society—a reminder of home." (p. 14)

As a celebrity, Richard's dark complexion becomes not the reason for ridicule as it is for working-class Mexican Americans, but as a "mark of his pleasure." The hotel clerk in London wants to know if he has just arrived from skiing in Switzerland. The bellhop in New York wants to know if he has been tanning in the Caribbean. His "complexion assumes its significance from the context of his life." If he had entered the hotel through the service door, his dark complexion would have been perceived differently. He would have been considered a working-class Mexican American, or a Chicano. But this new model of the celebrity fails to "fit" Richard's modern subjective experience of being torn between two cultures.

Thus, with the failure of this model, he is forced into a final impasse, which the text never resolves. When Richard the narrator appears on the lecture circuit as a celebrity, he is immediately historicized by members of the audience. He is confronted with the label of the minority, which he has rejected. Because he is "marked by indelible color," he is anointed by some white Americans "to play out for them some drama of ancestral reconciliation." (p. 5) They define him not as a celebrity but as a racial minority.

To be called a celebrity means that you are famous or known for something. Richard the narrator is not famous or known because he is a successful scholarship boy. There are many scholarship boys who are not known. Richard is a celebrity because he, a Mexican American, takes positions on such social issues as Affirmative Action, bilingual education, and cultural diversity which generate the official order, the ideological position of those Americans who take a single hegemonic approach to American life and culture. He, as a Mexican American, is a celebrity because he opposes those people of color and women who threaten the stability and sanctity of a Western, white, male-dominated literary canon and tradition: "In 1974 I published an essay admitting unease over becoming the beneficiary of affirmative action. There was another article against affirmative action in 1977. One more soon after. At times, I proposed contrary ideas; consistent always with the admission that I was no longer like socially disadvantaged Hispanic-Americans. But this admission, made in national magazines, only brought me a greater degree of success. A published minority student, I won a kind of celebrity. In my mail were admiring letters from right-wing politicians. There were also invitations to address conferences of college administrators or government officials. My essays served as my 'authority' to speak at the Marriot Something or the Sheraton Somewhere." (p. 148)

Richard the narrator's essays, which draw "admiring letters from right-wing politicians," echo the conservative American trend to repress, and therefore reestablish hegemony over, the dissenting voices of women, gays, and people of color who are demanding the right to speak for themselves, in their own voices, and have those voices accepted as legitimate.

Just as Richard the narrator in *Hunger of Memory* fails to ferret out a new life or style that would compliment his modern, subjective experience, Sarah Phillips in Andrea Lee's *Sarah Phillips* also fails in her attempt to have a successful unmediated encounter with the real, to refashion her consciousness, or to find a unique style that would be in harmony with her subjective lived experiences. She too will need a postmodern vision which recognizes, accepts, and incorporates America's diverse cultural forms and lifestyles to accommodate her subjective individuality.

Andrea Lee in *Sarah Phillips* revolts against the prevalent style of the old-fashioned black bourgeoisie—a style that attempts "poignant imitations of high society, acting with genuine gallantry in the struggle for Civil Rights."[8] Lee assaults the old-fashioned black bourgeoisie by incorporating themes such as interracial dating, interracial sex, easy nudity, communal living, the disdain for career, or any combination of these possibilities, which are antithetical to its ruling code, norms, values, and sensibilities. *Sarah Phillips* opens in Paris with a detailed description of a young black woman, Sarah Phillips, who is involved in a romantic relationship with a Frenchman, Henri. They clutch "a private exotic vision in the various beds where [they] made love." (p. 5) Although Sarah is Henri's girl, she, "in the spirit of *Bruderschaft*," spent nights with Alain and Roger, friends who have "grown up with Henri in the city of Nancy."

The novel's heroine, Sarah, revolts against the old-fashioned black bourgeoisie because it excludes her lived, subjective experiences. Therefore, to ferret out a new mode of perception, Sarah attempts to escape from historical imperatives. But, as with Richard Rodriguez in *Hunger of Memory,* Andrea Lee in *Sarah Phillips* lacks the vision to develop Sarah's own style, to refashion her consciousness, to live an existential, authentic existence. Therefore, by the end of the novel, Lee's Sarah returns precariously, knowledgeably, and more wisely to the values and conventions of the old-fashioned black bourgeoisie.

To show how Sarah Phillips comes to reject her past and seek out in Paris an authentic existence, Lee in *Sarah Phillips* presents Sarah's life as a series of moments, rather than as a planned progression of events or incidents moving toward a defined terminus. In dealing with the chaos of modern life, Lee's *Sarah Phillips* structurally takes on the appearance, and sometimes the substance, of that chaos. The text focuses on a series of moments that contribute to Sarah's expatriation to Paris.

Although Sarah grows up in the "hermetic world of the old-fashioned black bourgeoisie," she belongs to the first generation of African Americans who are "educated in newly integrated [or predominantly white] schools." The experience in the newly integrated schools alienates and cuts her off from the experience of her parents. Thus, like Richard Rodriguez the narrator, Sarah is caught between two worlds. Physically, she lives in one world, and cognitively and intellectually she lives in another. Thus, she becomes alienated from both worlds. As a modern subject who needs a temporal unification between the past and the future in the present, she finds herself without social identification and outside any historical tradition. This alienation and fragmentation, this lack of historical continuity constitute Sarah's subjective, modern experience. It is this modern experience that the text seeks to resolve.

Unlike her parents. who grew up in middle-class black neighborhoods in South Philadelphia, Sarah grows up on Franklin Place, in an insulated, black suburban community that has the appearance of being ahistorical. It is a neighborhood that "lay in a Philadelphia suburb. The town was green and pretty, but had the constrained, slightly unreal atmosphere of a colony or a foreign enclave; that was because the people who owned the rambling houses behind the shrubbery were black. For them—doctors, ministers, teachers who had grown up in Philadelphia row houses—the lawns and tree-lined streets represented the fulfillment of a fantasy long deferred, and acted as a barrier against the predictable cruelty of the world." (p. 39) She attends a predominantly white Quaker elementary school, preps at the prestigious Prescott school for girls, where she is the only black student, and attends Ivy League Harvard University. Through education, other social institutions, and her daily social contact with white members of the upper middle class, Sarah, like Richard the narrator in *Hunger of Memory,* internalizes the norms and values, the cognitive style, of this race and class. This newly acquired cognitive style, along with her enlightenment education, which embraces the ideas of progress and activity and seeks to break with history and tradition, alienates Sarah from the world of her parents.

The world of Sarah's parents consists of "prosperous, conservative, generally light skinned" blacks who spend much of their time and energy attempting "poignant imitations of [white] high society." Unlike Sarah, her parents attended all-black private schools and considered New African Baptist Church, where her father is the minister, their "spiritual home." They grew up in segregated black middle-class communities in Philadelphia and are very active in the Civil Rights movement—mostly because they see their present and future destiny as being inseparable from that of the rest of the African American communities.

In addition, Sarah's parents and the old-fashioned black bourgeoisie are materialistic and socially rigid. They are very conscious of class, with special concerns for such material possessions as houses, perfumes, clothes, food, etc. Because the old-fashioned black bourgeoisie is preoccupied with attaining or imitating the decorum of high society, it allows nothing creative or innovative or different (from high society) to enter its lifestyle. For example, New African Baptist Church is not the kind of traditional Baptist church where "shouting was a normal part of the service." New African, like any other high society church, considers shouting an "incomprehensibly barbarous behavior." Lastly, the old-fashioned black bourgeoisie is exclusionary in its opposition to interracial dating and interracial marriage. When Matthew brings his white Jewish girlfriend, Martha, home for dinner, his mother wants to know why they cannot date their own kind.

In addition, Sarah's insulated and almost ahistorical life in the suburb marginalizes her to her parents' historical tradition. She knows very little about the Civil Rights movement and African American history and life. Although her father is integrally involved in the 1963 March on Washington, Sarah has only vague ideas about the March. For her, it is something "happening at a distance." At Prescott, she is "embarrassed to have a parent [her father] who freely admitted to going to jail in Alabama." Sarah also finds it difficult to picture the slaves as her ancestors. When her parents tell her about "the perilous region below the Mason-Dixon Line," Sarah has—"beyond a self-conscious excitement"—"little idea of what they meant." (p. 39)

Sarah's suburban upbringing particularly insulates her from the darker realities of black life. It insulates her from what Cornel West calls "the ragged edges of the Real, of *Necessity,* not being able to eat, not having shelter, not having health care." She has no sense "of what it means to be impinged upon by structures of oppression."[9] She is living in what Barbara Ehrenreich calls the "final stage of material affluence—defined by cars, television, and backyard barbecue pits." Looking from the perspective of Franklin Place, Sarah sees "only an endless suburb, with no horizon, no frontier, in sight." She believes "that America had stepped outside of history."[10] But Sarah is not able to escape completely from history, or the ragged edges of the real. Sarah encounters, intermittently, characters and experiences that serve to historicize her; that is, that force her to at least make a symbolic acknowledgement of her place in a broader historical reality,[11] that invoke her cultural past or remind her of the harsher realities of life. She is completely overwhelmed when Mrs. Jeller, one of her father's parishioners, tells her and her mother about how by the time she was fourteen years old, she [Mrs. Jeller] had been raped, pregnant, married, and separated. Mrs. Jeller's story forces Sarah to deal with "the complicated possibilities of [her] own flesh—possibilities of corruption, confused pleasure, even death." (p. 85) Sarah's encounter with the Gypsies again forces her to acknowledge her connection with a larger, complicated world. "It was not that I had really feared being stolen: it was more, in fact, that [the Gypsies] seemed to have stolen something from me. Nothing looked different, yet everything was, and for the first time Franklin Place seemed geniunely connected to a world that was neither insulated nor serene." (p. 46)

And just as the Gypsies and Mrs. Jeller expose Sarah to a life and a world beyond her "insulated and serene" world, her trip to Camp Grayfeather also exposes her to the harsh realities of inner city life. At Camp, Sarah's norm is the "other black kids" who "are overprotected or horribly spoiled products of comfortable suburban childhoods." Sarah sees the arrival of the Thunderbirds, a black teenage gang from Wilmington, Delaware, at the Camp as a thrill. "For a day and a half, the Thunderbirds, like a small natural disaster, had given an edge of crazy danger to life at Grayfeather." (p. 79) But these encounters with the harsher realities of life remain "thrills" because Sarah is not able to integrate them into her vision of existence, into her insulated and serene world.

Furthermore, Sarah is equally misplaced in her parents' "spiritual home," New African Baptist Church. Sarah's enlightened education, which is a part of a secular progressive movement that has sought the demystification and desacralization of knowledge and social organization in order to liberate individuals, causes her to view New African Baptist Church as belonging to a "past that came to seem embarrassingly primitive" as she grows older. Because her education puts her on the margin, inside yet outside, she has a perspective that allows her to deconstruct the church's rituals as contrivance, as something that is functional. Therefore, she dispels "the mysteries of worship with a gleeful secular eye." She believes that "the decision to make a frightening and embarrassing backward plunge into a pool of sanctified water [means] that one [has] received a summons to Christianity as unmistakable as the blare of an automobile horn," but it is not a call she hears. (pp. 19–20)

Sarah's misplacement and alienation in New African Baptist Church force her to seek social identification and historical continuity and traditions elsewhere. She identifies with marginal heroines in the Bible—seeing herself as "a romantically isolated religious heroine, a sort of self-made Baptist martyr." (p. 29) She also seeks social identification through reading. "I would read with the kind of ferocious appetite that belongs only to garden shrews, bookish children. ... I plunged into fairy tales, adult novels, murder mysteries, poetry, and magazines." (p. 31)

Sarah's final break with New African Baptist Church, and the first step she takes in rejecting the values and conventions of the old-fashioned black bourgeoisie, comes with her refusal to accept baptism, which "fascinated and disturbed [her] more than anything else at church." (p. 23) Despite Aunt Bessie's physical attempts to take her body and "soul to the Lord," Sarah wins in her first battle with a grownup. When her father learns of her refusal, he recognizes her as different, as an individual for the first time. "I kept remembering the way my father had looked when he'd heard what had happened. He hadn't looked severe or angry, but merely puzzled, and he had regarded me with the same puzzled expression, as if he'd just discovered that I existed and didn't know what to do with me." (pp. 28–29) Later in life, Sarah reflects and acknowledges the "peculiar gift of freedom" her father had given her "through his silence" on the issue of baptism.

Although her parents give her this "peculiar gift of freedom," they also contribute to her misplacement, her alienation and fragmentation, her lack of social identification. They fail to integrate Sarah into their tradition. When Sarah expresses an interest in attending the March on Washington, her mother "immediately squelche[s] the idea for fear of stampedes and what she called 'exposures'—by which she meant not sun and wind but germs from possibly unwashed strangers." (p. 51.) Sarah and her brother, Matthew, watch the March on Washington on television. Again, Sarah, in watching the March on television, uses her imagination to ferret out a place for herself in a broader historical reality, to seek out a social identification. "Now, suddenly, a tremendous picture appeared in my mind, as clear and severe in its lighting as one of those old battle engravings that swarm with distinctly uniformed soldiers the size of fleas. I saw a million men, their faces various shades of black, white, and brown, marching together between the blazing marble monuments. It was glory, the millennium, an approaching revelation of wonder that made blood relatives of people like my father and the cab driver." (p. 50) Lastly, her parents, further contributing to her alienation from and misplacement in the larger, historical world, send her to exclusive upper-middle-class summer camps and to a predominantly upper-middle-class private school. They never try to understand her lived experiences in the newly integrated schools.

But, just as Sarah's insulated, suburban upbringing and enlightened education alienate her from the world of her parents and the old-fashioned black bourgeoisie, her skin color, and all that it represents, marginalizes and misplaces her in upper-middle-class white America. Sarah feels alienated at upper-middle class, white Prescott because she finds herself in a unique position in a system in which she does not understand the rules. Until her arrival, the unstated rule was: if you are black at Prescott, you are a servant; and if you are white, you are a student or teacher.

The unique status of being a black student at Prescott confuses Sarah because her association with Prescott is in conflict with the prevailing system that delegates whites to intellectual status and blacks to service. As in the world of her parents and the old-fashioned black bourgeoisie, at Prescott, she does not belong to a historical tradition. She does not find a social identity that complements or explains her lived experience. First, Sarah feels alienated from the white world of Prescott, which shuts her "off socially with a set of almost imperceptible closures and polite rejections." (p. 54) She becomes the "object of a discreet, relentless curiosity—a curiosity mingled with wariness on the part of some teachers, as if [she] were a very small unexploded bomb." (p. 53) She is not invited to the Friday Evening dance classes, and when she tries out for a leading role in the school play, Sarah, who prides herself on her light complexion, is given the stereotyped role of Rheba—"a colored maid ... a very dark girl somewhere in her thirties." (p. 58) And although she wants "to fit in, really fit it," Sarah is forced to align herself with a person of similar marginal status. She becomes friends with Gretchen Manning, who is marginal because her father is a Marxist Professor of History at Penn.

As in all other instances where Sarah fails to see herself or find social identification in the existing social milieu, she becomes romantic, or seeks social identification elsewhere or in the "other." In her exclusion from Prescott's normative society, Sarah joins Gretchen to become a "pair of hyper-educated, pre-adolescent misfits." They form "a two-member society of revolutionaries, who [sing] a backward version of the school song and with private signals [indicate] which members of the Prescott Athletic Association and Charity League would be executed in the first round of purges." (p. 56) And just as she sought role models in religious heroines who are martyrs when she felt misplaced at New African Baptist Church, Sarah deals with her alienation from the white world of Prescott by identifying with "a picture of a southern black girl making her way into a school through a jeering crowd of white students, a policeman at her side." (p. 54)

Second, Sarah's unique status of being a black student at previously all-white Prescott, where students and teachers are white and servants are black, also alienates her from the black staff, who belong to a different social reality than she. The members of the black staff know their social reality. They know the African American tradition to which they belong, and they live within its rules and norms. But Sarah belongs to a new phenomenon of African American social reality, which has not come to grip completely with its boundaries. It does not have clearly defined norms; the rules of its existence as the first generation of blacks "educated in newly integrated schools" have not been delineated and generalized clearly.

Therefore, when Sarah encounters a greeting from the black cook, she becomes uneasy. She is "filled with a mixture of confusion and embarrassment." She averts her eyes and ignores his greeting. "Thinking about the black people who worked at the school made me uncomfortable; I didn't know what to feel about them." (p. 57) When she ventures to the "top floor of the main tower of the Great Lodge" at Prescott and discovers how the black employees at Prescott live, Sarah realizes "that contiguous to the bright, prosperous outer life of the school was another existence, a dark mirror image, which ... was only a few steps off the path of daily routine." (p. 57) This "dark mirror image" reminds Sarah of "a print [her] brother had hanging in his room: it showed a flock of white geese flying on a strong diagonal against a dark sky—except if you looked at it another way it was a flock of dark geese heading in the opposite direction. You couldn't look at the poster and see both without a spinning feeling in your head." (p. 57) It is understandable, even predictable, as the poster's image indicates, for twelve-year-old Sarah to be confused by the mixed images and signals she encounters at Prescott. She does not know how to deal with such inconsistencies, and therefore she runs away from them. Again, she fails to integrate some of the harsher realities of life into her insulated and serene world.

Because the first "generation of [African American] children educated in newly integrated schools [is] impatient to escape the outworn rituals of their parents" and has no history or tradition of responding to racism, it has to grapple with ways of responding that are not incongruent with its social reality—a reality that knows very little about the structures of racial oppression. Sarah chooses to make light of it, to dismiss it, to lessen the threat. When she is given the role of the maid in the school play, she is seized by a "fit of giggling ... it was laughter that burned [her] insides like vinegar, and it felt different from any way [she] had ever laughed before." She chooses not to tell her parents, who are fully cognizant of racial oppression and therefore have their own response to racism, about this because "they would make a fuss." (p. 58) Instead, she develops a new laugh and keeps silent about the incident.

In all the vignettes that show Sarah's alienation not only from the world of the old-fashioned black bourgeoisie in which she is raised but also from the world of upper-middle-class white America in which she is educated, Andrea Lee, through Sarah, shows a modern inclination or impulse to experiment, to revolt against the normalizing functions of tradition, to disrupt Sarah's serene, insulated world. Sarah sees the arrival of the Thunderbirds at her summer camp as a thrill; the encounter with the Gypsies in Franklin Place is seen as a connection to a "world that was neither insulated nor serene," and the venture to the top floor of the main tower is seen as a revolutionary act because the top floor is "off limits to students."

Before she attends Harvard, we can conclude that Sarah possesses a hunger to break past the proprieties and self-containment, "to escape the outworn rituals," of not only the old-fashioned black bourgeoisie, but also of upper-middle-class white America. But she is unable to defy authority, to transcend the whole apparatus of cognition of both worlds that keeps the self stifled.

However, at Harvard, and later in Paris, Sarah begins to revolt against the insularity of her past, against the rigid conventions of the old-fashioned black bourgeoisie. At Harvard, Sarah becomes close friends with Curry Daniels, a family friend. Like Sarah, Curry is a product of a newly integrated education and has come from "a comfortable, insular, middle-class black neighborhood swathed in billiard green lawns." At Harvard, both Sarah and Curry decide to rebel against everything their parents represent. The two decide that they cannot be linked romantically because, first, it would fulfill Sarah's mother's wish, and second, the union would remind Sarah of the dullish, serene, insulated life she has chosen to abandon. Their rebellion is not of the surface. They spend "a lot of time talking about what it meant to come from the kind of earnest, prosperous black family in which Civil Rights and concern for the underprivileged are served up, so to speak, at breakfast, lunch, and dinner." (p. 89) The experience made them "naughty and perverse."

Both do proceed to live lives that "almost geometrically contravene anything of which [their] parents would approve." (p. 89) Sarah moves in "groups of friends" who "found constant excuses to have chaste, tingly nude encounters, all organized in the name of a specious artistic freedom." (p. 93) She exhausts her "thrill" in going "out with white boys"—"the forbidden fruit of [her] mother's generation"—which is required in the "arty circles" she frequents. To bring new thrills to her life, she envisions liaisons with "millionaires the age of [her] father, with alcoholic journalists, with moody filmmakers addicted to uppers ... [and with] members of the [Harvard] faculty." (p. 97) As with most insulated, protected, and bored American youths who do not want to be their parents, Sarah is looking for new thrills, new adventures. She is looking for suitors who could grant "every dangerous wish [she] had ever had."

Curry Daniels is equally as adventurous as Sarah. He is popular "with girls of any color," and he is a wonderful photographer, especially of nude women. The poster on his wall shows his "eccentric range of interests: a black and red notice for a Caribbean Marxist rally, a poster from a psychedelic minimalist exhibition that depicted what looked like a radioactive pea, and an enlarged reproduction of Burne-Jones angel." (p. 92)

Although Sarah and Curry want to be different from their parents, they do not want to commit class suicide. Both want to live by the values, not of the old-fashioned black bourgeoisie, but of upper-middle-class America. They accept and live within a concept of Western high art. Sarah and Curry are at home "in a lecture on *King Lear.*" (p. 88) They comfortably discuss "Spazzola's monograph 'Restructuring Relish.'" (p. 88) Sarah is at home at her "desk reading Donne and Herbert for seminar or writing poetry for Professor Hawks's versification class." (p. 97) They want to be individuals who are not weighed down by the political and social baggage of their parents. They want the upper-middle- class luxury to indulge themselves, to pursue their own whims. After graduation, Curry plans to spend a year travelling and taking pictures in northern Brazil where he will "eat *feijoada* among the Bahians." (p. 94) Sarah has "vague literary aspirations." Neither is concerned terribly with careers. In revolting against the style of the old-fashioned black bourgeoisie, Sarah and Curry are rejecting the past of the old-fashioned black bourgeoisie as a model, as a guiding example.

It is the death of Sarah's father that serves as the catalyst for her attempt at a total rejection of the old-fashioned black bourgeoisie. On the night during her senior year at Harvard on which her mother calls and informs her of her father's illness and impending death, Sarah witnesses a "change in everything, as inconspicuous and profound as the change a tincturing drop makes in a glass of water." (p. 105) The fact that she is finishing college and that her father is dying forces Sarah to see and understand the vulnerability of everything she has ever depended on. This revelation produces a "gradual but continuous sensation of removal, as if filament after filament of the ties that had bound [her] previous life of school and family were breaking." (p. 105) Sarah's only reliable ties to the world will be those she creates. The break with the past allows Sarah the option to take complete responsibility for her own existence, to devise her own rituals, to seek her own self-fulfillment, to, in short, create a *new* life. The modernist search for authenticity, argues Marshall Berman, "is bound up with a radical rejection of things as they are. It begins with an insistence that the social and political structures men live in are keeping the self stifled, chained down, locked up."[12]

On the train ride back to Boston after her father's funeral, Sarah becomes cognizant of her existence in the world, of her relationship to a broader historical reality. On the train, she encounters a fifteen-year-old boy who is on drugs and who is travelling to Las Vegas. She also sits next to an opera student who has just won a scholarship to study at the Salzburg Conservatory, and, looking out her window, she sees a black kid jogging on the sand of a Connecticut beach. She observes "that the world [was] a place full of kids in transit, people ... bound on excursions that might end up being glorious or stupid or violent, but that certainly moved in a direction away from anything they had ever known. I was one of them, and although I didn't know what direction I was heading in, and had only a faint idea yet of what I was leaving behind, the sense of being in motion was a thrill that made up for a lot." (p. 117) In the observation, Sarah understands that she is a part of a generation that is creating a society bound only by the common tie of their individuality.

Soon after, she leaves the United States for France, intending never to return. Her "lifelong impulse to discard Philadelphia had turned into a loathing of everything that made up [her] past." (p. 4) She wants "to cut off ties with the griefs, embarrassments, and constraints of a country, a family." (p. 15) Living with Alain, Roger, and Henri allows her to enter "a world where life [is] aimless and sometimes bizarre—a mixture that suited [her] desire for amnesia." (p. 5) Sarah wants to neutralize the standards of morality, the past, and utility by opening herself up to what Habermas, in his discussion of the avant garde, calls an "unknown territory ... an as yet unoccupied future."[13]

Certainly, Andrea Lee understands Sarah's existential freedom to define a new life. Modernity provides the context for the emergence of what Berman calls the metropolitan man who is "emancipated from all traditional and social roles and traditional modes of servitude" and who knows "how to dream a place for himself [or herself] in the world."[14] But, in Paris, Sarah fails to create a newer and better life. She is unable to dream a genuine place for herself in the world.

In Paris, Sarah learns very early that she cannot reject the past, "cut off ties with the griefs, embarrassments, and constraints of a country," or save the dignity and autonomy of life and art from the impurities of mass culture. Once considered a self-sufficient universe with its own rules, Paris, as textualized in *Sarah Phillips,* has been invaded by International capitalism. Multinational corporations and capital, which trangress the boundaries of nation-states, take mass production abroad. They have made it possible for many products and images to be mass marketed instantaneously over space. Therefore, Paris reminds Sarah constantly of the "portion of America"—the commodification and the commercialization of life and art— that she wants to abandon. First, as she watches French television, she is bombarded daily with French commericals and advertisements that are replicas of images of the American Wild West. One of the current hit songs being played on the radio is by the cartoon canary TiTi, who imitates the American cartoon Tweety. French women are wearing "rust-colored cavalier boots and skintight cigarette jeans … in imitation of Jane Birkin, the English movie star." (p. 7) American movies (*Gatsby* has just opened on the *Champs Elysees*) are quite visible, and current French movies reproduce "shootouts in the gold and ocher mock-western landscape." Sarah, along with Alain, Roger, and Henri, eats hamburgers at *Le Drugstore Saint-Germain.*

On a more personal level, Sarah is reminded of the family that she has thrown away when she encounters objects or has experiences that make her feel nostalgia for home. A wet leaf that affixed "itself squarely on [her] cheek or forehead like a airmail stamp" reminds her of "the letters [she] hadn't written home." (p. 8) In England, the "chemistry of [the] air, soil, and civilization filled [her] with unwilling nostalgia." Therefore, she looks for "certain types of tourists: prosperous black Americans, a little overdressed and a bit uneasy in hotel lobbies, who could instantly identify where [she] came from, and who might know [her] family." (p. 8)

In addition, Henri, Roger, and Alain will not let Sarah forget some of the "constraints of country," racism, or the griefs and embarrassments of being racially stereotyped. Just as in the United States, where she is marginalized by whites whose "complacent faces had surrounded [her] in prep school and in college" and who could see her only as a black, in Paris Sarah realizes that Henri does not see her as an individual, but only as a racial stereotype, and she does not try to understand him:

"Throughout our short romance we remained incomprehensible to each other, each of us clutching a private exotic vision in the various beds where we made love. ... He couldn't begin to imagine the America I came from, nor did I know, or even try to find out, what it was like to grow up in Lorraine, in a provincial city, where at school the other boys gang up on you, pull down your pants, and smear you with black shoe polish because you have no father." (p. 5) But this private, exotic vision that brought Sarah and Henri together begins to fail, and "the mutual fascination that had joined [them] suddenly and profoundly three months before had begun to break down into boredom and suspicion." (pp. 8–9)

The relationship between Sarah and Henri has been predicated on the myths and fantasies that characterize much of black/white relations in the West. The assumption is that blacks and whites come from different species. Therefore, they present each other with unknown and mysterious territories to be explored. But, once the myths have been explored and the fantasies acted out, Sarah and Henri are left with the antagonisms and "suspicion" that are endemic to race relations in the West. The dissolution of the relationship between Sarah and Henri comes when Henri tells Sarah a tale about her non-human pedigree or her "elegant pedigree." In the tale, Sarah is the offspring of an Irishwoman who is raped in the jungle by a monkey. The tale stirs a repressed "portion of America" in Sarah that she has tried desperately to discard.

Although Sarah has a hunger to break past the proprieties and the self-containment of the old-fashioned black bourgeoisie and the constraints of upper-middle-class white America, she is unable to move to a form of absolute personal speech, or to establish an alternative mode of perception. For a fleeting moment, she is able to just escape, to erase the past. But Sarah is never able to rework nature, refashion her consciousness, or remake the "self" and a new life outside the conventions and outworn rituals of the old-fashioned black bourgeoisie and upper-middle-class America. Sarah is unable to use her wit and imagination to create a place for herself in the world; she is incapable of defining and creating a life that is authentically her own. She fails at the existential moment to, as Irving Howe says in "The Idea of the Modern," "reinvent the terms of her own reality."[15] The "intensity of name-less emotions" and the inability to transcend the whole apparatus of cognition of the old-fashioned black bourgeoisie prevent her. Sarah fails to realize that coming to grips with her existential existence means not repressing, but confronting and accepting, one's past—including racism, racial stereotyping, commercial culture, and the ragged edges of the real. This means that she fails to create and sustain a newer and better life that "almost geometrically contravene[s] anything of which [her] parents would approve." (p. 89) Modernism fails, and Sarah becomes entrapped in a style that *Sarah Phillips* has already shown to be inadequate.

Rather than continue to exalt the present and anticipate an undefined future, Sarah, like Richard Rodriguez, reaches an impasse and capitulates. She interprets her decision to reject the past and escape to Paris not as an attempt to create a new existential life, but as a "slight hysteria, filled with the experimental naughtiness of [a child] reacting against [her] training." (p. 15) Her rebellion becomes not a desire for revolutionary change, but a youthful rebellion for the sake of youth, an upsurge that was not so much apolitical as opposed to all conventional versions of politics. We can say that Sarah's rebellion is a middle-class critique of affluence. She escaped to Paris because she found mass commercial culture, along with racism and racial stereotyping, squalid and deadening. Yet in Paris she is surrounded with mass commercial culture. She sees no way out, except possibly through a gradual upgrading of popular taste and the repression of racial stereotyping. But, in Paris, Sarah is unable to upgrade popular taste and escape racial stereotyping. Mass commercial culture, which appropriates forms of racial stereotyping, has colonized all the social and cultural spaces and has pushed high art to the margins. Therefore, realizing that her "sense of being in motion" does not take her to a new authentic life, she prepares to make the "complicated return" to America. But Sarah's return is different from Milkman's in *Song of Solomon*. Milkman rejects his and his parents's present and returns to a cultural and historical past. Sarah returns to a personal past and a particular class that she truly never ever rejected. Why the failure of literary modernism in *Sarah Phillips*? Why the failure to attain a newer and better modern life in *Sarah Phillips*?

Lee in *Sarah Phillips* takes a narrow view of literary modernism. She sees it as an endeavor to maintain the high standards of the old masters against the intrusion of commercialism and the impurities of mass culture. Lee's literary modernism in *Sarah Phillips* endeavors to stem the decline of aesthetic standards threatened by what Matei Calinescu calls the "relative democratizing of our culture under industrialism." "The overriding and innermost logic of modernism," Calinescu continues, "is to maintain the levels of the past in the face of an opposition that hadn't been present in the past."[16] In the case of Lee's *Sarah Phillips,* this means art and life withdraw from an ever-expanding commercial taste or reach an impasse, especially since the avant garde has been institutionalized. *Sarah Phillips* reaches an impasse and withdraws. Rather than standing as a promise of a new life, it becomes a symbol of alienation. In its passion for a formalistically conceived purity of standards, *Sarah Phillips* ends up offering little more than a rhetoric of aesthetic conservation. What we get instead of a dynamic of looking forward and innovation—the hallmark of modernism—is a paradoxical looking backward.

In addition, the increasingly categorical separation of art from reality pushes art and artists to the margins of society. The "complicated return" indicates that *Sarah Phillips* is bound to a one-way history of literary modernism that interprets it as a logical unfolding toward some imaginary goal and that is based on a whole series of exclusions. *Sarah Phillips's* literary modernism, which purports to save art and life from the vulgarities of mass culture, is out of tune with current sensibilities. And in adhering to this narrow, codified version of literary modernism, *Sarah Phillips,* as did *Hunger of Memory,* excludes the possibilities and options opened by the emergence of the various forms of "otherness" in the cultural sphere. In the years since the Civil Rights movement forced official integration, the dominant categories of black womanhood, which suggests certain cultural traits, and literary modernism have given way to a plurality of categories. The 1970s and 1980s produced, or allowed to emerge, other options. The traditional categories still exist, but they have become two of many categories. For example, now we have African American women who have African blood, but whose looks, experiences, and sensibilities are drawn from traditions that fit none of the established standards of African American womanhood. Despite the lingering racism, black women who grow up and attend predominantly white private and suburban public elementary and secondary schools, particularly in the

North, belong to a different tradition experientially and cognitively than their counterparts who grow up and attend elementary and secondary public schools in the inner city. Black women who grow up in countercultured families and adopt those values belong to a different tradition than their counterparts who grow up in traditional, southern Christian families. If Andrea Lee's vision had included some of these various options which Sarah's life experiences suggest, if Lee could have envisioned, at a higher plane, the emergence of these other traditions, she could have provided Sarah with other models to assist her in ferreting out a social identification.

In addition, as the different experiences of women and racial and sexual minorities emerge into the cultural and sociopolitical spheres, high modernism, which is modelled historically and primarily on white, middle-class, male experiences, is eroded, thereby opening the way for other forms of literary modernism to emerge. If Lee's version of literary modernism in *Sarah Phillips* could have become aware of these other emergent literary options and possibilities, it, along with the vision of black womanhood as one of a plurality of categories, could have provided the necessary structure for the positive articulation of a new modern life.

Furthermore, though Sarah is pushed to reject the old-fashioned black bourgeoisie by a feeling of "slight hysteria," she never transcends it. Sarah is unable to critique successfully the old-fashioned black bourgeoisie's obsession with color and class. Therefore, she and the novel are entrapped in the conventions of a particular class and color, in the conventions of the old-fashioned black bourgeoisie. In short, neither Sarah Phillips nor Andrea Lee is able to visualize a new social model outside the conventions and values of the black middle class. This limitation incapacitates the text so that it is unable to answer the question it poses and to realize its full potential.

Finally, although both *Hunger of Memory* and *Sarah Phillips* are entrapped ideologically in upper-middle-class American conventions and values that prevent them from realizing their modernist quest for authenticity, or for a newer life, they have been received differently by mainstream critics and basically the same by Chicano and African American critics. *Hunger of Memory* takes positions on volatile social issues such as Affirmative Action, bilingual education, and cultural diversity that generate the official order. Therefore, it can be easily appropriated, as I have discussed earlier, to generate the ideological position of those Americans who take a single hegemonic approach to American life and culture. This, perhaps, explains the enormous attention it has generated and its subsequent institutionalization. It is perhaps the first text written by an American of Mexican [and Hispanic] descent that has been reviewed and, sometimes, highly praised by reviewers *in The New York Times Book Review, The Atlantic Monthly, Time, Harper's, Newsweek, The American Scholar, Commentary,* and the *Harvard Educational Review.* In addition, selections from *Hunger of Memory* are included in anthologies used in freshman composition courses throughout the United States.

Sarah Phillips, on the other hand, received routine treatment by mainstream reviewers in the *New Republic, Essence,* the *Virginia Quarterly Review,* the *New Leader, The New York Times Book Review,* and *Ms.* But, outside of Valerie Smith's article, "Black Feminist Theory and the Representation of the 'Other,'" which deals with it in a general and secondary way, *Sarah Phillips* has been ignored by African American critics, including black women and black feminist critics. Why the silence around *Sarah Phillips?* Does it not fit into the current canon of black women authors, which features Zora Neale Hurston most prominently? Does it critique those values and conventions that most African American critics harbor? Or does it present a black woman's experience that most African Americans would rather ignore or repress? Does it not fit into the racially constructed paradigms that pervade African American critical practices? Does the modernist countertradition that animates *Sarah Phillip* put it outside the critical and aesthetic expectations of African American critics?

Because racial critical discourses, which tend to universalize their taste in or assumptions about literature, or minority critics, have the power of policing language, of "determining that certain statements [are permitted and others] must be excluded because they do not conform to what is acceptable," those modernist texts such as Lee's *Sarah Phillips* and Rodriquez's *Hunger of Memory* are rejected, ignored, and repressed because they do not generate or affirm codified, "timeless" versions of African American and Mexican American experiences. Sherley Anne Williams, in the lone review of *Sarah Phillips* by an African American critic, ignores the new phenomenon of African American social reality that *Sarah Phillips* attempts to articulate and criticizes it for not reproducing a permanent, "timeless" African American cultural tradition. First, Williams views *Sarah Phillips* as a recurrent aberration in this "timeless" African American tradition. Lee's *Sarah Phillips,* she argues, after fifty years returns the attention of African American literature to the black bourgeoisie of such Harlem Renaissance writers as Jessie Fauset and Nella Larsen. Williams welcomes the broadening of subject matter. But then, she criticizes *Sarah Phillips* for "literally and figuratively renouncing oral culture and black traditions of personal autonomy." Williams complains about *Sarah Phillips's* "rejection of black community rather than a renewed sense of identification with blacks."[17] Finally, Williams interprets *Sarah Phillips's* use of vignettes as showing not Sarah's legitimate historical alienation from blacks, but as Sarah's "own sense of distance from black people."[18] But what Williams' review ignores is *Sarah Phillips's* Otherness, which is the book's power. The protest of *Sarah Phillip,* its Otherness, goes beyond matters of social and racial ideology exclusively and addresses the modernist impulse or desire of an African American to reject the past and to move to refashion a new consciousness, a new existence that is outside of the existing hegemonic social and racial traditions.

Rodriguez's *Hunger of Memory* receives similar criticism from Mexican American or Chicano critics. They reject the text on ideological grounds. In his review, Tomás Rivera initially has wonderful things to say about *Hunger of Memory.* It is, he argues, "an exceptionally well written book. It is a profound book, a personal expression which one learns to respect for its sensibility."[19] But then, Rivera, using essentialist language, criticizes *Hunger of Memory* for its "negation of what is fundamentally the central element of the human being—the cultural root, the native tongue. As one reads each essay, one progressively recognizes that what is most surprising [is that] for Richard Rodriguez silence and his basic culture are negative elements, regressive ones."[20]

Finally, Rivera moves to repress *Hunger of Memory* because it does not "conform to what is acceptable" by Chicano essentialist and cultural nationalist standards, or by the standards of those who believe that there is only one "native tongue." "I want to place in opposition to Richard Rodriguez's work a body of Chicano literature which has precepts as profound and as well written. ... In these Chicano works there is little hunger of memory, and much hunger for community."[21]

Likewise, in his review, Arturo Madrid rejects *Hunger of Memory* for privileging individuality and ignoring collective Chicano cultural heritage. "Our coming of age took place when we understood that the reasons for our rejection did not lie in ourselves and therefore could not be overcome by any individual efforts, whether through accommodation or assimilation. Knowing that we could begin to fashion a new future for ourselves, this Richard has still to learn."[22] What Madrid does here is to universalize a concept of Chicano cultural nationalism and use it to measure the worth and value of literary texts written by Mexican Americans, including *Hunger of Memory*.

Even Ramon Saldivar's "Ideologies of the Self: Chicano Autobiography," which gives a brilliant analysis of the conflicts and contradictions of the self in *Hunger of Memory,* succumbs finally to criticizing *Hunger of Memory* on essentialist grounds. He criticizes *Hunger of Memory* for "locating subjectivity outside of socio-historical reality," and argues that Rodriguez cannot conceive of a "form of subjectivity that would draw upon existing social practice, the life of the collective folk (of la raza), for an alternative critical society.[23]

What is repressed in Rivera's, Madrid's and Saldivar's reviews and critical assessments of *Hunger of Memory* is its modernist impulse to reject the past, the "community," "the life of the collective," and to find a new life. Contrary to these critics' evaluation, however, if *Hunger of Memory* can be said to have committed a literary or philosophical crime, it is in its inability to allow Richard the narrator to come into his own voice, to refashion his consciousness, or to create a newer and better life, not in its failure to affirm old ways, or "existing social practice."

--- NOTES ---

1. Terry Eagleton, "Capitalism, Modernism, Postmodernism," in *Against the Grain: Selected Essays* (London: Verso, 1986), p. 139.

2. Irving Howe, "The Idea of the Modern," in *Literary Modernism,* edited by Irving Howe (Greenwich, Conn.: Fawcett Publications, 1967), p. 17.

3. Andreas Huyssen, *After the Great Divide: Modernism, Mass Culture, Postmodernism* (Bloomington: Indiana University Press, 1986), p. 172.

4. Paul de Man, *Blindness and Insight* (Minneapolis: University of Minnesota Press, 1983), p. 147.

5. Richard Rodriguez, *Hunger of Memory: The Education of Richard Rodriguez* (New York: Bantam Books, 1983), p. 46. All further references will be to this edition and will be given in the text.

6. Ramon Saldivar, "Ideologies of the Self: Chicano Autobiography," *Diacritics* 15 (Fall 1985): p. 27.

7. Andreas Huyssen, *After the Great Divide,* p. 198.

8. Andrea Lee, *Sarah Phillips* (New York: Penguin Books, 1985), p. 4. All further references will be to this edition and will be given in the text.

9. Anders Stephanson, "Interview with Cornel West," in *Universal Abandon? The Politics of Postmodernism,* edited by Andrew Ross (Minneapolis: University of Minnesota Press, 1988), p. 277.

10. Barbara Ehrenreich, *Fear of Falling: The Inner Life of the Middle Class* (New York: Harper Perennial, 1990), p. 17.

11. Valerie Smith, "Black Feminist Theory and the Representation of the 'Other,'" in *Changing Our Own Words: Essays on Criticism, Theory, and Writing by Black Women,* edited by Cheryl A. Wall (New Brunswick: Rutgers University Press, 1989), pp. 50–51.

12. Marshall Berman, *All That Is Solid Melts into Air: The Experience of Modernity* (New York: Penguin Books, 1988), p. xix.

13. Jurgen Habermas, "Modernity—An Incomplete Project," in *The Anti-Aesthetic: Essays in Postmodern Culture,* edited by Hal Foster (Port Townsend, Wash.: Bay Press, 1983), p. 59.

14. Marshall Berman, *The Politics of Authenticity: Radical Individualism and the Emergence of Modern Society* (New York: Atheneum, 1970), p. 115.

15. Irving Howe, "The Idea of the Modern," *Literary Modernism,* edited by Irving Howe (Greenwich, Conn.: Fawcett Publication, 1967), p. 17.

16. Matei Calinescu, *Five Faces of Modernity* (Durham, N.C.: Duke University Press, 1987), p. 290.

17. Sherley Anne Williams, "Roots of Privilege: New Black Fiction," *Ms.*, June 1985: p. 7.

18. *Ibid.*: p. 7.

19. Tomás Rivera, "Richard Rodriguez's *Hunger of Memory* as Humanistic Antithesis," *MELUS* 11 (Winter 1984): p. 5.

20. *Ibid.:* p. 6.

21. *Ibid.:* p. 11.

22. Arturo Madrid, "Review of *Hunger of Memory: The Education of Richard Rodriguez*," *La Red / The Net* No. 53 (April 1982): pp. 6–9.

23. Ramon Saldivar, "Ideologies of the Self: Chicano Autobiography," *Diacritics* 15 (Fall 1985): p. 33.

4

Problematizing the Historical Past:
Maxine Hong Kingston's *The Woman Warrior*
and David Bradley's *The Chaneysville Incident*

Song of Solomon and *House Made of Dawn* resolve the
modern condition—the alienation and fragmentation, the
lack of social identification, and the lack of historical
continuity—by rejecting modernity and retreating to the
values and conventions of the pre-modern past. They
reject modernist culture and give a nostalgic nod to the
golden age of the past. *Hunger of Memory* and *Sarah
Phillips* resolve the modern dilemma by rejecting the past
and reaching an impasse in the present, seeking unsuc-
cessfully a new life. *The Woman Warrior* (1976), by
Maxine Hong Kingston, and *The Chaneysville Incident*
(1981), by David Bradley, resolve the modern dilemma of
their modern heroine and postmodern protagonist respectively by transforming, or imagining, aspects of the
historical, personal, and cultural past into a contemporary constellation in order to validate, make coherent,
and give history and continuity to certain modern and
postmodern experiences. In the process of these transformations, these imaginings, the two texts problematize, or
undermine seriously, our traditional conception of history,
which assumes that history seeks to explain what happened
in the past by providing a precise and accurate reconstruction of the events reported in the documents. And in
the case of *The Chaneysville Incident,* these imaginings
liberate its protagonist from any external moral or tran-

111

scendental authority. This liberation allows him to act purely on desire and want.

The Woman Warrior and *The Chaneysville Incident,* unlike *Hunger of Memory* and *Sarah Phillips,* release their modern, existential narrator and postmodern protagonist respectively from metaphysical, absolute racial tradition or cultural narratives, from internally cohesive sets of perceptions or formal conventions, and from sanctioned notions of an ordered universe and of man's and woman's place in it. The two texts revolt against the prevalent, representational style that views history and culture in universal, essential terms, that subordinates the individual's subjective experience to the consolidated values and the socio-political mechanisms of a meta-narrative.

The kind of literature that *The Woman Warrior* and *The Chaneysville Incident* represent is what Linda Hutcheon in *A Poetics of Postmodernism* calls "historiographic metafiction" or "postmodern historicism," which is "unwillingly unencumbered by nostalgia in its critical dialogical review of the forms, contexts, and values of the past."[1] This kind of fiction is not "realistic" in the nineteenth-century sense of asking the reader to assume that there is a one-to-one correspondence between the textual real and the social real. Neither is it radically non-referential in the sense of experimental fiction. Historigraphic metafiction is intensely self-reflexive and yet, paradoxically, also lays claim to historical events. It rewrites history yet calls history as a referent into question. It is aware of its own fictionalizing processes. It has a theoretical self-awareness of history and fiction as human constructs. As historiographic metafiction, *The Woman Warrior* and *The Chaneysville Incident* blur the distinction between history and fiction. In the blurring of the two categories, the two texts aesthetically cross the boundaries between modern and postmodern fiction.

Unlike *Song of Solomon* and *House Made of Dawn, The Woman Warrior* and *The Chaneysville Incident* do not want to exhume, or even preserve, a revered past. Nor do they want to deny the existence of the past as some critics of postmodern fiction have claimed. Rather, they want, to use the words of Linda Hutcheon, "to revisit the past critically"; they want to problematize the past's values, contents, conventions, and aesthetic forms. They want a reevaluation of and a dialogue with the past that are informed by the present. Finally, they want to arrive at a conscious, functional, and intentional truth about the past that is socially and ideologically conditioned.[2]

Like Sarah Phillips in Lee's *Sarah Phillips* and Richard the narrator in Rodriguez's *Hunger of Memory,* the female narrator in Kingston's *The Woman Warrior* is educated in America's Eurocentric schools where she internalizes the Enlightenment ideas of progress. Yet the female narrator in *The Woman Warrior,* like Richard the narrator, grows up in a traditional home and culture, Chinese in this instance, whose values, whose conceptions of time and space, are in total contrast to the values of her integrated, secular American education. In school, she becomes conscious of a world beyond the confines of her home and traditional Chinese culture.

Like Richard the narrator and Sarah Phillips, *The Woman Warrior's* female narrator's modernity or modern experience exists because she is caught between cultures, two worlds. Her secular American education alienates her from her parents' transcendent and naturalized Chinese culture. Because she is racially and, somewhat, culturally Chinese, she is alienated from her middle-class white classmates. "Even now China wraps double binds around my feet."[3] Unlike Richard the narrator in *Hunger of Memory,* the female narrator does not reject her Chinese past and become entrapped in the conventions of the mainstream society. Rather, she synthesizes her American and Chinese parts to create a balanced Chinese American identity. The female narrator's subjective, modern experience is what Hutcheon calls ex-centric, "inside and yet outside"; it involves having an alien and critical perspective, one that is "always altering its focus," since it has no centering force.[4]

Unlike Richard the narrator in *Hunger of Memory,* the female narrator in Kingston's *The Woman Warrior* does not move from the margin to the center. Rather, she uses her paradoxical doubled position to critique the inside from both the outside and the inside. Her struggle is not to just reject the past or the present. It is instead to take certain traditional Chinese conceptions, myths, and legends, such as the woman warrior and certain determined historical events from her personal and family past, and subvert and alter their content and make them relevant to her own modern dilemma. This she accomplishes by means of her contemporary [American] feminist consciousness or sensibilities and her secular [American] education, which promotes individualism and equality and which is comprised of a rationalism that breaks with history and tradition, that demystifies and desacralizes knowledge. The female narrator's objective in resolving her modern condition—her alienation and fragmentation, her lack of social identification, and her lack of historical continuity—is to create a version of the Chinese past that can connect with and ratify her subjective Chinese American present.

Kingston also uses the metaphor of the Chinese knot-makers to inform the designs of her Chinese American narrative. In recounting the events of the story—which she receives from one of her sisters, who receives it from her brother—of her mother's and aunt's visit to Los Angeles to visit the aunt's long-lost husband, and in exposing her narrative technique, the female narrator states: "His version of the story may be better than mine because of its bareness, not twisted into designs. ... Long ago in China, knot-makers tied string into buttons and frogs, and rope into bell pulls. There was one knot so complicated that it blinded the knot-maker. Finally an emperor outlawed this cruel knot, and the nobles could not order it anymore. If I had lived in China, I would have been an outlaw knot-maker." (pp. 189–190) Thus, the female narrator takes the materials of her historical and personal past and twists them into designs.

The narrator of *The Woman Warrior,* who remains nameless throughout, belongs to "the first American generations [of Chinese Americans who] have had to figure out how the invisible world the emigrants built around [their] childhoods fits in solid America." (p. 6) The female narrator's initial problem is that her Chinese history and culture are not completely available to her. The confusion is due to the silence and misconceptions surrounding the Chinese in America. "The emigrants confused the gods by diverting their curses." They confused their offspring by becoming sojourners who take "new names when their lives change and guard their real names with silence." (p. 6) What the female narrator eventually learns about Chinese culture and history she learns from the stories her mother, Brave Orchid, tells.

But even if the female narrator and her generation had total access to, and knowledge of, Chinese culture, their secular American education would force them to cast doubt on its veracity.

Because they are the first generation of Chinese Americans who are "born among ghosts, were taught by ghosts, and were [themselves] ghostlike," the female narrator and her generation are alienated from their parents' traditional Chinese culture. Like Americans, they stare at people with whom they are talking—a practice that makes their newly arrived aunt, Moon Orchid, very uncomfortable. They watch American television, which is one of the great transmitters of modern consciousness. Like other Americans, they are vain. They "never denied a compliment." (p. 155) Contrary to Chinese practices, the female narrator and her siblings smile for photographs, and are, like Richard the narrator in *Hunger of Memory* with Spanish, embarrassed when they hear other Chinese speak the Chinese language loudly in public. For example, when Moon Orchid's daughter and Brave Orchid want to get Moon Orchid's attention upon her arrival at the airport, Brave Orchid asks her Chinese American children to "call out together," but they refuse. "Maybe that shame-face they so often wore was American politeness." (p. 136)

Furthermore, their secular American education does not allow the female narrator and other members of this first generation of Chinese Americans to accept readily certain non-rational or superstitious Chinese beliefs. When the female narrator's mother, Brave Orchid, hints that "during the next eclipse we slam pot lids together to scare the frog from swallowing the moon," the female narrator retorts: "On the other side of the world, they aren't having an eclipse Mama. That's just a shadow the earth makes when it comes between the moon and the sun." (p. 197) The exchange between mother and daughter is a clash between ontological systems, a clash between the mother's non-rational, mythical thought system, which "establishes homologies between natural and social conditions,"[5] and the daughter's scientific system in explaining the moon's disappearance, or the total obscuring of one celestial body by another.

The female narrator's secular education also clashes with her mother's transcendent, Chinese belief system on other occasions. Brave Orchid thinks that when the delivery person from the Rexall Drug brings mistakenly "a pale blue box of pills" to the laundry, he also brings a curse that will make the children sick, or that he is putting "a plague on the family." Therefore, Brave Orchid orders her daughter to go to the drugstore to "make them stop the curse." She wants her daughter to "swing stinky censers around the counter, at the druggist, at the customers. Throw dog blood on the druggist." (p. 197) To rescind the curse, the druggist has to give the family "reparation candy" for having "tainted [their] house with sick medicine." Brave Orchid believes that these actions will teach "the druggist ghost a lesson in good manners." But her daughter, the female narrator, who understands the presuppositions that govern everyday American life, knows that asking the druggist for "reparation candy" and her mother's non-rational explanation for wanting the candy are something "impossible to explain to the druggist." She knows that the druggist will think that they are "beggars without a home who [live] in back of the laundry."

Although this secular education and American socialization alienate the female narrator and her generation from traditional Chinese culture, they are not fully Americanized. They are also alienated from middle-class America. For example, the female narrator and the other Chinese American females have difficulty, to use Richard Rodriguez's term from *Hunger of Memory,* adopting a public language and a public American identity. In her early years, the narrator becomes silent when her voice is noticed by other non-Asian Americans: "When I went to kindergarden and had to speak English for the first time, I became silent. A dumbness—a shame—still cracks my voice in two, even when I want to say 'hello' casually, or ask any easy question in front of the check out counter, or ask directions of a bus driver. ... It spoils my day with self-disgust when I hear my broken voice come skittering out into the open. It makes people wince to hear it." (p. 191) When the female narrator recognizes that other Chinese American girls do not talk, especially in front of class, she knows that it is cultural, that the silence has to do with being a Chinese American girl and having "little squeaks" for voices, that Chinese Americans, coming from a communal culture, have difficulty asserting their individuality. Also, the female narrator and the other Chinese American girls are conscious of the fact, which further make them feel different from middle-class Americans, that Chinese sounds "chingching ugly to American ears." It has a gutteral peasant sound and is very loud. Therefore they whisper to make themselves American feminine and invent "an American feminine speaking personality."

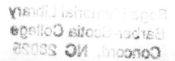

Because she is a part of the first generation of Chinese Americans who is not totally culturally and cognitively Chinese, though not yet fully American either, the female narrator in *The Woman Warrior,* to deal with her alienation and fragmentation, has to ferret out and define a sense of self. As a modern subject who needs a temporal unification between the past and future in the present, she needs a historical tradition and a social identification. First, she has to discern, "what is Chinese tradition and what is movies," and to figure out how "the invisible world the emigrants built around [her] childhood fits in solid America." Second, she has to find or devise a narrative that complements her present, subjective experience.

When *The Woman Warrior* opens, the female narrator has already emerged as a contemporary Chinese American feminist who wants to be a woman warrior. "If I could not-eat, perhaps I could make myself a warrior like the swordswoman who drives me." (p. 56) But she lacks social identification and historical continuity. The act of writing becomes her way of creating the self, of working out her relationship with the past and the present. The non-linear, chaotic, fragmented structure of *The Woman Warrior* and the voice movement from the second and third persons in the earlier chapters to the first person in the final chapter signify the difficult task confronting the female narrator. The fragmented narrative symbolizes the female narrator's search for her social identity and her voice. Thus, *The Woman Warrior* operates as a modern racial, feminist experience in search of its narrative.

In reconstructing her childhood, and in revisiting the personal, historical past, the female narrator uses specific values, her feminist sensibilities or consciousness and her secular education, to select, and to twist into designs, events from the past and to reinterpret her childhood. The female narrator's feminist consciousness is evident in the reconstruction of her childhood among the ghosts. She defines her childhood as one where she grows up in a patriarchal Chinese ethos that does not welcome daughters. In the "invisible world" the emigrants built around her, the narrator, because she is female, is judged as worthless. "'Girls are maggots in the rice.' 'It is more profitable to raise geese than daughters.'" (p. 51) In China, female babies are given away and bad daughters-in-law are "smeared ... with honey and tied ... naked on top of ant['s] nests." (p. 225) A husband can kill his "wife who disobeys him." (p. 225) When one of the emigrants, who preserves this patriarchal Chinese culture in America, observes the female narrator throwing a tantrum, she says: "I would hit her if she were mine. But then there's no use wasting all that discipline on a girl. 'When you raise girls, you're raising children for strangers.'" (p. 54) When her uncle calls to take the children shopping, he says "no girls" when he hears female voices. (p. 55) Finally, the female narrator raises many questions when her parents treat her differently than they do her brother, when they pay more attention to him: "Did you roll an egg on my face like that when I was born? Did you have a full-month party for *me*? Did you turn on all the lights? Did you send *my* picture to Grandmother?" (p. 55) For raising these questions, the female narrator is accused of being "bad."

Unlike the other Chinese girls, who resign themselves to being Chinese pretty and worthless, the female narrator, in using her feminist sensibilities and secular education to subvert and transform her childhood, challenges the image of the Chinese girl as a worthless slave. First, she is baffled and confused by the pronoun "I." The English "I," which is capitalized, does not correspond with the Chinese "I," which is the word for female slave: "I could not understand 'I.' The Chinese 'I' has seven strokes, intricacies. How could the American 'I,' assuredly wearing a hat like the Chinese, have only three strokes, the middle so straight? Was it out of politeness that this writer left off strokes the way a Chinese has to write her own name small and crooked? No, it was not politeness; 'I' is a 'capital' and 'you' is lower case. I stared at that middle line and waited so long for its black center to resolve into light strokes and dots that I forgot to pronounce it." (p. 193)

Second, in her challenge to the image of the Chinese girl as worthless, the female narrator rebels. She "ate up food and threw tantrums." Realizing that her actions or behavior could cause her to be returned to China where women are made a wife and slave, the female narrator decides to do "something big and fine." She becomes a good student. But her parents still refuse to see her as a worthy individual. They want to marry her off. In her challenge, the female narrator transforms the Chinese conception of "bad" into something positive and achieves freedom. First, she decides that she never wants a husband. Therefore, she puts on "shoes with the open flaps and [flaps] about like a wino Ghost. From then on, she wore those shoes to parties, whenever the mothers gathered to talk about marriages." (p. 226) Second, she refuses to cook and "when [she] had to wash dishes, [she] would crack one or two [plates]." When she is asked what she wants to do when she grows up, she says " a lumberjack in Oregon." She stops attending Chinese school, and, finally, she refuses to continue to live with the unexplained mysteries surrounding her and her parents' life. She tells her mother: "You lie with stories. You won't tell me a story and then say, 'This is a true story,' or 'This is just a story.' I can't tell the difference. I don't even know what your real names are. I can't tell what's real and what you make up." (p. 235)

Furthermore, realizing that her mother does not know her as an individual, the female narrator decides to force the issue: "I had grown inside me a list of over two hundred things that I had to tell my mother so that she would know the true things about me and to stop the pain in my throat." (p. 229) She wants validation of her own voice, her own individuality from her mother. But her mother refuses to listen. Unable to contain herself any longer, the female narrator's "throat burst open" and she screams at her mother, telling her that she will not be a traditional Chinese girl and become a wife and a slave, that she will be her own person: "I am going away ... I am. Do you hear me? I may be ugly and clumsy, but one thing I'm not, I'm not retarded. There's nothing wrong with my brain. Do you know what the Teacher Ghosts say about me? They tell me I'm smart, and I can win scholarships. I can get into colleges ... I'm smart. I can do all kinds of things. I know how to get A's, and they say I could be a scientist or a mathematician if I want. I can make a living and take care of myself. So you don't have to find me a keeper who's too dumb to know a bad bargain. ... Not everybody thinks I'm nothing. I am not going to be a slave or a wife. Even if I am stupid and talk funny and get sick, I won't let you turn me into a slave or a wife. I'm getting out of here. I can't stand living here anymore." (p. 234)

The outburst or scream constitutes the female narrator's rejection of her parents' past. To accept her parents' version of the past entails accepting a subtext that embraces sexist roles and values, that denies her her own individuality. To assert her own individuality, to find a new life, to fulfill her own human destiny, she has to abandon the past. Thus, breaking with the past becomes a prerequisite for finding an identity in the present. In writing *The Woman Warrior,* the female narrator articulates her own space. She decides to go to college where "it won't matter if [she is] not charming. And it doesn't matter if a person is ugly." (p. 237) At Berkeley in the Sixties, she studies and "marche[s] to change the world." As with Richard Rodriguez, leaving home gives her the necessary distance to understand critically and logically her family and culture. "I had to leave home in order to see the world logically, logic the new way of seeing. I learned to think that mysteries are for explanation. I enjoy the simplicity." (p. 237)

After college, the female narrator does not return home, where she will be surrounded by emigrants who still practice a patriarchal Chinese culture that embraces the sexist roles and values she finds oppressive. Instead, she chooses to live "where there are Chinese and Japanese, but no emigrants from [her] own village looking at [her] as if [she] had failed them. Living among one's own emigrant villagers can give a good Chinese far from China glory and a place. ... But I am useless, one more girl who couldn't be sold." (p. 62)

With her new freedom, the female narrator can return home only as a visitor; and even during these visits, her parents and the emigrants remind her of the oppressive patriarchal culture she has rejected. "When I visit the family now, I wrap my American successes around me like a private shawl; I *am* worthy of eating the food. From afar I can believe my family loves me fundamentally." (p. 62) But, on these visits home when she hears words like "when fishing for treasures in the flood, be careful not to pull in girls" coming from her parents, and when she looks at their "ink drawing of poor people snagging their neighbors' flotage with long flood hooks and pushing the girl babies on down the river," (p. 62) the female narrator is reminded of what her parents, the emigrant villagers, and the patriarchal Chinese culture think about women, and she has to get out of "hating range." Despite her mother's wishes, she never intends to return home permanently. She has found a place "in this country that is ghost free."

Having freed herself from the ascriptive ties of patriarchal Chinese culture, the narrator is free to define her own modern existence. But, as a modern subject who needs a certain temporal unification of the past and future with the present, she looks for a social model or narrative from the past that can validate, make coherent, and give a history to her contemporary feminist consciousness and existence. Unlike Sarah in Lee's *Sarah Phillips* and Richard the narrator in *Hunger of Memory,* the female narrator of *The Woman Warrior* looks for models in her historical and cultural past. She wants her modern, subjective existence to have a line to the past. But, unlike Milkman in *Song of Solomon* and Abel in *House Made of Dawn,* she does not recuperate, or even preserve, the historical and cultural past. With her contemporary feminist consciousness and secular American education, she revisits the past critically. She rethinks, reworks, and twists into designs the determined contents and events of the past.

First, the narrator turns to her father's sister, No Name Woman, to assist her in ferreting out a model. The narrator will rethink and rework the aunt's life, pregnancy, and death to make her her feminist forerunner. "Unless I see her life branching into mine, she gives me no ancestral help." (p. 10) In Brave Orchid's account of No Name Woman's pregnancy, the aunt is portrayed as a "wild woman" who was "free with sex" and who "kept rollicking company." (p. 9) She becomes pregnant while her husband is in America, and she "jump[s] into the family well" and "kill[s] herself." But the female narrator refuses to accept her mother's version of her aunt's pregnancy and death. First, using her secular education, she questions her mother's version. "My mother spoke about the raid as if she had seen it, when she and my aunt, a daughter-in-law to a different household, should not have been living together at all." (p. 8) Second, using her limited knowledge of patriarchal Chinese culture and her feminist consciousness to reflect critically on her aunt's story, the female narrator cannot imagine her aunt "free with sex" or as a "wild woman." The aunt, she reasons, could not have been the "lone romantic who gave up everything for sex" because "women in the old China did not choose." (p. 7)

Rethinking and twisting into designs the events of her aunt's life, pregnancy, and death, Kingston, or the female narrator, concludes that "some man had commanded [the aunt] to lie with him and be his secret evil." (p. 7) Abandoned by her family, the aunt, to assert her individuality, had "combed individuality into her bob." (p.10) Further, the female narrator reasons that the "villagers punished her for acting as if she could have a private life, secret and apart from them." (p. 14) Therefore, the narrator interprets the aunt's death not as suicide but as defiance. The aunt kills herself and her baby, interprets the female narrator, because "at [the baby's] birth the two of them had felt the same raw pain of separation, a wound that only the family pressing tight could close. A child with no descent line would not soften her life but only trail after her, ghostlike, begging her to give it purpose. ... Full of milk, the little ghost slept. When it awoke, she hardened her breasts against the milk that crying loosens. Toward morning she picked up the baby and walked to the well." (pp. 17–18) Just as Brave Orchid's version of the aunt's life, pregnancy, and death functions to validate her husband's patriarchal view of the aunt, the female narrator's rethought version functions to give her a forerunner, a feminist descent line. But the aunt, No Name Woman, cannot serve as a model for the narrator because she kills herself.

From the stories that her mother, Brave Orchid, tells her, the female narrator, in her search for social identification and historical continuity, finds a second possible model in a legendary Chinese woman warrior, Fa Mu Lan. Again, the female narrator uses her feminist consciousness to rethink and rework the legend of the Chinese woman warrior. At the same time that Brave Orchid tells her daughter the story of her nameless, forgotten aunt as a warning against getting pregnant, she also tells her "the song of the woman warrior," Fa Mu Lan, who goes out, avenges her people, finds a husband who soldiers with her, and returns "home to [her] parents-in-law and husband and son." (p. 53)

A traditional reading of the Fa Mu Lan legend focuses with admiration on Fa Mu Lan's temporary, ephemeral adoption of higher masculine traits and the way she, upon the completion of her masculine mission, sheds her unnatural male disguise and reverts back to her traditional female role.[6] With the female narrator reworking and retelling the ancient story, Fa Mu Lan emerges as a new figure, an avenger for women. She emerges as a new myth of female initiation in the wilderness: the new woman warrior acquires physical strength and mental acumen through solitary survival in nature.[7] The female narrator, who transforms the Fa Mu Lan legend into a personal myth of being herself the savior of her people ["The call would come from a bird that flew over our roof. ... I would be a little girl of seven the day I followed the bird away into the mountains." (p. 24)], includes within her retold tale certain elements that bring forth the injustices women suffer in patriarchal China. Hunting down the baron of her own village who has drafted her brother, the female narrator as Fa Mu Lan presents herself as the defender of the whole village: "I want your life in payment for your crimes against the villagers." (p. 51) But the baron—showing his sexism by quoting her the sayings she hates ("Girls are maggots in the rice" and "It is more profitable to raise geese than daughters." [p. 51])—tries to appeal to her "man to man," legally acknowledging his crimes against women in a misguided attempt at male bonding.[8] In addition, in subverting and transforming the legend of Fa Mu Lan, the female narrator valorizes things uniquely feminine, such as menstruation ("Menstrual days did not interrupt my training; I was as strong as on any other day." [p. 36]), pregnancy, and childbirth. "Marriage and childbirth strengthen the swordswoman." (p. 57) Finally, in her version of the Fa Mu Lan legend, she revises the dynamic between the old man and the woman, showing the woman as unsubmissive. The female narrator's version of Fa Mu Lan introduces a woman warrior who avenges sexism in her own village and further gives the female narrator a feminist descent line by giving her historical continuity. But the legend of Fa Mu Lan as a model proves inadequate because the narrator does not know how to transfer the legend into an American context.

In using her feminist consciousness to rework and to twist into designs the events of her aunt's life, pregnancy, and death, and of the legend of Fa Mu Lan, the female narrator of *The Woman Warrior* problematizes the entire notion of historical and legendary knowledge. She shows that there is no single, essentialized, transcendent concept of history, that history and legends are human constructs. She does not argue that historical events from the past do not exist. Rather, she questions whether we can *know* that past other than through its textualized remains. The meaning and shape of history are not in the events, but in the ideological or discursive systems that make these past events into present historical facts.

A third model that the female narrator uses to ferret out her social identification and establish historical continuity is her mother, Brave Orchid, who was a successful woman warrior in China. When her husband comes to America, Brave Orchid, after losing her two children in a fire, uses the money sent home by her

husband to become a doctor in a Western school in China, coura-
geously defying the Chinese taboo on education for women. She
leaves her village for Canton, where she becomes free of all family
obligations. "Free from families, my mother would live for two
years without servitude. She would not have to run errands for
my father's tryant mother with the bound feet or thread needles
for the old ladies." (p. 73)

The female narrator's account of her mother's life gives the
image of a woman warrior who is a part of the emergence of a
new woman in China. "The [women] students at the To Keung
School of Midwifery were new women, scientists who changed the
rituals. When she got scared as a child, one of my mother's three
mothers had held her and chanted their descent line, reeling the
frightened spirit back from the farthest deserts." (pp. 88–89) But,
at the midwifery school, when Brave Orchid loses her spirit, the
women do not call out "her real descent line" which entails calling
out "personal names and secrets about husbands, babies, [and]
renegades." Calling out personal names would lead Brave Orchid
back to her village. To bring her back to them, "they called out
their names, women's pretty names, haphazard names, horizontal
names of one generation. They pieced together new directions,
and [Brave Orchid's] spirit followed them instead of the old foot-
prints." (p. 89) This change in descent line causes Brave Orchid to
lose her home village, and she does not reach her husband in
America for fifteen years. Like her mother, the female narrator
will also have to change descent line.

After two years of study, Brave Orchid becomes a doctor.
According to the narrator's reconstructed version of her mother's
sojourn, Brave Orchid had gone away "ordinary" and had
returned home "miraculous like the ancient magicians who came
down from the mountains." When she joins her husband in
America, Brave Orchid is no longer a warrior; she is only a worker.
"This is terrible ghost country, where a human being works her
life away," she said. "Even the ghosts work, no time for acrobatics.
I have not stopped working since the day the ship landed. I was
on my feet the moment the babies were out. In China I never ever
had to hang up my clothes." (p. 122) In America, Brave Orchid
spends her life working in the family's laundry business, which is
later torn down for urban renewal. At the age of eighty, she is
catching the day truck to pick tomatoes with the Mexican workers.

In addition, she fails to reunite Moon Orchid with her husband. Thus, Brave Orchid is a woman warrior only in a Chinese context. Therefore, she is limited as a model for her daughter. In addition, the female narrator is also aware of Brave Orchid's partial Chinese acceptance of female inferiority, demonstrated in her purchase of a girl slave, and in her acceptance of the status quo, which is shown in her refusal to treat the dying or to save a mad-woman from a communal murder when challenging the community's values was personally dangerous.[9] "'The midwife or a relative would take the back of a girl baby's head in her hand and turn her face into the ashes,' said my mother. 'It was very easy.' She never said she herself killed babies," but it remains a possibility. (p. 101)

Comparing her own life story to that of the magnificent story of Fa Mu Lan and her mother's earlier warrior life, the female narrator admits that her life is not as fullfilling. She is having difficulty becoming a warrior in America. Her mother "talk-stories" about a girl who saved her village, but the female narrator "couldn't figure out" what her own village was. How can she become an effective woman warrior in America? When urban renewal tore down her parents' laundry business, she could only make up gun and knife fantasies. How can she conquer the enemy?

But the female narrator does come to learn who the enemies are. They are "stupid racists" and men who are "business-suited in their modern American executive guise." But she is impotent when face to face with them. Once when she worked in an art supply house and her boss told her to order "more of that nigger yellow," she replied that she did not like the word. Her complaint had no impact, for her boss never responded. In another situation, she is fired from a land developer's association when she, in her squeaky voice, informs her boss that the restaurant he chose for the banquet is being picketed by Civil Rights organizations such as CORE and the NAACP. Again, the female narrator, who can identify the enemy, fails as a warrior against "stupid racists" or against the "tyrants who for whatever reason can deny [her] family food and drink." (p. 58)

These abortive attempts at being a woman warrior show the female narrator the enormous task she would have to undertake if she were to become a warrior in America who has the avenging magnitude of Fa Mu Lan: "To avenge my family, I'd have to storm across China to take back our farm from the Communists; I'd have to rage across the United States to take back the laundry in New York and the one in California. Nobody in history has conquered and united both North America and Asia. ... I mustn't feel bad that I haven't done as well as the swordswoman did; after all, no bird called me, no wise old people tutored me. I have no magic beads, no water gourd sight, no rabbit that will jump in the fire when I'm hungry. I dislike armies." (pp. 58–59) Despite the enormous task faced by the swordswoman, the female narrator also realizes that she and the swordswoman are "not too dissimilar." What they have in common are the "words at [their] backs. The idioms for *revenge* are 'report a crime' and 'report to five families.' The reporting is the vengeance—not the beheading, not the gutting, but the words. And I have so many words—'chink' words and 'gook' words too—that they do not fit on my skin." (p. 62–63)

Unable to be a swordswoman in the traditional Chinese way, the female narrator, after a critical review of the history of the swordswoman in China, again transforms the values and reinterprets the events of the swordswoman into a contemporary context. Like the historical swordswoman, the female narrator knows her enemies and wants vengeance upon them. But whereas the historical swordswoman uses the sword to behead and achieves her vengeance thus, the female narrator recognizes that a woman warrior's power can lie in words, that the reporting of the crime can be the vengeance.

The female narrator's first vengeance is upon those who have repressed the existence of her aunt, who act as "if she [the aunt] had never been born." When her mother tells her about her aunt, she also tells her that she "must not tell anyone. ... Don't tell anyone you had an aunt. Your father doesn't want to hear her name." (p. 18) Initially, the female narrator agrees to remain silent because her parents "needed to clear their names, and a wrong word would incite the kinspeople even here." (p. 18) But later she becomes aware that her parents want more than silence from her. They want her to participate in her aunt's punishment; they want her to uphold a patriarchal system that has denied her aunt life and individuality. She decides that the "real punishment was not the raid swiftly inflicted by the villagers, but the family's deliberately forgetting her. Her betrayal so maddened them, they saw to it that she would suffer forever, even after death." (p. 18)

By writing *The Woman Warrior,* Kingston or the female narrator uses words and reporting for vengeance. She moves to rectify the aunt's punishment, to return her life and her own history to her by telling everybody her story. She devotes many pages of paper to making her aunt come alive. And in going against her father's command, in rethinking and re-creating her aunt as a feminist forerunner to herself, the female narrator creates her own feminist descent line.

The female narrator also creates a transcendental feminist narrative. This feminist narrative counters the existing patriarchal Chinese narrative and establishes its own hierarchy. The female narrator uses this narrative to measure the worth of other women in her personal and historical past. She thinks little of weak, sickly women such as her aunt, Moon Orchid, who goes crazy and is committed to an asylum because she cannot adjust to America. Also, because her feminist narrative hates "fragility" and dislikes women who do not have a voice or a personality, the female narrator tortures the passive, "quiet" Chinese American girl in her school. Thus we see how a totalized feminist narrative, like a totalized patriarchal narrative, becomes repressive and exclusionary.

In rethinking and reworking certain events from her childhood, from her aunt's life and death, from the legend of Fa Mu Lan, and from her mother's life, thereby making them relevant to the self the narrator wants to create, Kingston's *The Woman Warrior* is taking what Raymond Williams calls an innovative approach to tradition. In using a feminist consciousness or ideology to rethink and rework the past, *The Woman Warrior* offers a "version of the past which is intended to connect with and ratify the present. What it offers in practice is a sense of *predisposed* continuity."[10]

Also, Kingston in *The Woman Warrior* transforms the tales, her mother's "talk-stories," from an aesthetic form of the past into one of the present, making them serve much more than the moralistic, didactic function utilized by Brave Orchid. In telling her own story, the female narrator uses talk-storying to synthesize her Chinese and American heritages and, finally, to create a myth or an individual narrative that is in harmony with her own contemporary lived experience, that allows her to articulate her own subjective individuality. The story of Ts'ai Yen expresses the possibility of cultural integration that the female narrator yearns for as a woman warrior who can use her Chinese voice to harmonize with the music of another culture.

In the conscious manipulation of events from the past and in revealing the specific values that structure the writing, *The Woman Warrior* arrives at a truth that is socially and ideologically conditioned, thereby exposing the process of performativity. The reader is able to see the process by which notions of truth gain power and authority over others. "The performativity of the text," argues Linda Hutcheon, "questions whose notion of truth gains power and authority over others."[11] It also examines the "process of how it does so." In *The Woman Warrior,* a feminist notion of truth gains power and authority over an old Chinese patriarchal one.

Finally, in problematizing the notion of historical knowledge, *The Woman Warrior* self-consciously reminds us that while events did and do occur in the real empirical past, we name and constitute those events as historical facts by selection and narrative positioning, and that we only know of those past events through their discursive inscription, through their traces in the present.

The female narrator in *The Woman Warrior* achieves existential freedom and self-realization not by rejecting the past but by subverting and transforming the past into the present. In using her feminist consciousness to reflect critically on the past, the female narrator is able to resolve her modern condition. She is able to rethink and reconstruct a past that validates her present, subjective lived experience. Likewise, John Washington, the protagonist in David Bradley's *The Chaneysville Incident* cannot overcome his alienation and fragmentation, his lack of social identification, and his lack of historical continuity because he is trapped in his father's, Moses Washington's, naturalized narrative, his values, conventions, and definitions—values and definitions that are relevant to Moses Washington's existence but are incongruent with John Washington's existence in the present. John Washington learns eventually that if he is going to find truth in history, he has to think of history critically and contextually. To achieve the freedom to live his life in the present and according to his own desires and wants, he has to accept the presupposition that history, like fiction, constitutes a system of signification by which we make sense of the past, that our readings and interpretations of the historical past are vitally dependent on our experience of the present.

At its opening, *The Chaneysville Incident* presents immediately John Washington's modern dilemma. His present living situation alienates him from the values and views of his father. John, who is a Professor of History at a university in Philadelphia, has been living with Judith, a white psychiatrist, for the past five years. It appears to be a genuine relationship. They have developed the sort of esoteric codes of communication usually reserved for lovers. Judith has concern in her voice when she speaks to John, and the relationship is filled with human warmth, humor, and love.

Yet the five-year relationship has reached an impasse; it has not been finalized. John and Judith are not "legally espoused," and marriage does not appear imminent. Despite the fact that Judith's biological clock is running down, they have no children and there is no talk of children. John has not taken Judith home to meet his mother, and he refuses to discuss with her his childhood, or his inability to reconcile his father's values, which he has adopted and internalized, with his present living situation. Why the failure at finalizing this relationship?

The five-year relationship has not been finalized because Judith is white, and interracial marriages and interracial babies are excluded from, or are repressed in, John Washington's conception of the social real given to him by his father. What Judith's white skin represents for John is growing up with a father who had an essentialized narrative, a conception of time and space, that was not only distrusting of white people, but was also antithetical to a Judeo-Christian society. Basically, Moses Washington believes that man should be "natural." He believes that a man must be able to live in the wilderness. He "has to be able to make a fire, has to know how to make it in the wind an' the rain an' the dark."[12] Moses Washington believes that a man must know how to hunt, fish, curse, and drink whiskey. He must be independent—that is, not dependent on mother, Jesus, or the government.

After forty years of living naturally, or in nature, in the mountains and making and selling illegal whiskey, Moses Washington comes down into the small southwestern Pennsylvania town to live. But he does not become a conventional man; he continues to live by his own rules. He marries Yvette Stanton, the daughter of a prominent black historian in town. But there is no love or companionship in this marriage. It is not a conventional marriage; it is a marriage between allies. She wants children and he wants two sons to carry on his legacy.

But Moses Washington's marriage is not the only thing unconventional about his stay in society. In society, he remains a "natural" man. He continues to live by his own rules—totally disregarding the laws and mores of society. He pays bribes to the sheriff to sell his whiskey. He keeps a "folio" of illegal doings by prominent white citizens for blackmail purposes. He has "far-reaching theological discussions" with preachers about "certain Christian assumptions concerning the afterlife." (p. 128) He continues to mistrust white people. Jack Crawley narrates to John: " ... Moses didn't have no love for whitefolks. He'd sell to 'em, an' he'd buy from 'em when he had to, an' he'd talk to 'em if there wasn't no way around it, but he sure as hell wasn't goin' to think too much of John fallin' in love with one of 'em." (p. 87)

This is the narrative or way of life that John Washington inherits from his father. On his death bed, Moses solicits a promise from Jack Crawley that he will teach his son John "to be a man." (p. 36) Fulfilling his promise, Crawley teaches John how to be a "natural," independent man. He teaches him how to survive in the woods, how to aim a rifle, how to hunt and fish, how to "bring [his] breathing under control; to still [his] own fear, to be methodical; to accept [his] limitations and compensate." (p. 45) Like the men in his family who have come before him, John Washington is taught to be both rational and instinctive.

In asking Jack Crawley to teach his son to be a "natural" man, Moses Washington is taking the necessary action to continue the universalization, or transcendence, of his particular definition of manhood—a definition that he receives from his grandfather C. K. and that he accepts uncritically and imposes upon his subjective lived experiences. In Crawley's action, we see the process by which one notion of manhood gains power and authority over another. We also see the limitations of this definition when we witness how it becomes ineffectual for John. It arrests John Washington emotionally, not allowing him to live his life in the present. It fails to explain and validate John's contemporary lived experiences and, therefore, represses his desires and wants.

For a while, Moses Washington's way of life, or vision of man, becomes what his son John Washington wants out of life: "to get up in the morning, build a fire and go to the spring and pay a visit to the privy, and then cook my breakfast." (p. 47) In short, John accepts Moses Washington's definition of manhood as a part of an absolute racial tradition or cultural narrative. At this moment in his life, John does not realize that either Moses and C. K. have taken the raw material of history and made it relevant to them, or have imposed an external narrative upon their subjective lived experiences.

But somewhere along the way, John Washington abandons the natural, independent lifestyle of his father for the American success story. He accepts and internalizes some of the cognitive styles of the mainstream society. A "neat, clean-cut" appearance, the image of a "nice, gentle, shy Negro," and his passion for reading indicate that he has internalized the values of a secular American education and the behavior and appearance of middle- class America. John's competitive American spirit and his Protestant work ethic show as he reads the summer before college "the things that [his] soon-to-be classmates would have cut their intellectual teeth on." (p. 139) He becomes the local success story with his name and picture in the paper and his scholarship to college.

In addition to a father who held views and practiced values that are contradictory to his present living arrangement, John Washington's attitudes, especially about race, have also been shaped by his own experiences. He grows up in a small southwestern Pennsylvania town that was basically *de-facto* segregated. He learns early "many of the little assumptions and presumptions that go with dormant racism or well-meaning liberalism." (p. 68) Although never understanding why, John and other black males had to travel forty miles to another town to get haircuts. They could not swim in the city's public swimming pool and they were not welcomed in the town's coffee shop. John is aware that in this small southwestern Pennsylvania town blacks are buried in a segregated cemetery and black males are always drafted in the armed services before their white counterparts. More overt and more conscious are those incidents where John is "pursued by white boys from the town, shouting names and curses; [he] would make the climb imagining that all the house windows were eyes staring at [him]; that they knew, somehow, that that day someone had called [him] a name or threatened [him], and [he] had done nothing besides close [his] eyes and ears, trying to pretend it was not happening." (pp. 15–16) Finally, there is the experience that John has with a white friend, Robert, from high school, whose mother does not want John to visit the house any more because he is black. These experiences of racism explain John's mistrust, or even hatred, at times, of whites. They also generate or affirm his father's racial views.

Finally, John Washington's racial attitudes are further hardened by the circumstances surrounding his brother Bill's induction into the Army and his eventual death. Because of his athletic abilities in football and wrestling, Bill is passed academically through high school. When he has played out his four-year option and is of no more use to the school, he is flunked. Without school, Bill is eligible for the draft. Against John's advice and knowledge and through his mother's coercion, Bill is drafted into the Army and is sent to Vietnam where he is killed. John never forgives his mother for Bill's death. In fact, after Bill's death, he cuts off all communication with her.

The racial incidents he experiences in his home town, along with the circumstances surrounding his brother's death and his obvious desire for a middle-class American lifestyle, make John want to escape physically his family's past. He comes to hate his mother, perhaps for her choice of Bill as her favorite; he hates his father and was never close to his brother. He "promised [himself] that someday [he] would go where [the trucks] were going." (p. 14) John does go away and does not return until he receives the call from his mother announcing Jack Crawley's sickness and impending death. In going away, he had hoped both to abandon his life on the hill and to repress his father's definitions of manhood and of cultural life. Reflecting on this promise as he returns for Jack's death and funeral, John thinks: "I knew nothing about the Hill any longer, I had made it my business not to know." (p. 17)

Physically, John Washington is successful in escaping his family's past, but ideologically and psychologically he is still very much his father's son. He continues to accept Moses Washington's definition of manhood as a part of an absolute racial tradition or cultural narrative, despite the fact that it contradicts his present living arrangement and choice of lifestyle. His entrapment in many of the values and conventions of his father's essentialized narrative is amplified clearly in two poignant moments. The first moment comes after he has learned of Jack Crawley's illness. On the bus ride home, John grapples with the difficulty of abandoning his father's narrative. "And so I settled myself in my seat and took another pull on my flask and looked out the window at the mountainsides black with pine, and thought about how strange home is: a place to which you belong and which belongs to you even if you don't particularly like it or want it, a place you cannot escape, no matter how far you go or how furiously you run." (p. 13) The second moment comes in a conversation where Judith asks him why he is with her if he hates white people. "You're the man with the logic," she said. "Here's some for you. You hate white people. I am a white person. Therefore you hate me. Only you say you don't; you say you love me. Which seems like a contradiction. So I guess you must be lying about something. Either you can't hate so much or you can't love—." (p. 287) John's response is that "it's not that simple." John still views the world through his father's lens and by the experiences of his personal past.

Judith, who takes a practical approach to the situation, does not understand the complexity of John's contradictory predicament.[13] She does not understand how, on the one hand, John is in love with her, and how, on the other hand, he is tied, or is entrapped historically and ideologically, to a version of history that mistrusts white people. For Judith, the situation is rather simple: either John loves her or he hates her. But because he is unable to articulate his complex, contradictory feelings to Judith, John becomes silent.

The event, that forces him to confront both his father's essentialized narrative and his tenuous and unsettled relationship with Judith, who is growing impatient with him, comes with the illness and eventual death of Jack Crawley. After burying Jack Crawley, John becomes obsessed, again, with finding the truth about his father's life and death, which he has been pursuing since he was thirteen. Obviously, as a modern subject, he needs answers from his family's past to function as a whole person in the present. He needs a historical line from the past to the present, and he hopes to find it in his father's past. John first pursued the truth of his father's life and death three years after Moses Washington's death. He entered his father's attic and found "the chair, the table, the book, the lamp, the empty fireplace ... the keys to a man's mind, laid bare to [him], clues to a mystery, the answer to every question there. All [he] had to do was interpret them. It was the greatest thrill [he] had ever known." (pp. 144–145)

But this approach to history works from the assumption that history itself consists of a congeries of lived stories, individual and collective, and that the principal task of historians is to uncover these stories and retell them in a narrative.[14] John, the traditional novice historian, believes that history seeks to explain what happened in the past by providing a precise and accurate recon-struction of the events reported in the documents. In taking this approach to finding truth in history, John falls prey to one of the "greatest fallacies" that surrounds the study of the past: "the notion that there is such a thing as a detached researcher, that it is possible to discover and analyze and interpret without getting caught up and swept away." (p. 145) This first attempt to find truth in history ends in failure, for he refuses to accept the fact that our readings and interpretations of the historical past are vitally dependent on our experience of the present or that history constitutes a system of signification by which we make sense of the past.

After John buries Jack, he returns again to his father's attic. This time his interest is sparked because he is bewildered by certain facts found in his father's portfolio. Again, he is seeking the truth of his father's life and death. But this time, he is not a naive boy struggling to give shape to amorphous data, hoping to discover the truth of a legend—at least that is what he thinks. Now he is a Professor of History who has been trained to order facts, to control data. John organizes his facts on color-coded index cards. The organization of Moses Washington's books, John surmises, indicates that Moses had been researching something, that what had happened was not, as everybody thought, that Moses Washington had given up hunting but rather that he had transferred his energies and efforts to a different pursuit.

The question that plagues John is, why did Moses Washington leave his books and take up his gun after ten years? For clues to his father's action, John traces his biblical research, examining all the facts and documents. But in acting still as a traditional historian who refuses to imagine, or to think of history critically and contextually, he is still unable to unravel "the whys and wherefores" of Moses Washington. "I had put the facts together, all of them, everything I could cull from those books and his notebooks and my notebooks: everything. I had put it together and I had studied it until I could command every fact, and then I had stepped back and looked at the whole and seen ... nothing. Not a thing. Oh, I had seen the facts, there was no shortage of facts; but I could not discern the shape that they filled in." (pp. 151–152)

Still, in his endless search to find the truth about his father's life and death, John seeks information and knowledge from other sources. He has a rare conversation with his mother and he talks with Judge Scott, his father's friend. His mother reaffirms his knowledge that his father's marriage was one of convenience and that he lived an unconventional life. From Judge Scott, John learns about his father's business, his payment of bribes, and the portfolio he used for blackmail purposes. John also learns from Judge Scott that Moses Washington was both methodical and instinctive. But neither John's mother nor Judge Scott is able to shed any additional insight into why Moses Washington killed himself.

John moves into Jack Crawley's cabin, which is innocent of modern appliances and of an indoor bathroom, and which is literally very close to nature and the wilderness. He cleans the cabin of the "[stink] of dying," moves his belongings in from his mother's house, and adjusts to the meagre comforts that Jack's cabin provides. Obviously, he has clear intentions of staying for a while in the cabin. The letter to Judith and the hunting trip in the woods indicate John's rejection of his present condition—his relationship with Judith and his job as a historian—and his return to, or reenactment of, Jack's and Moses Washington's natural way of life.[15] But, in absorbing the full implication of John's letter, Judith comes to the Hill and disrupts John's reenactment. Her arrival brings John back to the present, which includes his dealing with his own existential existence, his relationship with her, and the mystery of his father's suicide.

With Judith, John visits Chaneysville—the place where the twelve slaves are buried and where C. K. and Moses Washington committed suicide. But because he still refuses to be intuitive, or imagine—which is an integral part of interpreting history and which is a prerequisite for his giving "shape" and "pattern" to the facts in his possession—John still cannot find the truth about Moses Washington's suicide. "Bit by bit the thoughts came slipping in, the facts and the calculations, the dates and the suspicions.

There was no pattern to them, nothing I could grab on to: it was just random cerebration; a mind chuckling to itself." (p. 336) The provisionality and uncertainty of John Washington the historian do not cast doubt upon his seriousness. All of his actions indicate his complete devotion to finding the truth about his father. Rather, they define the new postmodern seriousness that acknowledges the limits and powers of writing about the past. He is forced to grapple with the possibility that we can only know the past through discursive systems.

Simultaneous with John Washington's search for the truth of his father's suicide are repeated flashbacks to his unrealized relationship with Judith. Obviously, resolving the historical dilemma concerning his family's past, which has been narra- tivized into an essentialized truth by Moses Washington, also means resolving his personal one. But Moses Washington's truth in history does not satisfy or explain adequately John's present wants and desires. It does not give him a viable narrative by which to live in the present. In addition, John continues to view history as something that is objective, as something that is external to his subjective reality, or his own ideology. Again in Judith's company, John recognizes her love and warmth. He also acknowl- edges his attraction to her. "She stepped closer to me and thrust my hands into her armpits and held them there with her own. Slowly I felt the sensation come back, felt the warmth and the pressure from her, the swell of her breasts against my wrists ... seeing her cheek and belly and the faint hint of thigh beneath the material of her slacks, and I remembered how it felt to have the cheek against my chest, the belly and thighs solid and warm against mine." (p. 266) Yet, despite the acknowledged love and warmth, John still refuses to tell Judith about himself or his family's past. He still refuses to give himself completely to the relationship.

But later, when Judith asks John how he got here, John, for the first time in their five-year relationship, begins to tell Judith about his family's past. He tells her about the history of the Hill where he grew up, about the role the Methodist Church played in the slave trade. He tells Judith about the Underground Railroad. Then in a radical turn of events, John, pulling his father's portfolio from the shelf, reconstructs for Judith the history of the Stantons, his mother's side of the family. Then, he proceeds to reconstruct the history of the Washingtons, his father's side of the family.

In all of these stories about, and reconstructions of, the family's past, John is working only with facts. From the facts of his family's history, John sees a parallel in the lives of his father, Moses Washington, and his great-grandfather, C. K. Washington. Both C. K. and Moses were methodical and instinctive. For example, although C. K. was a "natural" man, he hunted the man down who killed his father and murdered him. Likewise, Moses is a natural man, but he also calculates how to manipulate the whites in town. Moses Washington had loved a woman because C. K. had loved a woman. Moses wanted sons because his grandfather had a son, Lamen Washington, who became "a fairly prominent black mortician." (p. 385) (Although *The Chaneysville Incident* does not consciously critique it, it shows unconsciously that John, like C. K. and Moses, sees women as objects. C. K. indifferently fathers a son. He "never ever mentions the fact that sometime during the winter she [Bijou, who is the mother of Lamen Washington] became his mistress." Moses, also, uses Yvette to bear him two sons; then he abandons her. John, even in his transformation in the end, does not engage his response to Judith as an object.) Both C. K. and Moses Washington had moved to the mountains of western Pennsylvania and had become bootleggers. He also reasons that knowledge of death had a significance for Moses that it did not have for most men.

But the facts in John's possession do not lead to a complete satisfactory history for him. The facts, and the system of signfica-tion that presents them, do not give him a history that will allow him to explain his present living situation. John does not know why death is so important to Moses and why Moses commits suicide; he does not know what happened to C. K., and that means he does not know anything. John does know that C. K.'s death and his father's death happened in Chaneysville where twelve slaves are buried. He knows that C. K. was in love with Harriette Brewer, who was "educated and intelligent" and who helped to "take escapees [from slavery] who had made it as far as Philadelphia on north." (p. 372) But he does not know the "details of the affair." (p. 372) He also knows that F. H. Pettis, who might have known C. K., "had seen the lucrative possibilities represented by fugitive slaves, and he had begun to advertise in Southern newspapers, offering to track down and return fugitive property." (p. 378) But he does not know if Pettis is the one who is responsible for C.K.'s murder.

In his visit to Chaneysville with Judith, John learns other

things. He learns that Moses had killed himself in "close proximity" to Richard Iiames's remains and in a family graveyard belonging to a family named Iiames. He also discovers an unmarked thirteenth grave. "It was like the others, the same size and shape, and it had nothing written on it, but it was not in the pattern at all, it was above it, closer to the southeast corner of the Iiames family plot, almost exactly where [Moses] would have been when he killed himself." (p. 398) John knows the facts of the history he is trying to know. He knows names and places and people. In short, he knows "what Moses Washington [and C. K.] knew when [they] got this far." But what John does not know are the connections between these facts, between these names and places and people, and so he does not know their meaning. He does not know how to make these names and places and people relevant to his own subjective reality. He does not know how to establish a historical line from the past to the present. That is, until he takes a non-rational leap of faith.

As Judith gets the toddies, John begins to reconstruct imaginatively a historical past and a truth of his father's life and death. He stops "wondering and worrying and start[s] doing what he should have been doing all along: thinking. Really thinking. Not just gathering facts and ordering them; not just trying to follow them along; *really* thinking, looking at the overall patterns of things and figuring out what the facts *had* to be." (p. 413) Unlike Moses Washington and C. K., when John Washington reaches the limit of his factual knowledge of his father's and great-grandfather's lives and deaths, he goes on beyond reconstruction into pure speculation. The signs of the narrative act fall away and with them all questions of authority and reliability: "'Facts,' I said. 'Don't you understand? There aren't any facts. All that about the runaway slaves and Moses Washington, that's extrapolation. It's not facts. I've used the facts.'" (p. 408)

In addition, John begins to trust Judith, and it is within this trust that he can "imagine" the truth of his father's death and resolve his unrealized relationship with Judith. "[Judith] brought the cup to me and pressed it into my hands, letting her hands linger there for a moment, holding the warmth of the cup against mine. I knew then that I had underestimated her, and had done it in a way that cheated us both. ... And then I realized that something strange was happening. Because I was no longer cold.

... I saw that she was leaning forward, her eyes shining in the light, fixed on the candle. And I looked at it too, at the steady flame, hardly a flame at all now, but a round, warm, even glow that seemed to grow as I looked at it, expanding until it filled my sight." (pp. 421, 430, 431).

The shift from reconstructed history based on facts to speculation is manifested in the sounds, and a voice, that John, and not Judith, hears through the wind. These sounds put John squarely in the non-rational, non-Western African tradition of C. K. and Moses. And just as C. K. and Moses, in committing suicide, had taken non-rational leaps, John takes a non-rational leap. With a drink and Judith's acceptance, John "imagines" and imposes a meaning on the historical past, on what had to happen to C.K. Washington and the slaves on the fateful night they went running through the woods of South County. In choosing to imagine, he has finally realized that the meaning and shape of history are not in the events, but in the ideological or discursive systems that make these past events into present historical facts. Thus, he begins to use his subjective reality and his wants and desires to shape the historical past.

Therefore, he imagines that C. K.'s life had included a lost love, a woman named Harriette Brewer. C. K. had fallen in love with Harriette some years after his first wife was killed in a race riot. Before they could consummate the relationship, C. K. had gone back to the mountains to run his whiskey business, and Harriette, who believed not only in financing slave escapees but also in leading them out, had gone South. The discovery of her action led C. K. to his many daring rescues of slaves. Pursued by Pettis, whose business is catching runaway slaves, and half the men of South County, C. K. and Harriette, John imagines, are reunited a few hours before they face death together. C. K. arrives at their hiding place to bring them supplies and realizes that the slaves are "watching him" and "waiting for him to lead them." (p. 448) Cornered by Pettis and his men, C. K., Harriette, and the twelve slaves sing the song: "And before I'll be a slave I'll be buried in my grave and go home to my God, and be free." (p. 448) Then they kill themselves.

In John's "imagined" history, the warmth that C. K. experiences with Harriette and the warmth that John is simultaneously experiencing in his life with Judith are more than physical warmth. It is a human warmth of two people in love. "But [John] had not known about the other cold, the cold inside, the glacier in his guts that had been growing and moving, inch by inch, year by year, grinding at him, freezing him. He had not known that. But he knew it now. Because he could feel it melting. The heat that melted it did not come from the fire, it came from her, from the warmth of her body that pressed against his back, the warmth of her arms around him, the warmth of her hands that cupped the base of his belly. He lay there, feeling the warmth filling him, feeling the fatigue draining from him, feeling the aching in his ribs easing, becoming almost pleasant, and wishing that he would never have to move." (p. 431) As John nears the completion of C. K.'s imagined history, Judith's warmth begins the melting of his "other cold"—the cold that has prevented him from sharing his past, his present, and his future with her because she is white.

Completing his imagined history, John imagines other things. After the slaves kill themselves they are buried next to a family graveyard. Richard Iiames, a white man who had come to Chaneysville, the "oldest continuous settlement in the County," (p. 395) in 1728, had taken "the time to bury them like that, to figure out who loved who." (p. 444) This reconstructed event allows John to believe that there are some good white people. John also concludes that Moses did not commit suicide, as C. K. had not committed suicide. Since he was sixteen, Moses had been on the search to prove the Christians wrong. He spends endless hours doing biblical research. He even goes to war because "he want[s] to understand dying," and he becomes a hero in the war because "he want[s] to take chances, [to] get closer to death." (p. 405) Finally, John reasons, Moses understands C. K.'s life and death. Going to Chaneysville, Moses was on a hunting trip—looking for his "Ancestors." Unlike Christians, C. K and Moses saw death, reasons John, not as the end of life, but as an extension of life. In "imagining" the historical past, John Washington recognizes that history depends as much upon intuition as upon analytical methods. Expressing his attitude toward history in an interview, David Bradley states: "History to me is raw material, the past is raw material. We can't be governed by it."[16]

In "imagining," in rewriting and re-presenting the contents and events of C. K.'s and Moses's lives and deaths, John Washington, like the female narrator in *The Woman Warrior*, produces a version of the past that validates and makes coherent his present existence. In producing his own narrative, John becomes aware of and rejects the naturalized narrative and tradition of his father and great-grandfather as a construct and becomes postmodern. His narrative becomes what Lyotard in *The Postmodern Condition* calls a language game, which has its own rules and has no recourse to a larger metanarrative or external principle of justice or authority. In this situation, the function of John's self-conscious and self-aware postmodern narrative, which is self-legitimating, is no longer truth but "performativity."[17] He does what he does not because there is an external truth or metanarrative to legitimate it, but because that is what he wants to do, that is what he desires. This postmodern narrative gives John the *option* of marrying Judith, which he hopes she understands. "As I struck the match it came to me how strange it would all look to someone else, someone from far away. And as I dropped the match to the wood and watched the flames go twisting, I wondered if that someone would understand. Not just someone; Judith. I wondered if she would understand when she saw the smoke go rising from the far side of the Hill." (p. 450) And in the conscious manipulation and interpretation of events from the past, he arrives at a truth that is socially and ideologically conditioned. It is a truth that is vitally dependent on his own subjective reality for its shape and pattern. In this truth, *The Chaneysville Incident* admits that the past is real and does exist, but it also suggests that there is no direct access to that past unmediated by the structures of our various discourses about it. John Washington has to use a discourse of his personal experience to make sense out of the past.

Therefore, as he and Judith prepare to leave Jack Crawley's cabin and return to Philadelphia, John seals the "folio up with candle wax, as [his] father had done for [him]" and puts it under his arm. Then, he puts "the books and pamphlets and diaries and maps back where they belonged, ready for the next man who would need them." (p. 450) Finally, he burns all the "pads and cards" he has accumulated. With the portfolio and the books and pamphlets and diaries and maps, and a copy of *The Chaneysville Incident,* whose chapters' headings are the same as John Washington's note cards, *his* son (and, hopefully, his daughter), in years to come will have to rethink and rework the contents and facts of the past. He, like John, will have to make the raw material of history relevant to himself. It is this constant rewriting and rethinking of history that prevent it from being conclusive and teleological.

In moving beyond reconstruction of facts into "imagining" or pure speculation, *The Chaneysville Incident* passes from mimesis of facts, rumors, documents, information gathered from a graveyard visit, Moses Washington's "personal memoirs," and the various characters'—Jack Crawley's, Judge Scott's, and Yvette Washington's—accounts to what Brian McHale in *Postmodernist Fiction* calls "unmediated diegesis, from characters 'telling' to the author directly 'showing' us what happened" between the various characters.[18] John Washington's mystery about his father's death and his great-grandfather's disappearance is solved not through epistemological processes of weighing evidence and making deductions—as traditional modern history is conceived and written—but through the imaginative projection of what could—and what *The Chaneysville Incident* insists *must*—have happened. Abandoning the intractable problems of attaining a reliable knowledge of the historical past, John Washington improvises a possible historical past. At this point, *The Chaneysville Incident* crosses the boundary between modernist and postmodernist writing.

In problematizing the entire notion of historical knowledge, Kingston in *The Woman Warrior* and Bradley in *The Chaneysville Incident* put into question the authority of any act of writing, by, to use the terms of Linda Hutcheon, "locating the discourses of both history and fiction within an ever-expanding intertextual network that mocks any notion of singularity."[19] Kingston and Bradley use the two texts to make us aware that historical truths are socially and ideologically conditioned, that history itself depends on the conventions of narrative, language, discourse, and ideology in order to present what happened.

Although both *The Woman Warrior* and *The Chaneysville Incident* give their modern heroine and postmodern protagonist, respectively, the individual freedom to ferret out their own existences without the burden of a codified and naturalized racial history on their shoulders and at the same time problematize history (both novel and innovative feats), they have been received and appropriated differently by critics and scholars.

Mainstream American and minority critical practices either reject Kingston's *The Woman Warrior* and Bradley's *The Chaneysville Incident* because they do not appropriate or ideologically reflect hegemonically contrived notions of the social real, or they appropriate them by rewriting them, making them amenable to certain institutionalized norms of the literary. In this rejection and appropriation, these critics and scholars ignore these books' innovative feat of problematizing history and presenting a postmodern subject who is outside of any external principle or authority. Instead, they read into these texts traditional racial, cultural, and feminist narratives. As Michel Foucault points out in *The Archaeology of Knowledge,* the notion of tradition allows critics and scholars or general historians to reduce difference and innovation proper to every beginning. It allows them to isolate and repress the new against a background of permanence.[20] It makes it possible for them to rethink the dispersion of history [and experience] in the form of the same.

An examination of the critical responses to *The Woman Warrior* will illustrate these points. Frank Chin's and Jeff Paul Chan's attack on and rejection of *The Woman Warrior* can be explained in term of its inability to reproduce or reflect their ideologically constructed notion of Chinese history and culture. They accuse the author of distorting traditional Chinese culture. Chin writes: "In *The Woman Warrior,* Kingston takes a childhood chant, the Ballad of Mulan, ... and re-writes the heroine, Fa Mulan, to the specs of the stereotype of the Chinese woman as a pathological white supremacist victimized and trapped in a hideous Chinese civilization. ... Kingston, [Henry David] Hwang, and [Amy] Tan are the first writers of Asian ancestry, to so boldly fake the best-known works from the most universally known body of Asian literature and lore in history. And to legitimate their faking, they have to fake all of Asian American history and literature, and argue that the immigrants who settled and established Chinese America lost touch with Chinese culture, and that a faulty memory combined with new experience produced new versions of these traditional stories."[21] Jeff Paul Chan faults Kingston for mistranslating the Cantonese term "ghost" and giving a distorted picture of Chinese American culture based on her subjective experiences.[22]

But Kingston is aware that she is distorting or twisting into designs certain traditional Chinese myths and legends. As Sau-ling Cynthia Wong states in her response to Chan's attack, "Kingston has never made any claims, explicit or implicit, to historical veracity."[23] The fact that she exposes this process of distortion in *The Woman Warrior* renders Chin's and Chan's attacks moot. However, the problem with Chin's and Chan's arguments is that they assume that there is some "real" Chinese culture that can be reflected accurately, that traditional Chinese myths and legends are universal and absolute and therefore transcend historical matrices such as patriarchal Chinese history. What they fail to understand is that there is no direct access either to the Chinese historical past or to social reality that is unmediated by the structures of our various ideological discourses, which distort, about them. The creators of these traditional Chinese myths and legends, which are human constructs, did the same things that Kingston does in *The Woman Warrior:* twist into designs, and therefore distort, the historical past or the social real to generate narratives or belief systems to explain their own subjective experiences and realities.

But despite its rejection by Chin and Chan, *The Woman Warrior* was immediately, and continues to be, canonized by mainstream, Asian American, and feminist literary scholarship, which keep it in print and visible. This scholarship rewrites *The Woman Warrior* to serve its political and ideological needs. First, traditional Chinese critics read *The Woman Warrior* into traditional Chinese culture. From Lucien Miller and Hui-Chuan Chang's "Fiction and Autobiography: Spatial Form in The Golden Gangue and *The Woman Warrior*," to Alfred S. Wang's "Lu Hsun and Maxine Hong Kingston: Medicine as a Symbol in Chinese And Chinese American Literature," to David Li's "The Naming of a Chinese American 'I': Cross-Cultural Sign/ifications in *The Woman Warrior*," to Linda Hunt's "I could not figure out what was my village: Gender vs. Ethnicity in Maxine Hong Kingston's *The Woman Warrior*," Kingston's *The Woman Warrior* is canonized racially and culturally. And in this racial and cultural canonization, *The Woman Warrior's* innovative and postmodern strategies of problematizing history are repressed.

Second, mainstream American critics also rewrite *The Woman Warrior* into their institutionalized norms of the literary. Writing in *The New York Times,* critic John Leonard, as Sau-ling Cynthia

Wong reports, calls it "one of the best [books] I've read in years."[24] Sara Blackburn places *The Woman Warrior* in the traditional, universal American immigrant experience: "In this searing, beautiful memoir of growing up as the first-generation American daughter of Chinese immigrant parents, Maxine Hong Kingston illuminates the experience of everyone who has ever felt the terror of being an emotional outsider."[25] Paul Gray of *Time* magazine calls *The Woman Warrior* an "astonishingly accomplished first book by an American-born Chinese woman. ... Though it is drenched in alienation, *The Woman Warrior* never whines. Author Kingston avoids rhetoric for a wealth of details—old customs and legends, the feel of Chinese enclaves transported to the California of her childhood. Even at their most poignant, her stories sing. Thousands of books have bubbled up out of the American melting pot. This should be one of those that will be remembered."[26] In *The New York Times Book Review*, Jane Kramer writes: "*[The Woman Warrior]* is a brilliant memoir. It shocks us out of our facile rhetoric, past the cliches of our obtuseness, back to the mystery of a stubbornly, utterly foreign sensibility, and I cannot think of another book since Andre Malraux's melancholy artifice, *La Tentation de l'Occident,* that even starts to do this."[27] *The Woman Warrior* won the National Book Critics Award for nonfiction in 1976 and was rated by *Time* magazine as one of the ten best works of nonfiction in the 1970s.

Again, in interpreting and defining *The Woman Warrior* within the context of certain institutionalized norms of the literary, Leonard, Blackburn, Gray, Kramer, and other mainstream critics repress that which is different and innovative about the text, namely its postmodern view, its conscious effort to show how historical truths are socially and ideologically conditioned. They also ignore completely *The Woman Warrior's* attempt to name a new social space, that of Chinese American.

The Woman Warrior is further canonized by Asian American Studies, particularly Asian American women scholars. Amy Ling sees Kingston as "not an isolated Athena," but as belonging to "a line of Chinese American women writers dating back nearly a century."[28] Critic Elaine Kim defends *The Woman Warrior* against Frank Chin's accusation of distortion. She writes that "it is impossible for Asian American women to interpret their own experiences as women without airing the 'dirty laundry.' For the women, the heroic [Chinese] past [Frank] Chin is recalling is a sham."[29] Although Ling, Wong, and Kim successfully defend Kingston's *The Woman Warrior* against the essentialism of Chin and Chan, they repress that which is most innovative about the text, namely its postmodern view, when they read it into a tradition. However, Asian American critic Shirley Geok-lin Lim recognizes this view when she writes: "Kingston's books are marked by intertextuality, that is, by layers of reinterpretations of earlier literatures, and consequently by a deliberate stylistic inventiveness."[30]

Finally, *The Woman Warrior* is appropriated into mainstream white feminist scholarship, which adds further to its canonization. From Leslie W. Rabine's "No Lost Paradise: Social Gender and Symbolic Gender in the Writings of Maxine Hong Kingston," to Joanne S. Frye's *"The Woman Warrior*: Claiming Narrative Power, Recreating Female Selfhood," to Jeanne Barker-Nunn's "Telling the Mother's story: History and Connection in the Autobiographies of Maxine Hong Kingston and Kim Chernin," to Mara E. Donaldson's "Woman as Hero in Margaret Atwood's *Surfacing* and Maxine Hong Kingston's *The Woman Warrior,"* we see how Kingston's *The Woman Warrior,* through feminist reading after feminist reading and through comparisons with other (white) feminist texts, is read into the canon of an established, feminist literary scholarship. Once canonized, *The Woman Warrior* has very little chance of being read through the strategies of poststructuralism or postmodernism.

Likewise, Bradley's *The Chaneysville Incident* receives a similar kind of rejection and rewriting by critics, making it amenable to certain ideological and institutionalized norms of the literary. First, mainstream critics and reviewers received *The Chaneysville Incident* favorably. Writing in the *Christian Science Monitor,* Bruce Allen states that, "for [him], *The Chaneysville Incident* rivals Toni Morrison's *Song of Solomon* as the best novel about the black experience in America since Ellison's *Invisible Man* nearly 30 years ago." Discussing its American and African American "literary echoes," Allen places *The Chaneysville Incident* in the tradition of Faulkner, Baldwin, Ellison, and Warren and focuses in on the sanctioned literary theme of black people's "experience and their suffering."[31] Vance Bourjaily further appropriates *The Chaneysville Incident* into the instutionalized norms of the literary by focusing on Bradley's ability to write a particular kind of fiction: "Whatever else may be said, and there's apt to be a lot said about David Bradley and his second novel, *The Chaneysville Incident,* the man's a writer. What he can do, at a pretty high level of energy, is synchronize five different kinds of rhetoric, control a complicated plot, manage a good-sized cast of characters, convey a lot of information, handle an intricate time scheme, pull off a couple of final tricks that dramatize provocative ideas, and generally keep things going for 200,000 words."[32] Typical of mainstream reviewers of African American novels, Bourjaily interprets the individual actions of the protagonist generically. "What blacks must do, John Washington feels, is recover belief in a religion, and particularly a view of death, suited to their African natures. The voodoo beliefs of Haiti perhaps come closest."[33] These reviews of *The Chaneysville Incident* repress the novel's innovation of producing a new postmodern subject. They generate and reaffirm conventional sterotypes of notions of aesthetic beauty or they generate and affirm the sanctioned literary convention of the African American as a suffering victim. All fail to deal with the most revolutionary thing about *The Chaneysville Incident:* the fact that a black man rejects essentialized narratives, from both his race and the white society, and chooses to live by his own wants and desires.

Other mainstream and African American critics continue rewriting *The Chaneysville Incident,* making it amenable to certain ideological and instutionalized norms of the literary. Klaus Ensslen interprets *The Chaneysville Incident* not as the textualization of an emergent postmodern racial individual who comes to exist outside of any absolute racial or cultural narrative, but as the working out of racial conflicts between blacks and whites in the late twentieth century. He argues that Bradley in *The Chaneysville Incident* "has created a new narrative space for representing the recurring referent of Afro-American literature— the so-called black experience." In doing so, Bradley has "added to what some critics see as the outstanding features of late twentieth century Western culture—its ongoing reconciliation with black culture."[34] In her discussion of *The Chaneysville Incident,* Trudier Harris reads it into the tradition of James Baldwin's *Another Country,* comparing Bradley's Judith to Baldwin's Vivaldo, who is initiated into a black world "that whites so seldom see with their black friends."[35] In reading and interpreting *The Chaneysville*

Incident against a background of permanence or tradition, Ensslen and Harris repress the new in this text. They totally ignore Bradley's problematizing of history and how that problematization signifies a new world view and a new social subject.

But despite the favorable reception by some mainstream critics, it is *The Chaneysville Incident's* newness that causes it to be ignored and repressed by most African American critics. Its themes of individualism and of problematizing historical knowledge and the prevailing interracial relationship between John Washington and Judith marginalize it from dominant African American critical discourses, which are basically essentialist and which involve varying degrees of cultural nationalism. Historical cultural nationalism tends to repress or subordinate issues of individualism and interracial relationship and focuses on codified and collective notions of history and traditions. Perhaps this explains the paucity of criticism on *The Chaneysville Incident* by African American critics. This inattention to *The Chaneysville Incident* can best explain its struggle to remain in print.

NOTES

1. Linda Hutcheon, *A Poetics of Postmodernism: History, Theory, Fiction* (New York: Routledge, 1988), p. 90.

2. *Ibid.,* p. 18.

3. Maxine Hong Kingston, *The Woman Warrior: Memoirs of a Girlhood among Ghosts* (New York: Vintage Books, 1977), p. 57. All further references will be to this edition and will be given in the text.

4. Linda Hutcheon, *A Poetics of Postmodernism,* p. 69.

5. Claude Levi-Strauss, *The Savage Mind* (Chicago: University of Chicago Press, 1966), p. 22.

6. Elizabeth J. Ordonez, "Narrative Texts by Ethnic Women: Rereading the Past, Reshaping the Future," *MELUS* IX (1982): p. 26.

7. *Ibid.,* p. 26.

8. Joanne S. Frye, "The Woman Warrior: Claiming Narrative Power, Recreating Female Selfhood," in *Faith of a (Woman) Writer,*

edited by Alice Kissler-Harris and William McBrien (Westport, Conn.: Greenwood Press, 1988), p. 295.

9. Majorie J. Lightfoot, "Hunting the Dragon in Kingston's *The Woman Warrior*," *MELUS* 13 (Fall-Winter 1986): p. 61.

10. Raymond Williams, *Marxism and Literature* (Oxford: Oxford University Press, 1977), p. 116.

11. Linda Hutcheon, *A Poetics of Postmodernism: History, Theory, Fiction* (New York: Routledge, 1988), p. 18.

12. David Bradley, *The Chaneysville Incident* (New York: Avon Books, 1982), p. 43. All further references will be to this edition and will be given in the text.

13. Of course, she should, for she is a trained psychiatrist. This is one of four technical flaws in *The Chaneysville Incident*. The other three are the scaling of the catfish, the lack of an explanation for John's absence from his job, and Jack's talking, despite his sickness, without interruption or pause.

14. Hayden White, *The Content of the Form: Narrative Discourse and Historical Representation* (Baltimore: John Hopkins University Press, 1987), pp. ix–x.

15. Klaus Enssler, "Fictionalizing History: David Bradley's *The Chaneysville Incident*," *Callaloo* 11 (Spring 1988): p. 285.

16. Susan L. Blake and James A. Miller, "The Business of Writing: An Interview with David Bradley," *MELUS* 7 (Spring-Summer 1984): p. 33.

17. Jean Francois Lyotard, *The Postmodern Condition*, p. 46.

18. Brian McHale, *Postmodernist Fiction* (New York: Methuen, 1987), p. 10.

19. Linda Hutcheon, *A Poetics of Postmodernism*, p. 129.

20. Michel Foucault, *The Archaeology of Knowledge* (New York: Harper Colophon Books, 1972), p. 21

21. Frank Chin, "Introduction," in *The Big Aiiieeeee!: An Anthology of Chinese American and Japanese American Literature,* edited by Jeffrey Paul Chan, Frank Chin, Lawson Fusado Inada, and Shawn Wong (New York: A Meridian Book, 1991), p. 3.

22. "Jeff Chan, Chairman of San Francisco State Asian American Studies, Attacks Review," *The San Francisco Journal*, May 4, 1977, p. 3.

23. Sau-ling Cynthia Wong, "Necessity and Extravagance In Maxine Hong Kingston's *The Woman Warrior:* Art and the Ethnic Experience," *MELUS* 15 (Spring 1988), p. 7.

24. Sau-ling Cynthia Wong, "Necessity and Extravagance in Maxine Hong Kingston's *The Woman Warrior:* Art and the Ethnic Experience," p. 25.

25. Sara Blackburn, "Notes of a Chinese Daughter," *Ms* 5 (January 1977), p. 39.

26. Paul Gray, "Book of Changes," *Time* 108 (December 6, 1976): p. 91.

27. Jane Kramer, "On being Chinese in China and America," *The New York Times Book Review* (November 7, 1976): p. 1.

28. Amy Ling, "Chinese American Women Writers: The Tradition behind Maxine Hong Kingston," in *Redefining American Literary History,* edited by A. Ruoff, LaVonne Brown, and Jerry W. Ward (New York: Modern Language Association of America, 1990), p. 219.

29. Elaine Kim, "'Such Opposite Creatures': Men and Women in Asian American Literature," *Michigan Quarterly Review* 29 (Winter 1990): p. 78.

30. Lim, Shirley Goek-lin, "Twelve Asian American Writers: In Search of Self-Definition," *MELUS* 13 (Spring-Summer 1986): p. 69.

31. Bruce Allen, "Well-made Novel sifts Black History," *Christian Science Monitor,* May 20, 1981, p. 17

32. Vance Bourjaily, "Thirteen Runaway Slaves and David Bradley," *The New York Times Book Review,* April 19, 1981: p. 7.

33. Vance Bourjaily, "Thirteen Runaway Slaves and David Bradley": p. 20.

34. Klaus Ensslen, "Fictionalizing History: David Bradley's *The Chaneysville Incident,"* *Callaloo* 11 (Spring 1988): pp. 294–295.

35. Trudier Harris, *Exorcising Blackness: Historical and Literary Lynching and Burning Rituals* (Bloomington: Indiana University Press, 1984), p. 166.

5

The Postmodern Subject:
Maxine Hong Kingston's *Tripmaster Monkey* and Richard Perry's *Montgomery's Children*

This chapter focuses on postmodernity and the postmodern subject and the ways American writers of color since the 1960s have engaged and textualized postmodern experiences in their respective racial groups. Postmodernity, as a new social formation, is a social, economic, and philosophical condition, which emerged in the United States in the 1960s. It not only critiques and dispenses with positivism and Marxism, but humanism as well, since it calls into question Enlightenment notions of the modern subject. The term "postmodernism" in literary criticism has been traced to the 1950s, when it was used by Irving Howe and Harry Levin to describe or lament the levelling off of the modernist movement in American poetry. Howe and Levin were looking back nostalgically to what already seemed like a richer past.[1] "Postmodernism" was used again in the 1960s by such literary critics and artists as Leslie Fiedler, Ihab Hassan, and Susan Sontag who held widely divergent views of what a postmodern literature was. Generally, for them postmodern literature was that literature which derided the pretensions of modern art and attempted to close the gap between elite and mass culture. It was only during the 1970s that the term gained acceptance in such other disciplines as architecture, dance, theater, painting, film, and music.[2]

By the 1970s, however, as Andreas Huyssen argues, postmodernism had developed two strains. One strain became quite eclectic and esoteric in its attempt to abandon the struggle for metaphysical meaning and to show us, without moralizing, the tone and the manners of an emerging postmodern society. This strain abandoned any notion of critique. A second strain of postmodernism rejected the version of modernism that attempts to rescue authentic life and art from the vulgarities and impurities of mass culture. It moved to close the gap between elite culture and mass culture.[3]

In the 1980s, Postmodernism joined with poststructuralism in rejecting any postulates that were considered totalizing, metaphysical, and/or essentialist. This means that we can consider as postmodern fiction that literature which consciously exposes those narrative strategies, or the process, which would lead to totality, that would advocate an essence, a metaphysics, or a meta-narrative. Finally, we can consider as postmodern fiction that literature which constructs the subject as decentered, as possessing various subjective positions, or as a network of desires. Unlike the alienated, modern subject who seeks temporal unification of the past and the future with the present, the postmodern subject is free from all metaphysical narratives, free to simply desire and want. He or she no longer seeks social change; he or she exists only to satisfy his or her desires.

The postmodern subject is not new to the cultures and literatures of people of color in the United States. The trickster, who exists as a marginal figure in Native American, African American, and Asian American histories and cultures is a postmodern subject, with his multiple identities existing without a conflict. In the literatures of people of color, the postmodern subject has existed as a part of a repressed discourse in modern texts that sought totality, closure, metaphysical meaning, and historical continuity. The minor character, Rinehart, in Ralph Ellison's *Invisible Man*, published in 1952, is constructed as a postmodern subject. He has many subjective positions. Encountering this new phenomenon of African American urban reality, the invisible man questions and ponders: "Can it be, I thought, can it actually be? And I knew that it was. I had heard of it before but I'd never come so close. Still, could he be all of them: Rine the runner and Rine the gambler and Rine the briber and Rine the lover and Rinehart the Reverend?"[4] Rinehart has many identities superimposed upon each other, and we never know, in the modern sense, which identity is the "real" Rinehart. Rinehart exists to satisfy his many desires, and, therefore, a moral, rational narrative has not been imposed upon his various subjective positions. He is not a centered subject. Likewise, the minor character, Arnold Tippis, in Charles Johnson's *Faith and The Good Thing* (1975), is also constructed as a postmodern character. He appears to Faith and the reader as a retired dentist, a peddler of medical dictionaries, a porter, an insurance salesman, and later as a male nurse. And Faith and the reader never know who is the "real" Arnold. As I have discussed earlier, Tosamiah in Momaday's *House Made of Dawn* is a postmodern subject. Andrea Lee in *Sarah Phillips* acknowledges aspects of this postmodern experience in Sarah's nihilism, particularly during her stay in Paris, where Sarah wants to reject the past and live in a "world where life [is] aimless and sometimes bizarre." But in *Sarah Phillips* this postmodern experience never comes to fruition, and instead is repressed, because the text remains entrapped in modern literary conventions. The minor character, Huero, in Guy Garcia's *Skin Deep* is constructed as a postmodern subject in that he apparently exists without being a centered subject. There are many Hueros: "Huero the professor, Huero the cynical preacher, Huero the revolutionary, Huero the gangleader."[5] Huero has no desire or inclination to solidify the various conflicting selves into a whole subject.

Finally, Marita Golden in *Long Distance Life* presents a postmodern subject as a minor character. There is the middle-class dope dealer ("freelance business"), Nathaniel, who has "created a small universe in which he sets the rules." Nathaniel's life becomes a performance that seeks no outside authority or narrative for validation or legitimation. He lives in the here and now, totally disconnected from a narrative about history. Nathaniel "thought the only moments he was really alive were when he was nearly losing his life." He is decentered in that the thought of being "both a [dope] pusher and a dutiful son inflamed [his] imagination."[6] His two contradictory subjective positions or desires coexist in the same space. The agony and doubt over choices, self-worth, career, and family that plague others are foreign to Nathaniel.

In the modern novels mentioned above, the postmodern experience is subordinated or repressed. Ellison's invisible man, Garcia's David, Johnson's Faith, and Momaday's Abel—the centers of their authors' morality—reject the postmodern Rinehart,

Arnold, Huero, and Tosamiah, implying that their existences are not acceptable options for these searching modern protagonists. Garcia defines Huero in the negative: his life is not a viable option for the middle-class, educated, modern protagonist David Loya. The solution to the modern dilemma of Abel and David Loya is not the acceptance of a fragmented existence, but a retreat to a romantic past where wholeness and historical continuity and notions of the unified subject are considered the norm. Lastly, in making Nathaniel's postmodern life into a tragedy, Marita Golden in *Long Distance Life* denies it its validity.

But, unlike the above mentioned modern novels, Maxine Hong Kingston's *Tripmaster Monkey* (1989), Richard Perry's *Montgomery's Children* (1984), Alejandro Morales's *Reto en el paraiso* (1983), John Edgar Wideman's *Philadelphia Fire* (1990), Al Young's *Who is Angelina?* (1975), Don Belton's *Almost Midnight* (1986), Arturo Islas's *Migrant Souls* (1990), Ana Castillo's *The Mixquiahuala Letters* (1986), Theresa Hak Kyung Cha's *Dict ee* (1982), Ishmael Reed's *Mumbo Jumbo* (1972), Gerald Vizenor's *The Heirs of Columbus* (1992), Gloria Anzaldua's *Borderlands / La Frontera* (1987), and Charles Johnson's *Faith and The Good Thing* (1974) and *The Middle Passage* (1990) bring the repressed discourses of postmodernity and of the postmodern subject to the forefront, or to the center of the text—either at the narrative level or at the subject level. They accept and privilege the logic of postmodernity.

Yet all of the abovementioned texts, except Perry's *Montgomery's Children,* Cha's *Dict ee,* Ishmael Reed's *Mumbo Jumbo,* Gerald Vizenor's *The Heirs of Columbus,* Anzaldua's *Borderlands / La Frontera,* and Belton's *Almost Midnight,* see the need to either repress their main heroines' and protagonists' multiple selves, their various contradictory subjective positions, or to bring closure to the text. In short, they see a need to impose a structure on the contradictory impulses and desires that make up their postmodern characters, usually under the pretense of making them socially responsible. In this chapter, I will discuss Maxine Hong Kingston's *Tripmaster Monkey,* which imposes a structure on her protagonist's desires and impulses, and Richard Perry's *Montgomery's Children,* which does not.

There are three subtexts informing the production of Kingston's *Tripmaster Monkey.* The first is the legend of Gwan

Goong. The references to this figure can be seen as either multi-faceted or ambiguous, invoked alternately as the god of readers, theater, "gamblers, beautiful Hong Kong girls, faery girls who float among birds and bats and flowers, kids riding on deer."[7] The legendary Gwan Goong figure has various subjective positions and participates in many mini-narratives without conflict.

A second subtext that informs *Tripmaster Monkey* is the legend of the Chinese Monkey god, who is an archetypal trickster king. This character is drawn from *The Journey to the West,* a one-hundred-dred-chapter Chinese epic consolidated from various ancient texts in the fourteenth century. He has considerable powers, an exuberant sense of humor, and many rebellious antics and tricks. The mythical Monkey can transform himself into seventy-two different incarnations, allowing him to rescue Tripitaka from a variety of perils during the pilgrimage to the West.

Finally, the mythical Monkey wields a magic staff, formed from a slab of iron that no one, not even "the high immortal himself" can lift. Monkey can cause it to grow until "its top reached the thirty-third Heaven and its bottom the eighteenth layer of Hell," and he can shrink it "into a tiny embroidery needle stored behind his ear."[8] Monkey is therefore able to defeat almost all enemies simply by enlarging his staff and crushing them. The figures Gwan Goong and Monkey, who can incarnate themselves into different subjective positions or can participate in several mini-narratives without conflict, allow Kingston to use them to generate and reinforce Wittman's postmodern life.

A third and final subtext that informs the production of *Tripmaster Monkey* is *The Notebooks of Malte Laurids Brigge,* by Rainer Marie Rilke, which carries with it a modern sense of existential angst. Without the slightest hint of a pattern, the novel is the story of a young Dane, Malte Laurids Brigge, who leaves Denmark, his country, and journeys to Paris. At the beginning, the novel's action alternates between Malte's life in Paris and his childhood in Denmark, where the decisive event is the death of his paternal grandfather. In Paris, Malte feels himself to be the last representative of his race, and senses that his blood is becoming thin. His consciousness flares up in an agony of suscep-tibility. Although he has not been reduced completely to poverty, he lives in the Latin Quarter, like some beachcomber. He lives in the dark of Paris, among the castaways and the street people.

Despite the fact that he believes that God cannot be a part of this reality, he yearns for the love of God. In the second part of the novel, there is an endless procession of historical figures. The novel ends with a version of the tale of the Prodigal Son, whose escape and return is bound up with an exploration of the meaning of love. Did he himself not know how to love? Or had he forgotten? But Rilke is less concerned with the Son's ability to give than his refusal to accept what he saw as the wrong kind of love. Malte's existential journey becomes a longing for home, for the collective and for the love of God. Rilke's *The Notebooks of Malte Laurids Brigge* becomes a deep structure underlying Kingston's seemingly chaotic postmodern tableau. It can assist us in explaining her establishment of a modern narrative at the conclusion of the novel.

Tripmaster Monkey: A Fake Book gives us a decentered, postmodern subject in Wittman Ah Sing whose, to use the terms of Deleuze and Guattari in *Anti-Oedipus,* "desiring-machines," which are "binary machines, obeying a binary law or set of rules governing association," or flows of desire, have not been reduced to the Oedipal codes or any other symbol, image, or representation.[9] In a decentered subject, the ego is disarmed. "To be anti-oedipal is to be anti-ego as well as anti-homo, willfully attacking all reductive psychanalytic and political analyses that remain caught within the sphere of totality and unity; in order to free the multiplicity of desire from the deadly neurotic and Oedipal yoke."[10] Since desire flows, there is no need for an unconscious, which is the effect of a banishment from consciousness of conflicting and contradictory desires by a symbolic order.

Like Rilke's Malte in *The Notebooks of Malte Laurids Brigge,* Wittman Ah Sing is not able to sustain his "desiring-machines." Alienation and existential anguish eventually cause him to give up the notion of living a free-spirited, here-and-now existence. Eventually, he accepts an order of representation or meta-narrative. In literary terms, this means that Wittman Ah Sing is characterized by a contradictory combination of modernist (the longing for a meta-narrative) and postmodernist (an acceptance of the decentered self) notions. This contradictory combination is embodied not only in *Tripmaster Monkey's* protagonist, Wittman, but also in its structure, where language games and a self-reflexive narrative give way to a single narrative in the end. But the narrator, who knows more than Wittman, remains distant from and ironic toward meta-narrative throughout, even after Wittman succumbs to a narrative at the end.

The Wittman Ah Sing we encounter at the opening of *Tripmaster Monkey* is different from the people in his surroundings, especially the people on the streets. Just as Rilke's Malte feels that the castaways, those figures of the lowest depths far beneath society who seem to emerge from the underground into the streets of Paris to haunt him, beckon him to follow them into an inconceivable abyss, Wittman feels that he will be hurt by the creatures from the "land of the wasted" that he encounters on the streets of San Francisco. When he opens up, he sees an old white woman sitting on a bench selling trivets. From the look of her feet, he can tell that she is one of the "crazy people who have no place to go." After watching on the streets a pigeon and a squatting man, both puking, a man fighting with his dog ["Who do you think you are bitch? Huh, bitch? You listening to me?" (p. 6)], and a Black man "pushing a shopping cart transporting one red apple and a red bull from Tijuana," Wittman decides that it is time to "stop letting it all come in." (p. 7) In seeing these creatures on the streets of San Francisco, his horror is at mankind's failure to grasp that ultimate reality is, and must be, free, utterly individual, unrepeatable, and unique. "The trouble with most people is that they don't think about the meaning of life." (p. 74)

The Wittman we encounter during the first three-fourths of the novel is free, and his freedom originates from both America and China. He considers himself the late-twentieth-century reincarnation of the Chinese King of Monkeys. Also, he, like Walt Whitman, is an organic being. He has not allowed his desires to be displaced from the level of pure mechanical functioning to the level of signifying.[11] He is the absolute individual in whom and through whom he experiences and reveals his subjectivity as true being. Unlike individuals in his surroundings, he is not a centered subject because he has not allowed a single perspective or representation to represent his desire and craving. "One of his rules for maintaining sincerity used to be: Never tell the same story twice. He changed that to: Don't say the same thing in the same way to the same person twice. Better to be dead than boring." (p. 19)

He has no fixed subject status, only subject positions. He does not posit overtly grand schemes of social change; only the body and immediate desire and satisfaction matter. He does not behave according to some external cultural narrative. Instead, he behaves according to his own immediate desire and whim. One year out of Berkeley's English Department, he is a clerk in a toy store, a visionary playwright who is writing a play, a self-conscious poet, an uneasy street stylist, the Chinese American Walt Whitman, and the present day incarnation of Monkey. (He moves and behaves like a monkey. When Nanci attempts to leave him, "Wittman jump[s] off the table to the mattress, trampoline[s] off that to the Gold Mountain trunk and onto the chair."[p. 33])

He operates in an eclectic, self-validating, postmodern way by freely drawing from any of these various subjective positions or mini-narratives without conflict among them. Like the legendary Chinese Monkey who springs out of the trap on his somersault whenever anyone thinks that he is caught, Wittman exists as many selves within himself: "The monkey, using one of his seventy-two transformations, was changed into a working stiff on his way to his paying job." (p. 44) Conversing with Nanci Lee, Wittman talks of having spent four years at Berkeley "building worlds, inventing selves." (p. 19) He changes from a man to a woman. Staring at his genitals in the reflection of a sword handgun, he sees a "gigantic purple penis, which ends in a slit, like a vagina." In addition to these various subject and gender positions, Wittman has two names. Wittman Ah Sing is his American name; his other name is Joang Fu. All of Wittman's various subject positions coexist in the same space.

As a postmodern subject who does not have the experience of temporal continuity, he lives in a perpetual present. He has a "principle about spontaneity." He never looks, or plans his life, beyond a year at a time. For example, he only plans for twenty-six weeks of unemployment because he believes the "bomb could very well fall before unemployment runs out." (pp. 247–248) In fact, there is a sense that even filling out the next Claim Card takes him from his "true life" of being free.

Wittman Ah Sing has no home. Although his parents, who are free spirits, located in Sacramento in order to give him a home, Wittman believes that "people who have gone to college—people [his and Nanci's] age with their attee-tood—well, there are reasons—people who wear black turtleneck sweaters have no place." (pp. 10–11) Therefore, after graduating from Berkeley, he does not return to Sacramento because he does not belong. When he does return home with Tana to visit his mother, he returns because "he has access to a car." He thought he "might as well take advantage to see how the Aged Parents and Grandparent are doing." (p. 175)

In his daily life, Wittman's movements represent liberated "desiring-machines." He is the revolutionary par excellence, or the "representative bearer of all the forbidden desires and archaically thronging cravings that in their very nature have to be inimical to order, rebellious, and subversive."[12] There is no single order in the movement of his life. As *Tripmaster Monkey* opens, he moves from a long walk in Golden Gate Park, to San Francisco, to Oakland, to Sacramento, to Reno (Nevada), and back to San Francisco. His "hip" attitude and approach to life and his refusal to take anything—himself, his family, or the world— seriously, allow him to be rebellious and subversive, to debunk every image, or representation. Walking through Golden Gate Park, Wittman indicates that he considers "suicide everyday ... whose mind is it that doesn't suffer a loud takeover once in a while?" (p. 3) Yet immediately Wittman undermines the seriousness of his suicide attempt by stating that he is not making plans to do himself in. If he really were going to commit suicide, he would take a "big leap off the Golden Gate" bridge where "the wind or shock knocks you out before impact." (p. 3)

Although Wittman Ah Sing is an American of Chinese descent, he deconstructs or debunks the styles or images of other Chinese, showing them for precisely what they are: images. Walking in the park, he meets FOBs (Fresh Off the Boats) who are "so uncool" because they "didn't know how to walk together." (p. 5) He exposes the FOB fashions as "highwater" or "puddle cuffs." On his bus ride to Oakland to attend Lance's party, he sees a Chinese American girl and he wishes "she weren't Chinese, the kind who works hard and doesn't fix herself up." (p. 73) He debunks the engineering major from Fresno with a slide rule on his belt, the dental student from Stockton, and the pre-optometry majors from Gilroy and Vallejo and Lodi. They are unacceptable to him because they live cliched existences; they represent the repression of "desiring-machines," or the free spirit.

In addition, his own existence undermines racial stereotyping of Chinese Americans. He shows, as Elaine Kim argues, that

Chinese Americans are not exotic, inscrutable foreigners who are all alike, good in mathematics and bad in English. Wittman hates numbers, has "no sense of direction," and never stops talking.[13]

To elude becoming entrapped in cliched existence, or a meta-narrative, and thereby to remain free, Wittman Ah Sing uses and then subverts meta-narratives. He plays language games with the business world, various occupations, and the condition of unemployment. Although he is in the Management Training Program at the department store where he works, he is unsuccessful and is eventually demoted because he, unlike his co-worker Louise, cannot accept and abide by the Program's business philosophy. He becomes subversive when he asks management: "Do you give any goods, furniture, clothes, candy to the poor?" (p. 60) Seeing how Louise is successful in playing the role of the Management Trainee, he, in showing how the program can accept only controlled individuals, decides that "you have to be dumb to be happy on this earth." (p. 62) Unable to repress his production flow and adjust to an image, Wittman is fired from his job as Management Trainee.

Wittman Ah Sing uses and then subverts other social spaces he moves into as well. Although he has been invited to Lance's and Sunny's party, he meant to turn it down. Though he does end up attending the party, afterward he refuses Lance's attempt to show him the business ropes, to show him how to get a job. For Lance, the purpose of the party, or of parties, is to establish business contacts. But Wittman subverts Lance's purpose by making friends instead of contacts: "'Do you throw these parties for the sake of business deals? You go around assessing our connections? Why cultivate me? What good am I to you and your associates?' Wittman meant that he didn't want to do [any] business whatsoever. There has got to be a way to live and never do business." (p. 116) In exposing the strategies of Lance's business operation, Wittman accuses Lance of belonging, even if belonging does not serve his best interest: "You take their shit like they're not dishing out any. You act like you're having the best time no matter what kind of racist go-away signals they're flashing at you. And you keep it up and keep it up all along. I spot your technique, see? You A. J. A.s are really good at belonging, you belong to the Lions, the Masons, the V.F.W., the AMA, the American Dental Association. That's why they locked you up, man." (p. 118) Since he cannot belong to a narrative, Wittman decides that he is "going to start living the life of an artist now." (p. 84)

Perhaps, the best example of a Wittman Ah Sing who refuses to take anything seriously, who sees representations for precisely what they are, is his marriage to Tana. Without much thought, Wittman marries Tana to avoid the draft. But his and Tana's notion of marriage undermines immediately the conventional institution of marriage. They agree the night before that they will part company if they meet someone else they love. Unlike conventional married couples, they continue to live separately. When Wittman and Tana, newly married, return from Reno after looking for his grandmother Popo, Wittman drops Tana off at her place, for "if you don't get back to your own pok-mun alone when the weekend is over, you start becoming the husband part of a long term living-together couple." (p. 217)

For Wittman, marriage is not to prevent him from living his free life. It cannot become a narrative that denies the flows of desire. He asks: "How to break the news to a wife that she's married a Chang? Don't worry; she's going to be supported but in a way that isn't going to sacrifice his free life. She's going to have to help out. He'll teach her how to live on nothing, and she'll always be able to get along, with or without him. For her birthday and anniversary, take her out to the dining rooms that feed any old body, such as the Salvation Army and the Baptist mission." (p. 205)

Wittman's hip attitude is a kind of ironic nihilism in which ironic distance is offered as the only reasonable relation to take to a reality which is no longer reasonable. This estrangement from the familiar and the familiarization of the estranged mean that the lines separating the comic and the terrifying, the mundane and the exotic, the boring and the exciting, and the ordinary and the extraordinary disappear.[14] Deconstructing and establishing an ironic stance against all images and representations in the first three-fourths of *Tripmaster Monkey* allow Wittman's escape from them. The ironic stance allows him to remain free of all metaphysical traps, free to simply desire, which best describes postmodern subjectivity.

The structure of *Tripmaster Monkey* reinforces Wittman's ironic stance. In the first three-fourths of *Tripmaster Monkey*, the narrative is disjointed and freewheeling, thereby preventing it and the reader from establishing a unified, coherent myth or narrative. First, in the tradition of the beat poets and Rilke's Malte in *The Notebooks of Malte Laurids Brigge,* Wittman's journey is erratic. In capturing his movement, the structure shows a Wittman who wanders through the parks and streets of San Francisco, meets beautiful Nanci Lee, his Berkeley classmate, for lunch, marries Tana, visits his mother and aunts in Sacramento, rescues his grandmother Popo from slow death by abandonment, gets fired from his job in a department store, and fills in an unemployment form. In this erratic, somewhat haphazard, directionless journey, the reader is looking for an underlying coherent meaning. He or she is looking for a center, an imposed structure. But the randomness of the episodes, like Wittman's ironic eye, undermines the notion of a coherent narrative.

Furthermore, the sense of a coherent narrative is further undermined by interruptions by Wittman and the narrator in the already episodic narrative. In the middle of these random episodes, Wittman provides the reader with quotes from Rilke's *Notebooks* that, on the one hand, undermine the text's narrative and, on the other hand, reinforce the sense of Wittman's existential struggle, or his struggle to maintain his free spirit in a social reality where people live cliched lives. On the Muni bus ride, he, feeling his fear and alienation from other passengers, pulls the *Notebooks* from his pocket and reads a long quote in which Malte resists the castaways who beckon him away. He offers chunks of his play-in-progress. In the middle of the party episode at Lance's, Wittman takes out a sheaf of manuscript, the next part of his play, and *Tripmaster Monkey* changes from an episodic novel with narration to a play where characters are transformed into actors playing various roles in the play. "Taking the stance of Gwan Goong the Reader, who read in armor during battle, who read to enemies, who read loud when no one listened, Wittman Ah Sing read." (p. 134) In the play-in-progress, Wittman is transformed from a character in *Tripmaster Monkey* to Gwan Goong in the play. This is another way by which *Tripmaster Monkey* shows that Wittman is a construct, or a postmodern subject with many selves.

But even in putting the play-in-progress within the novel, which exposes the novel as artifact, *Tripmaster Monkey* also exposes the play-in-progress in the novel as, also, a process. " 'In war, we will fight side by side.' Wittman Goong [multiple identities coexisting in the same textual space] gave the next part. But Lance chimed in, and made this up: 'Wherever we find a sit-in, we'll sit. A salt march along the coast? We'll march. A spinning wheel, we'll spin.'" (p. 144) The play, open here to Lance's spontaneous revision, is discovered to have an unfixed shape.

A similar point is made, about the novel, when the narrator of *Tripmaster Monkey* interrupts the episodic narrative and speaks directly to the reader. Chapter One ends with Wittman working on his play "the rest of the night." Then the narrator interrupts the narrative and tells the reader "if you want to see whether he will get the play up, and how a poor monkey makes a living so he can afford to spend the weekday afternoon drinking coffee and hanging out, go on to the next chapter." (p. 35) At the end of Chapter Two, the narrator again interrupts the narrative to remind the reader to go on to the next chapter to see how "*our* monkey man will live—he parties, he plays—though unemployed. To see how he does it, go on to the next chapter." (p. 65) The narrator's interruptions expose *Tripmaster Monkey* as performativity, as a process. They force the reader to see it as a construct. In addition to interrupting its narrative to insert parts of a play-in-progress, *Tripmaster Monkey* tells movie plots blow by blow for pages at a time. There are detailed summaries of "War of the Worlds" and "Invasion of the Body Snatchers." In being self-conscious about the way it makes itself out of junk from other discourses, and in forcing the reader to be aware of its process, *Tripmaster Monkey,* to use the terms of Robert Alter, "flaunts its own condition of artifice and ... by doing so probes into the problematic relationships between real-seeming artifice and reality."[15]

But, despite the fact that Wittman Ah Sing uses and then subverts images and representations and social cliches to keep his "desiring-machines" free, to prevent himself from becoming entrapped in a metaphysics, at the end of *Tripmaster Monkey,* he becomes entrapped. His desire is displaced from the level of pure mechanical functioning to the level of signifying. Explaining how she gives Wittman the modern challenge to make the world a better place, Kingston states: "I wanted to see whether Wittman can take all this wonderful literature and make the world a better place, given what he knows."[16]

There are situations, responses, and feelings earlier in the text to indicate that it has a repressed unconscious and that Wittman is also an alienated modern subject who craves a narrative. Discussing the death of the Chinese theater with Nanci Lee, Wittman asks: "So what do we have in the way of a culture besides Chinese hand laundries ... Where's our jazz? Where's our blues? Where's our ain't-taking-no-shit-from-nobody street-strutting language? I want so bad to be the first bad-jazz China Man bluesman of America." (p. 27) In looking forward to becoming the "first bad-jazz China Man bluesman of America," Wittman wants to become the representative of the social. He desires a community. Wittman Ah Sing also sees the Beat poet as a model, as a potential representation. When he is in high school in Sacramento, he goes to City Lights Pocket Book Shop in San Francisco "looking for others of his kind." (p. 21) In the Beat poets, "he had seen for himself what an older generation of poets was like." (p. 113)

Finally, Wittman also has a repressed desire to belong to a tribe, or a collective. When Mr. Sanchez requests that he see the movie about going on a job interview, Wittman expresses a desire to belong to a tribe. "[Wittman] got lonely for that tribesman that said to the Peace Corps volunteer, 'We don't need a reading class, we've already got a guy who can read.' That's the tribe where he wants to belong, and the job he wants, to be the reader of the tribe. O right livelihood." (pp. 246–247) In another instance, Wittman ponders and admits his longing for a home and a tribe when, as a child in the theater, he encountered the cleaning man, an immigrant from a South Sea Island. The cleaning man had the job, but his wife and children helped, and his family provided him with a sense of belonging to something larger than himself. He "had people to have his breaks with, eating home-popped popcorn and drinking sodas. [The man] wasn't at all lonely working. Jobs ought to be like that." (p. 247)

Of course, Wittman, in his desire, on the one hand, for total freedom and, on the other, for a community, is aware that he is living a contradiction, that he is participating in two different narratives. He realizes that for a man "who wanted badly to be a free man," he was "promising quite a few people that he would help them out. He had to create for Nanci Lee a theater. And find his Popo. And keep Tana for richer, for poorer." (p. 223) But he immediately disarms this position, this awareness of his contradictory position, by stating that he has no philosophy of life. "Do the right thing by whoever crosses your path. These coincidental people are your people." (p. 223)

Yet Wittman still craves for a metanarrative. Like Malte in Rilke's *Notebooks,* he wants a community; he wants a theater. In the *Notebooks,* Malte's conformity with the Dionysian principle, to which the theater seems to point, is based upon the collective.[17] If Wittman's craving for a theater is one of his many flows of desire, his "desiring-machines" are not threatened. But, if, like Malte, his craving means that he, the individual who has contradictory desires and wants and impulses, is negated as absolute reality, Wittman sacrifices his desiring production in order to become a representation of the collective.

For a number of reasons, the ending supports the understanding that Wittman is sacrificing his desiring production, his individuality. In an interview, Kingston talks of this change: "He starts out in the book as a poet. ... And then, he wants to make a difference, socially. And he wants to form community."[18] First, Wittman believes he will have the "right livelihood" when the theater comes alive again. "For a century, every night somewhere in America, we had had a show. But our theater went dark. Something happened ten years ago, I don't know what, but. We'll cook and blast again. We have so much story, if we can't tell it entirely on the first night, we['ll] continue on the second night, the third, a week if we have to." (p. 277) Wittman begins the revival of the Chinese theater by staging a successful phantas-magorical street theater piece, complete with diving monkeys and realistic thousand-man battle scenes before his community. Second, at the end of the text, Wittman becomes a centered sub-ject with one perspective, with one conscious desire. He sacrifices his individuality, his options to participate in several narratives simultaneously or take many subjective positions. He is not a monkey, or a clerk in the toy section of a department store; he is a playwright whose job it is to tell our "story." "A Job can't be the plot of life, and not a soapy love-marriage-divorce-and hell no, not Viet Nam. To entertain and educate the solitaries that make up a community, the play will be a combination of revue-lecture." (p. 288) He is a playwright who will use the theater to build a com-munity. "Wittman was learning that one big bang-up show has to be followed up with a second show, a third show, shows until something takes hold. He was defining a community, which will meet every night for a season. Community is not built once-and-for-all; people have to imagine, practice, and re-create it." (p. 306) His theater will be organic and in the tradition of Walt Whitman:

"As playwright and producer and director, I'm casting blind. That means the actors can be any race. ... I'm including every thing that is being left out, and everybody who has no place." (p. 52) Taking on the job of telling our "story" and building a community means Wittman's desiring-machines are displaced by an image, a signification. Because the desiring-machines counter single perspective, order, and rationality and all forms of signification, they become incongruent with the new playwright who wants to build a community. They become repressed and unconscious.

This transformation of Wittman from a free-spirited, postmodern subject who has many subjective positions, who takes an ironic view of the world, and who deconstructs all social spaces he encounters to a modern subject who wants a single perspective, historical continuity, and a collective community culminates in the final scene. At the end of the play, Wittman as playwright-director appears on stage and delivers, virtually uninterrupted, a thirty-three page monologue where he vents his anger against Vietnam, cosmetic surgery among Asian women, and the racism of an America that refuses to see and acknowledge him and other Chinese Americans as Americans. "They want us to go back to China where we belong. They think that Americans are either white or Black. ... There is no East here. West is meeting West. ... I am so fucking offended. Why aren't you offended?" (pp. 307, 308)

Although the performance of his play has been very successful, Wittman is insulted by the culturally biased, condescending, and short-sighted praise of the reviewers. He takes the opportunity to address his audience and the reader directly and attempts to impose his new narrative as a force for change. In the monologue, there is no quoting of Rilke, which means that the search might be over. He has found wholeness and historical continuity and a social identification. Also, he presents himself only as a playwright. Finally, the monologue, unlike the first three-fourths of *Tripmaster Monkey,* has no linguistic acrobatics, parody, or irony to undermine its sincerity, to inform the reader that the monologue is not gospel. In this culmination of events we see a postmodern character seeking a collective and modern narrative.

However, it is the narrator in *Tripmaster Monkey* who is smarter than Wittman and who is most consistently aware of the danger of illusions, images, shadows, and significations—forms or representations—and who embraces at the end a skeptical and ironic view toward Wittman, introducing subtly a narrative distance from Wittman in the last third of the novel. In the first two-thirds, the narrative point of view is usually the third person's limited (Wittman's). But it occasionally shifts into Tana's perceptions, or Kingston will offer omniscient commentary, or she will inject an authorial first person pronoun. The subtle shifts occur in close proximity with Wittman's unfortunate expression of his own racial and sexual prejudices. When Wittman asks Tana: "Are you a loose white girl? Where do you live, loose white girl? I want to take you home. I want you to invite me in," the narrator comments: "She ought to have slapped his hands away, and dumped him for acting racist." (p. 151) When Wittman tells Tana a sexist "wedding story from the tradition of the Heroic Couple on the Battlefield that will turn [her] into a Chinese," the narrator retorts: "Wittman thought that with this story he was praising his lady, and teaching her to call him Beloved. Unbeknownst to him, Tana was getting feminist ideas to apply to his backass self." (p. 175)

In the end, Kingston becomes uncomfortable with the Wittman she has created, and she feels the need to critique him from a distance. At the conclusion, when Wittman finds collectivity in the theater and is delivering his monologue, the narrator states distantly: "Now, Wittman was giving out what he thought was his craziest riff, the weirdest take of his life at the movies. But the audience stayed with him. His community was madder than he was." (p. 314) The final line of *Tripmaster Monkey* reads, "Dear American monkey, don't be afraid. Here, let us tweak your ear, and kiss your other ear." (p. 340) Here, the narrator adopts the ironic distance that Wittman practiced in the first two-thirds of the novel, but has repudiated. But she tempers her irony with affection. She, unlike Wittman, does not become entrapped in an illusion, a symbolic order. This ear-tweaking gesture functions to return the reader, if not Wittman, to reality. His play is just a performance, not a transformation of America. Even members of his chosen audience are beginning to leave.

Whereas at the subject and narrative levels *Tripmaster Monkey* is transformed from a postmodern to a modern text, Richard Perry's *Montgomery's Children* at the narrative and subject levels, is transformed from a modern text to a postmodern text.

Montgomery's Children—in offering multiple, provisional alternatives to traditional, fixed concepts—critiques the metaphysical
nostalgia for truth, meaning, and history which is the cornerstone
of modernism. Unlike *Song of Solomon, House Made of Dawn,
Sarah Phillips,* and other modernist texts, *Montgomery's
Children* abandons the struggle for metaphysical meaning,
abstains from a moral or pathological reading of contemporary
African American and American society, and tells us about the
tone, the manners, and the social patterns of recent American
life. *Montgomery's Children* gives us something of the focused
desire, the quick apprehension and notation. Then, at the end, it
exposes itself as a construct.

In *Montgomery's Children,* Perry portrays the small town of
Montgomery, and specifically its African American community, as
it is being transformed, as a result of the modernization process,
from a modern to a postmodern society. Within the African
American community of Montgomery, Perry, early in the novel,
juxtaposes the modern narrative, defined mostly by the church,
with the lingering pre-modern, traditional African narrative. The
postmodern narrative emerges half way through the novel. But
by the novel's end, the traditional African narrative is killed off,
the modern narrative is fragmented and the postmodern narrative
becomes hegemonic. In putting the modernization process to work
within the text, Perry shows its effects on individuals and the
community in general. He examines the conditions of modernity
and postmodernity and privileges postmodernity.

In a postmodern mode, *Montgomery's Children* recognizes that
the "fantasy of interiority," the "pathological itch to scratch surfaces
for concealed depths," and the need for wholeness and transcendence have become obsolete according to the rules or social patterns
of postmodernity, which question concepts of subjective consciousness, continuity, or any totalizing or homogenizing
system.[19] Postmodernity recognizes that desire is here and now,
that fragments and surfaces are all that we have, and that kitsch
is as good as the real thing because there is no real thing.
Whereas the modern subject forges unity through a temporal
unification of the past and the future with the present, the postmodern subject is decentered, has many subjective positions, and
is also disconnected from past and future.

The first half of *Montgomery's Children* gives us a traditional, fixed concept of community where shared standards of excellence, expressed through the church, impose restraints on its members. The second half of *Montgomery's Children* gives us three narratives that do not reject modern elements such as unity, coherence, and meaning. But the three different narratives do subvert *Montgomery's Children's* uniformity. In the second half, there is a discursive pluralizing where the text's center is dispersed and margins and edges gain value. Only those individuals who are ex-centric, whose marginality has given them different perspectives, making them less susceptible to master narratives, survive.

Before 1948, *Montgomery's Children* portrays the black community of Montgomery as having a single, dominant mode of representation, united as a means of defense and survival against the town's majority white population and its Christlessness: "[The Negroes in Montgomery] viewed their relationship to the world as one between 'it' and 'us.' If they came to exaggerate the world's viciousness, it was because they feared that to do otherwise would leave their children susceptible to disillusion. ... The world was wicked less because of white men than because of its failure to embrace Christ."[20] It has an internally cohesive set of common-sense perceptions of formal conventions. Although the black community in Montgomery is "repelled by the white world," it is "drawn to it, share[s] some of its values, [chooses] from it the symbols of success and beauty to covet in their not-so-secret hearts. Prosperous white men [are] held up as models." (p. 14)

1948 is a crucial and strategic year in *Montgomery's Children.* It signifies the crisis moment when the black community in Montgomery ceases being a community restrained by the narrative of the church. Until 1948, the people of Montgomery assumed that there exists a single, correct mode of representation, which would provide the means to happiness. Members of this community were thrifty and industrious people who had come to Montgomery because of the promise of jobs and a better life for their children. Once they had settled, they raised their children to have respect for their elders and a fear of God. The church, which explained to them their existence and gave them standards to live by, was at the center of their lives. They seldom smoked or indulged in alcohol since most belonged to a church which forbade it. The few individuals who did not belong to church practiced Christian values. For example, when Soapsud uses foul language in the supermarket, his mother, Edna, who does not belong to church, drags him home "where she poured half a cup of Tide in his mouth and followed it with water." (p. 50)

With the church at the center of the people's lives, its pastor, Melinda Mclain, becomes an influential member of Montgomery, for the white townpeople are "respectful of the size of her bank account and the black vote she control[s]." (p. 15) Pastor Mclain is a counselor and spiritual leader for the people. When Claire notices Norman's behavior and senses that "something was obviously wrong with him," Claire suggests that he talk to Pastor Mclain. When Meredith kills and buries her blind, deformed son and later feels guilty, she turns to Pastor Mclain for counselling. And when Norman's behavior becomes aberrant from the community's norms, or from what is expected of Christians, Pastor Mclain commits him to an asylum.

The African Americans of Montgomery are able to maintain a cohesive community and to continue to live by the principles and virtues of Christianity and the guidance of Pastor Mclain because they are isolated geographically and communicatively from the rest of the United States. They do not have television and they do not read newspapers from New York and Philadelphia. Montgomery is a "town in which, before 1948, pornography would have been the mispronunciation of the machine on which records are played, and a prostitute having the whole of the metropolis to herself would have starved to death. So would a dope dealer." (pp. 3–4) The people of Montgomery are also content with, and protective of, their insulated world. They are "a cautious people, who [find] it difficult to experiment with anything so different as another brand of tuna fish, they [succeed] in avoiding all but the most minor of accidents. The illnesses that [afflict] them [are] ordinary; the children [endure] mumps and measles and chicken pox, the adults their periodic colds, the old folks the rheumatism and diminished memory which are to be expected." (pp. 15–16)

This cautious and protective approach to life has a price. It causes the people of Montgomery to accept naively and uncritically certain assumptions about white people and certain longstanding stereotypes about themselves. The belief that the majority of the people in the world are white, that the stone of "civilization" came from Europe, and that Egypt is a part of Europe went unchallenged by the black people in Montgomery. Likewise, they knew nothing about their African heritage, and, if they knew they "recently descended from slaves," they never thought about it. They were not aware that there were prominent, white social scientists who made a "living demonstrating their inferiority," or that they "operated in the national imagination as the ultimate in the comic, and the darkest, most labyrinthine symbol of evil." (p. 12) Without black newspapers such as the *Amsterdam News,* the *Pittsburgh Courier, Jet Magazine, Negro Digest, Essence,* or Black Studies programs and departments to counter or deconstruct these myths and stereotypes about both blacks and whites, "nearly a generation [of African Americans] would pass before they seriously questioned what they had been taught." (p. 13)

By 1948, progress, or the modernization process and its subsequent modernist culture, has come to Montgomery and the idea that there is only one possible mode of representation begins to be undermined. It becomes harder and harder for the people of Montgomery to know how and what to choose, or how to defend or validate one's choice. In their reactions to the modernization process, Gerald, Norman, Hosea, and Josephine become symbols of modernism, magical realism, and postmodernism respectively. They allow the reader to see the options, and the positionality and viability of these options, within the social formation in Montgomery, which after 1948 is rapidly propelling itself toward postmodernity.

The presence of the modernization process in Montgomery has immediate effects. People begin to die. Meredith Malone, Hosea Malone's former wife, kills and buries her blind and deformed son, causing the first death in Montgomery. By 1949, other African Americans begin to die. In May, Sam "Big Boy" Richardson chokes to death on a fishbone. Jonah drowns in July, and Christopher Silas, Montgomery's oldest black citizen, dies in September.

The arrival of progress or the modernization process is followed by the devastation of nature and of Norman Fellis's lingering traditional African beliefs. The forest near Montgomery, which Norman uses to "prove the existence of God," is razed to build a race track. With the destruction of the forest, Norman's transcedental realm is interrupted. Also, modernist culture, which contrasts greatly with the modalities of the Christian narrative, appears in Montgomery. Sexual desires that had been repressed by Christian teaching are liberated. To exploit commercially these desires, entrepreneurs build motels that feature waterbeds and X-rated movies, along with X-rated theaters. The number of prostitutes increases in Montgomery. "You can find in almost any bar men and women who for a price will indulge the most complicated of your sexual fantasies." (p. 3) Stores that once sold overalls and nails by the weight are converted to boutiques featuring designer jeans and jewelry that are interchangeable between the sexes. Montgomery's children congregate at street's corners "where they [smoke] marijuana and [listen] to music that their elders find unfathomable." (p. 11) The modernization process also brings economic expansion, economic prosperity, and racial integration. And by 1960, Alice Simineski and her partner and lover, Hosea Malone, establish an illegal, but prosperous, drug industry in Montgomery.

But more importantly, the arrival of progress, or the modernization process and its subsequent modernist culture—alienation, fragmentation, the lack of historical continuity, and the lack of social identification—in Montgomery begins to undermine the church. The categorical fixity of Christian thought is challenged. In 1948, when the "rash of deaths" begins in Montgomery, Pastor Mclain and her congregation accept evil as imminent and begin to "point a collective finger" toward the racetrack. (p. 16) Although the Pastor's instincts tell her that the racetrack has no causal relations to evil, she, to be on the safe side of the Lord's wrath, strengthens the dress code for women, banning open-toed shoes and short-sleeved dresses. She orders everyone to take a thirty-day fast during which he or she consumes only soda crackers and organic juice. She invites an evangelist up from South Carolina who runs a "two-week revival meeting so intense it left everyone limp." (p. 16) In short, Pastor Mclain's actions—her reactions against the racetrack, her attempts to get Norman back in the church, and her attempts to solidify the African American community into a whole—are modernist responses to the disintegration and fragmentation caused by the modernization process.

Other uncontrollable and mysterious events begin to happen to members of Pastor Mclain's congregation. Claire, Norman Fellis's wife, makes an appointment with the Pastor for Norman when he develops erratic behavior after the razing of the forest. Meredith goes to the Pastor because she feels remorseful for killing her son. When Meredith finishes relating her story, the Pastor "sigh[s] and wonder[s] why the Lord [is] testing her." The Lord is testing her in a number of ways. First, there is Hosea's return to Montgomery with Alice, and the Pastor's instincts tell her that he is "up to no good." Second, her cousin, who moves next door, has a husband who is "a roaring drunk" and a daughter who has a "missing hand and a phony Southern accent." Third, there is rumor that one of her deacons' wives is having extramarital affairs. Fourth and last, there is an abundance of earthworms in Montgomery, "which had only recently disappeared, the visitation of which signaled impending disaster." (p. 151)

For all of these uncontrollable and mysterious occurrences, Pastor Mclain and the church fail to offer competent and plausible rationales; they fail to meet any of these challenges successfully. For example, despite the precautions taken to prevent the "rash of deaths" and the presence of the racetrack, black people in Montgomery continue to die and the racetrack and other forms of gambling flourish financially. Furthermore, Pastor Mclain's prayers do not stop Norman's erratic behavior, and she is forced to put him in an asylum. Pastor Mclain is never able to intercede and terminate her cousin's husband, Percy Moore's, drinking or to prevent him from raping his stepdaughter, and her niece, Josephine. The physical abuse of Gerald by his father, Alexander, who is a deacon, continues, and the Pastor never receives a disclosure from God for the presence of, or the frequent visits of, the earthworms.

Finally, despite the fact that she "faithfully [seeks] assistance in the matter of Meredith Malone," Pastor Mclain, in her daily talk with God, never receives any assistance. "He never mention[s] the subject." (The reader, on the other hand, knows that for twenty years Meredith waits for her pastor to counsel her about the murder of her son, and finally turns herself in to the police.) Unable to use their shared standards of Christian virtue to counteract the fragmented nature of modern society, to restrain the hedonism, the loss of social identification, and the secularization of culture in Montgomery, Pastor Mclain and the surviving faithfuls presage the end of the world: "All the signs were right, the prophecies fulfilled—war and rumors of war, earthquakes in divers places, the great, great falling away from God. People were going crazy all over the place. They'd even shot the President and the Pope." (p. 217)

Thus, the church's authority to maintain a cohesive community is seriously undermined. It cannot explain adequately and realistically the new experiences produced by the modernization process and modernist culture. The demands placed on modern life in Montgomery, the fast-paced rhythm of the modern social system, and the freedom that accompany the modernization process force many people to live in a perpetual present, to live in a perpetual change where traditions from the past and history become obsolete. In short, the church does not adequately address or explain modernity, or this new phenomenon of social reality. Therefore, good Christians begin to leave the church. Gerald leaves the church "not because his conversion had not succeeded in containing his father's wrath, but because [he] could not keep his hands off himself," which the church forbade (p. 99) and which modern culture and adult bookstores around him cultivated and tolerated. Hosea leaves the church because Christianity prevents him from dealing with his own existential existence.

But the church is not the only tradition or practice that is seriously undermined, or made obsolete, by the arrival of modernity in Montgomery. With the arrival of modernity in Montgomery, black magic, or traditional, pre-modern African culture is finally put to rest. Black magic, embodied in Norman Fellis, assumes that blacks have an intimate affinity with the earth. According to Norman, black people "in the olden days ... used to fly." At the beginning of time black people "developed tremendous control of their bodies. This control came from the only place it could have—the mind—and was yet apparent in the grace with which colored people moved, in their walk and dance, and in their athletic abilities." (p. 108) The razing of the forest, which Norman used to prove the existence of God, and the building of the racetrack disrupt this non-rational way that Norman made sense out of his existence. The clearing of the trees for the racetrack brings a certain death to the earth: "They began clearing the trees on a Monday in March. When the crew entered the forest they were greeted by a stillness deeper than death." (p. 3) The destruction of the trees leaves animals homeless; their livelihood—"their food and water and safety"—is destroyed. Blacks such as Norman are left without a symbol to represent their transcendent beliefs.

But, this decline in black magic began long before 1948. Blacks in Montgomery have been disconnected from their traditional, non-rational African culture for a stretch of time that predates their ancestors' indoctrination by Christian teachings. The crisis in 1948 exposes the absence of the traditional culture. They cannot use their historical black magic to withstand the negative consequences of modernity or the modernization process. By 1948, blacks can no longer read earth signs; they have lost touch with their bodies. They have also lost the ability to fly. Parents have long ceased teaching their children "who they [are] and where they'd come from." Instead, they have come to teach "them what they couldn't be and the place they must not hope to enter." Lastly, despite the facts that the earthworms have come and that the forest was sacred, Blacks in Montgomery, with the exception of Norman and the Professor, voice no opposition to the building of the racetrack, "none of [their] energy was directed to the preservation of trees."

If the people of Montgomery do not read the earth signs and act accordingly—that is, protest the destruction of the trees—the earth certainly shows its displeasure by sending forth the earthworms. The appearance and disappearance of the earthworms are warnings that Montgomery will be visited by calamity and strife. In 1948, they appear and disappear when Meredith Malone murders her son and when the trees are destroyed. In 1960, after the earthworms again visit and disappear, the children of Montgomery begin to exhibit behavior that goes against the norm. It begins in November, when the black captain of the basketball team begins to date a white cheerleader. By December, "interracial dating had become epidemic" in Montgomery. Also in 1960, Hosea arrives in Montgomery with Alice and establishes a prosperous illegal drug operation.

In their decline, the church and traditional African culture are superseded by political and modern secular institutions and practices. The NAACP comes to Montgomery and establishes a new kind of leadership. Greed and the acquisition of money become the religion of many. Drug dealers become new icons in the community. By the novel's end in 1980, Pastor Mclain's power, influence, and visibility in Montgomery have all but dissipated. In the postmodern world of Montgomery, the end has come for the church, which has been reduced to feeding and caring for the elderly. For example, the church sisters bring Gertrude, the Pastor's sister and Josephine's mother, who has been restricted to a wheelchair, her dinner, and "every night one of the deacons came to take her upstairs." When Josephine looks over at Pastor Mclain's house during her last visit to Montgomery, "all the lights were off" in her house. By 1980, Montgomery has lost the moral standards that kept it such a stronghold of modernism.

The arrival of progress, or the modernization process, in Montgomery brings about a new social formation, which has its own conceptions of time and space. In this new social formation, the Christian narrative—the standards and rules that generated the center—is seen as a contrivance with its own limitations. This means that Montgomery's children, the generation born after 1948, are raised in a new social and cultural milieu. With the decline of the church and the end of traditional African culture, a commercial culture emerges and permeates the communicative infrastructure, intensifying a relation of exchange that regulates everyday life in Montgomery. After 1948, parents increasingly internalize many of the economic and social values of the surrounding white people who "were so deep in money." (p. 187) They pursue their freedom through the acquisition of middle-class status, property, and wealth—thereby relinquishing any responsibility or obligation to pass on their Christian values to their children.

The acquisition of wealth and property by the parents and the relinquishing of their responsibility to pass on their Christian values elevate Montgomery's children almost completely into America's commercial culture. Only a few black families in Montgomery cannot afford to purchase high-topped Converse sneakers for their children, or spend the extra dollar for bells on the back of chinos. Montgomery's children begin attending the dentist regularly, and they are seldom disappointed on Christmas morning when living rooms are filled with bicycles, electric trains, and sports equipment. Occasionally, some ecstatic black teenager looks out the window and finds a "secondhand Chevrolet, which needed only a little body work." (p. 187)

One of the realities of the secular, modern world is that within it, it becomes virtually impossible to raise serious questions about the existence of God or any transcendental realm. "As modern technological rationality penetrates a traditional society," argue Berger, Berger, and Kellner in *The Homeless Mind*, "the archaic unity of being is broken. The cosmic connection between beings and all objects is severed."[21] The absence of a faith in transcendence and the lack of respect for an authority larger than they make Montgomery's children isolated and anxious and deny them the certainty of being part of some larger purpose.

Therefore, Montgomery's children become truly modern and postmodern American children. The impact of mass culture, especially through radio and television, becomes hegemonic. The distinction between "images" and "real life" can no longer be regarded as tenable. Social representations come to constitute social identities. Freed from the ascriptive ties of the modern church and traditional African culture, some come to embody a modern culture characterized by alienation and fragmentation, the lack of social identification, and the lack of historical continuity. Others come to embody a postmodern culture that is characterized by a disconnectedness from anything human, as it is defined by the Age of Enlightenment, and by the freeing of their desiring machines. They live in the here and now, without having nostalgia for the past. First, Montgomery's children reject the past familially and culturally. They bear "only the slightest resemblance to their grandparents." They refuse to "follow the example of their ancestors." (p.11) They "grew up mistaking mask for matter, never wondering at where the marvelous grace in their bodies came from, never questioning its possibilities. So they only danced, when they could have flown." (p. 109)

Second, Montgomery's children have grown up with and internalized the perspectives, values, and behavior of the majority popular culture. "Sometimes [black children] made [Meredith Malone] feel like white people made her feel. This has less to do with what the children did, than with what they didn't. [They] didn't tip their hats, or speak, or move courteously out of her path. Most didn't even look at her, and those who did regarded her with the same indifference with which they watched the sky." (p. 221) Third, for many of Montgomery's children, the drug culture becomes an integral part of their existence. They begin to "drink beer and smoke cigarettes." They stand on street corners and smoke hashish and marijuana. Some of the more adventurous ones begin to sniff the white powder they refer to mysteriously as "horse." Black teenage girls who are "willing to make love to keep their boyfriends," eschew the Christian principles that had restrained their parents, and become sexually active.

By 1959, Montgomery's children have traversed all the institutions of American social, military, economic, and educational life. Refraining from bemoaning the loss of religious and cultural narratives and giving a pathological reading of African American life and abstaining from moral criticism, Richard Perry in *Montgomery's Children* shows us the here and now, the tones, the manners, and the diverse social patterns and systems of representation of Montgomery's children as they make sense out of their lives, or just live, in the absence of grand narratives. In 1959, Hosea Malone's daughter, Rachael Malone, is arrested for "underselling the other prostitutes out at the racetrack." In the same year, Soapsuds takes his doctorate in linguistics from Howard University. He is later killed working in the Civil Rights movement in Mississippi. (Soapsuds joins with Gerald, Jesus Mclain, who changes his name to "Muhammed Something or Other" and becomes a Black Muslim, and Iceman, who moves from a passion for Navajo Indians to Eastern Philosophy and the non-violent philosophy of Martin Luther King, in becoming existential characters in search of authentic existences.) In 1960, Rachael Malone moves to Atlantic City, where she finds a good job. Andre Fellis, Norman's first born, is promoted to Staff Sergeant by the Army. Daisy Madison gets married and moves with her husband to New Mexico. Gerald continues to be beaten by his father. Later, he goes to graduate school at Columbia University in New York City. Josephine murders her rapist stepfather and goes to prison for six years. Jesus Mclain, who grows up spoiled, goes to Harvard, where he tapes sex sessions with white girls. For many of Montgomery's children there is no transcended logic to their existence, there is no longer a narrative they can use to evaluate their worth. For many, there is no subjective consciousness that will make them seek out meaning in their lives. Most just exist in the here and now.

In *Montgomery's Children's* emerging postmodern world, a hierarchy is established where there is a bias toward postmodernity, toward existential and postmodern characters. Modern characters such as Meredith Malone, Pastor Mclain, and Norman Fellis, who use external narratives to validate their existence, either end tragically or experience a decrease in their power and influence in society. Prior to 1948, Meredith Malone is the wife in a stable Christian marriage. When Hosea leaves her, she finds herself "husbandless, parent to six children, a woman still young and attractive, but shouldering a burden no man in his right mind would leap to assume." (p. 117) Hosea's leaving produces a "wall that had confined her ... , that had limited her vision and bent her memory out of shape." (p. 143) Meredith is frozen in time: she is unable to make any progress forward from Hosea's abandonment. But this frozen state does not cause Meredith to question the Christianity that defines and guides her life and action. Rather, Meredith becomes entrapped in her Christian narrative. She feels guilty for killing her son. "This was her punishment, twelve years lost, and with them her youth and beauty. ... So this was her punishment, and it was just, and she accepted. But she lived in the world, and there were two laws that governed it, God's law and man's law, and she had yet to answer to the latter." (pp. 149, 150) In 1980, at sixty-seven, Meredith has held her life in abeyance waiting for her pastor to tell her what to do about murdering her son. God has already punished her. Now Meredith turns herself in to the police for man to punish her. In a postmodern world where the Christian narrative has become obsolete, her fate is imprisonment.

Norman Fellis also needs a transcendent narrative to define his life and existence. Without one he goes mad. Norman is "driven by the human need to believe in things greater than himself." (p. 17) Before 1948, Norman is "ordinary" and stable. He and his wife Claire have three children. He is "conscientious about his family and faithful to his God," but in neither relationship is there any "passion." He has been a practicing Christian since 1930, but he "still [finds] the question of the Godhead incomprehensible." Therefore, he uses "trees to prove the existence of God."

The arrival of modernity in Montgomery in 1948 and the subsequent destruction of the forest to build a racetrack force Norman to change his passion from trees to fire. His discovery of the properties of fire gives him a vision, "make[s] him see." Staring into fire, Norman's vision and insight have intensity and clarity— allowing him to know not only the past, but also the future. Sitting in the barbershop one day, a voice informs Norman of his past, of "where [he] comes from." (33) He knows about Gerald's beatings "when they happened, how long, and for what purported reason. The birds who fed in his yard sang of it." (p. 80) He knows that Iceman is not the chosen one to whom he should pass on his knowledge because through the fire he sees Iceman's future death.

In addition, Norman, through some mystical process, becomes imbued with knowledge of African traditions and history. "There leaped into his imagination a series of images, fragmented, yet connected, all of them with such stunning clarity as to suggest an experience recently his own. A snatch of song, the clank of metal. FIRE. A stake, a black man burning, stains redder than flame where his thighs met ... " (p. 21) Norman develops mysterious mystical insights and becomes one with nature. Unlike other blacks in Montgomery, he knows African history and culture. He, along with the Professor, is the only Black who is aware that the beginning of the deaths of Blacks and the destruction of trees in 1948 mark the beginning of the Dispensation of Earthworms. He is aware that "death and disorder had marked its dominion," (p. 272) and he believes that soon Montgomery will return to peace and the Dispensation of flight will begin.

But in the heterogeneous, postmodern world of Montgomery after 1960, Norman's narrative for defining Black history and reality becomes problematic. Norman is having difficulty passing this cultural and historical knowledge on to the next generation. His "anxiety came from not yet knowing whom he was to protect and pass on his knowledge to." (p. 55) He is living with the terror of a man alone in the "wilderness clinging to a cliff." Earlier, he observes Meredith bury her son and their eyes meet, and he thinks that Meredith might be the chosen one—the one he is to protect and pass on his knowledge, the pre-Christian, African history and culture, to. Next, he thinks that Gerald Fletcher, who has a distinct, magical mark in his eye, is the chosen one. Norman encounters Gerald, age thirteen, on the beach and informs him of his specialness. Gerald rejects Norman. But later, Norman rejects Gerald, calling him an "impostor," when he sees Gerald's "third eye" has been removed. Gerald, through an operation (certainly a representation of the "modern" world's removing the magic from Gerald and the future of African Americans), becomes invalid as a chosen one. Unable to find a progeny to whom to pass on the culture and history of African Americans, Norman's "anxiety" pushes him over the cliff, where he goes mad and finds himself "dripping water all over Abigal

Fletcher's kitchen floor, and ... butt naked except for the lilies that had wrapped around his penis." (p. 57)

Although Norman is still in Montgomery at the end of the novel, Montgomery does not return to "peace and liberty." The destruction of the trees remains a fact and the disrespect for animals continues. Black people do not "once more follow the example of their ancestors," and they continue to die. (p. 272) The dispensation of flight does begin, but only for him. But his flight ends when "one of the star points" of the "new synagogue (which had failed to recognize him when he had come as a messiah) ... detach[es] itself and [flies] to stick in his skull." (p. 281) Again, as with Jesus, Jews have failed to recognize the coming of a messiah. In short, Norman's traditional African religion fails to protect him from this postmodern world of Montgomery: "He summoned all the strength that was left in his seventy-one-year-old body, a body he'd trained all his adult life to respond in a crisis. There was nothing left but weakness and terror." (p. 281) Norman dies as a result of his fall. The death of Norman signals the end of the pre-modern African narrative in modern and postmodern society. Meredith, Pastor Mclain, and Norman—all those who need grand narratives to define their lives and existence—either die tragically or have their influence decreased in Montgomery over the course of the novel. They cannot relinquish their epistemological paranoia; nor can they abandon a concept of the modern subject that requires a temporal unification of a past and future with the present.

Simultaneously, and in addition to showing the tone and contemporary manners, *Montgomery's Children's* second half privileges those individuals either who take existential responsibility for their existence or who live postmodern lives. They are the only ones who survive. In *Montgomery's Children's* discursive pluralism, the center is dispersed and its margins and edges gain value. The margins and edges are comprised of individuals such as Josephine, Gerald, and Hosea, who, according to the definitions Linda Hutcheon offers in *A Poetics of Postmodernism,* are ex-centric. They exist inside and outside the community at once, and therefore are able to gain a critical distance.[22]

Each of these characters is represented by a narrative. The first of the three narratives is that of Josephine, who comes to understand that to live healthily and freely, she has to break with the past and devise her own existential ritual. Because of her early traumatic life experiences—deformity, rape, and imprisonment—Josephine has to reject established social conventions—conventions that do not validate her existence—before she can refashion her consciousness and remake herself. When her hand is cut off by her stepfather, she becomes a "freak," a social outcast. As the beautiful girl without a hand, she is ostracized by her classmates. But she takes a liking to Gerald because he had given her hope, because the "depth of suffering in his eyes approached her own." But peer pressure causes Gerald to renege on the friendship. Also, Gerald's father does not want him to have anything to do with Percy Moore's daughter, "lest the Fletcher name be dragged in the mud by association." (p. 139) Feeling alienated, Josephine uses her crippled arm as a shield to keep a cruel world at a distance. She carries it in "front of her, held waist high, like a weapon or a portable barrier." (p. 127) Without social rituals such as family, church, or social network to give her life meaning and coherence, Josephine, alone, withdraws from the world.

But a new relationship with Gerald allows Josephine to focus on her own inwardness until she finds within what she is compelled to accept about herself. After Iceman's death, Josephine notices a change in Gerald. Again, she begins to trust and to confide in him. In their exchange, Gerald forces Josephine to re-examine her repressed past, especially her life during the time she was raped repeatedly by her stepfather. "She struggled to re-create the parts of her life that were missing. Something was wrong with her memory; it had been cut off—everything before the age of nine was darkness except for her father's touch and the one-handed clock whose bird had gone away." (pp. 193–194) With Gerald's assistance, she begins to concentrate on her life before the lapse in her memory. She "peeled layers of darkness only to find more darkness still."

Nineteen years later, in 1980, Josephine emerges in *Montgomery's Children* resembling a postmodern character who accepts her fragmentation and lives in the here and now. In prison, she comes to accept her fragmentation, to accept fragmented authority as the norm. In prison, she learns to live not in a continuum, but in fragmented moments: "Prison life had taught her the futility of thinking in blocks of time longer than a day. She preferred operating in hours, and was most alive on the few occasions when life provided the opportunity to live by the minute." (p. 269)

Before Josephine can free herself from a recurring violent dream and become truly postmodern, she has to confront her mother and force her to relate the events that led to the loss of her hand. "Only one thing caused her discontent, brought her wide-eyed and gasping from a tortured sleep. She still dreamed of the axe, the airplane, the chicken pulsing across the yard. And there was only one way to stop its bloody dance." (p. 241) In her final trip to Montgomery, Josephine finds her mother old and sick. She confronts her and learns that Percy Moore was not her father. Josephine's reaction to the information reveals her postmodernity. "Josephine was thinking that now she knew, and so what? What difference did it make? Still, she struggled to discover her reaction to Percy's violation now that she knew he wasn't her father. There didn't seem to be a difference, although she thought there should be." (p. 265) As a postmodern character, Josephine does not attempt to construct a rational, coherent narrative to explain the events of the past; she rejects coherence and the past. She rejects the modern gesture of being the daughter who cares for her mother and concludes that blood tie is just another prison that will entrap her: "Gertrude was her mother, but she had not *acted* like a mother. ... The blood made you prisoner as long as you lived; the death of the parents did not free you. Only the death of the children broke the bonds of blood." (pp. 266–267) In the end, Josephine also realizes that home is not in Montgomery, but is dispersed. She is totally disconnected from a traditional concept of home. Home is "in a prison and the gilded room of a strange old white man's mansion. These were the places she would have to return if she ever wanted to go home again."

In rejecting her mother, Josephine becomes truly postmodern. She is now free to live a life of unlimited options; she can act on all of her desires and wants: "It came to her again that she could go anywhere, to China, say, or Africa; money was no problem." (p. 269) And after she leaves Montgomery for Georgia to "play" with the mind of her real white father, Josephine remembers Gerald, her last friend in the world, and "shrug[s]." She has become a dispersed, decentered network of libidinal attachments, emptied of ethical substance and psychic interiority.

But Josephine strives not for wholeness, as a modern character would, but for the acceptance of her fragmentation. She is willing to accept and to live with her various subjective positions: "'This is me I accept it.' When the bile of self-loathing rose in her throat, she choked it back and repeated: 'This is me. I accept it. ...' Self-acceptance meant self-discovery: her beauty and ability to think, her fundamental value as a living, breathing form. But it also meant confronting the putrid side of her humanness. ... She also came upon the contradiction—on the one hand, peace, on the other, a restlessness that could only be calmed by bending people to her will. ... She declined to judge herself, or ask questions, kept self-examination and doubt outside the circle of her consciousness; her decisions were snap. She demanded only that she not be bored, and she'd found that the surest way to avoid boredom was to fuck with people's minds." (pp. 240–241) Josephine has many subjective positions and identities that logically contradict each other. She is poised on the precipice of living an ironic existence. She is prepared to live a full life of post-modern role-playing.

Montgomery's Children's advocacy of embracing the brute objectivity of random subjectivity is shown further in its juxtaposition of Josephine's postmodern subjectivity in the same textual space with Gerald Fletcher's modern experience. Unlike Josephine, Gerald is caught up in the struggle for meaning. He is never able to relinquish the rationality of bourgeois humanism. Gerald grows up with a father, Alexander, who beats him because he fears Gerald will become a man who, like his grandfather, will refuse "to take responsibility." Therefore, with the slightest sign of weakness or provocation, Alexander beats Gerald: "And in a rhythm as predictable as the one that brought light in the morning and darkness at night, at the height of his sense of power, [Gerald] would somehow manage to inspire his father's wrath: he had not hung up his clothes the right way, or had not hung them up at all; he'd neglected to take out the garbage; he'd failed math or talked in Sunday school; he'd looked at his father the wrong way, or there was insolence in his decision not to look. And then would come the beatings ... " (p. 70) What Gerald does not understand is that it is his person, with a mark in his eye that reminds Alexander of his father, that Alexander hates. This means that Gerald mistakenly believes that a change in behavior will cause his father to love him.

But, despite the constant beatings, Gerald still wants and needs his father's love. He still needs an external validation of his life. When Gerald falls from grace because he "could not keep his hands off himself" and has to leave the church, he decides that he will always be a failure until Alexander loves him. Even when Gerald is "punishing Alexander by refusing to accept his attempts at reconciliation," he does not give up on the hope that through some miracle, Alexander will come to love him. After college, Gerald realizes that the lack of his father's love had "unforgivingly perverted his life." It had affected all of his relationships, especially those with women: "This conviction express[es] itself in the flatness of his eyes, in his aloofness, and in the frequency with which he slept with women he felt nothing more than lust for. His reputation grew: he was a failure as a lover. He was controlled, impenetrable, selfish, but mostly he was rigidly controlled." (p. 246) When Alexander is on his death bed, Gerald still hopes to solicit some semblance of affection by telling his father he loves him. But Alexander talks only of responsibility. "I'm bending over [Alexander's] bed, crying like a baby, saying, 'Daddy, Daddy, I love you.' You know what he did? He looked at me and told me to be sure to take care of my mother and sister. Dying, and his last words to me are about responsibility. ... If he could have made himself say he loved me, he could have freed me to love." (p. 276) But Gerald never gets his father's love.

Yet, despite the fact that he yearns for his father's love and that he becomes "rigidly controlled," Gerald does make an abortive attempt to create himself, to define his own existential existence. After his friend Iceman's death, Gerald begins to focus on his own existence. He becomes aware that he has a life that does not belong to family, church, or school, but to himself. "Even though it could be made miserable, as his father had made it, though it could be taken, as Iceman had had his taken, still it was his own; he must control it. He [does] not experience joy or hope at this understanding; on the contrary, it [makes] him solemn. He resolve[s] to take care of his life, to respect it." (p. 175)

He begins to see himself differently, his life as something "special." Prior to this, there had been only three other people whom he considered as "special"—his grandfather, Iceman, and Norman Fellis. He had loved his grandfather and Iceman; now both are dead. Later, when Josephine returns, he tries to make her understand that he is "willing to learn how to love." But Josephine leaves him for Georgia without a message or without even saying goodbye. He is reminded, again, about how everybody he loves, or tries to love, is always leaving. He wonders if loving things or people makes them die, and deciding to take no chances, resolves to love no one. Although Gerald, coming to certain revelations after Iceman's death, assumes his own narrative, it is not radically different from the one his father has tried to impose upon him. Even though Gerald has himself resolved never to love anyone, he is still controlled by his father. "The truth was that he did not want to kill his father at all. Despite his heart's quiet insistence that it would never be, he had not given up hope that through some miracle, or mystery, one day his father would come to love him. ... Then Gerald could do anything: fly, or strike out Henry Aaron, or go fifteen rounds with the heavyweight champ." (pp. 201–202) But Gerald's realization that he controls his own life does not free him to become his own person, to take control over his life.

Still living an unfulfilled life, he passes through life distant and aloof. He feels incomplete and disconnected. He gets involved romantically with women not because he loves them, but because he lusts for them. During his college days at Columbia in the sixties, where he had been among those shouting obscenities at the system, "[Gerald] had done it from a distance, with the perspective of a man engaged in an important task and accomplishing his objective simply by going through the motions. To be a full participant meant that he would have to join something, and he did not want to surrender his separateness." (p. 244) His nine-year marriage to Margaret fails because he never tells her he loves her.

It is only later—after college and after breaking up with his wife Margaret—when he visits Iceman's grave, that Gerald discovers that he cannot be a disconnected, fragmented individual. He wants to be a unified subject. He, unlike Josephine, needs social rituals such as family and friends. He needs social identification and historical continuity. At Iceman's grave, he acknowledges that his "rigid control" is really a "lack of control." He comes to accept the fact that "people die or leave all the time, whether you love them or not." (p. 277) He realizes that he has been blaming his father his entire life for his own miserable condition. "All his death did was leave me blaming a dead man for what had happened to my life." (p. 276) Therefore, he decides to find his estranged wife, because she is the only person, besides his mother and sister, who [has] a history with him. He decides to "start again. Not all over. Just again." (p. 277)

Finally, he comes to an understanding of his past actions and behaviors and decides that he wants to change. For the first time in his life, Gerald looks forward to his future, rather than backward to his father. Unlike Josephine, Gerald remains a modern subject. He is never able to abandon the struggle for metaphysical meaning. He is caught up in what Terry Eagleton calls "metaphysical depth and wretchedness, still able to experience fragmentation and social alienation as spiritually wounding."[23] As a result, he fails to escape the bourgeois humanism that is an integral part of modernity.

The third of the three narratives is that of Hosea Malone. Whereas Hosea's subjectivity, along with the subjectivities of Josephine and Gerald, gives *Montgomery's Children* a pluralistic landscape, his life's content epitomizes postmodernity. Until 1948, Hosea is an exemplary member of Montgomery's black community. He is a deacon in the church, a good husband to Meredith, and a father to his six daughters. Although he loves his daughters, he wants a son to carry on his name. He and Meredith are successful in conceiving a son, but the son is born blind and deformed. The son's deformity causes Hosea to ask the most fundamental of human questions: Why?

Hosea is forced to reexamine and critique the narrative, Christianity, that he has used to define his life. When his son is born deformed, Hosea discovers that Christianity does not explain adequately everything, that life is chance. The moment he feels he has a grip on life, chance raises its head and shows how a totalized narrative cannot account for the ambiguities, possibilities, probabilities, contradictions, conflicts, and chances that life possesses. At this moment, Hosea has a paralyzing existential realization: "that life had no meaning, that it was empty, that he had filled it with the fathering of children and his obsession with work, and, in the few hours left between these and sleeping, with the church. None of the tremendous energy he exerted *went* anyplace, nothing could be affected, all was chance. Despite his paralysis, he felt a momentary triumph. He'd done it. He'd peeped life's hole card." (p. 7) He realizes that he has used duties of family, church, and work to deny or repress his own existence. The birth of the deformed son forces him to confront the *nothingness* of his existence. With this realization, he ceases building the addition to his house and gives up working overtime. He leaves home and family and work, only to return three weeks later for twenty-seven minutes to retrieve his clothes.

In rejecting family and past, Hosea experiences freedom and becomes afraid: "Hosea understood his options. He could rail against it or he could close his eyes. Or he could stand there, looking." (p. 8) He opts for privacy. He feels that he needs to be "alone, to be responsible to no one but himself, to have space that he [can] turn in without bumping against the edges of things." (p. 8)

Hosea does not achieve total freedom or postmodern existence until twelve years later, when he severs all ties with any transcendent realm. Although in 1948 he runs headlong into life's well-kept secret, upon his return in 1960 with Alice Simineski as his wife and partner, Hosea has not totally escaped "the effects of his long, intimate relationship with religion." (p. 146) He uses his refusal to have sexual relations with Alice as the "one thing [that] would be taboo, which he would not violate until he was certain life really was as he'd seen it." (p. 146) The day Hosea learns that Meredith has murdered their son and has not been punished by God, he knows completely and emphatically that there are no limits in the universe, that life has no meaning: "Now he knew. He was not bound except by himself; he could go beyond his limit. He was free." (p. 146)

Realizing that desire is here and now, he comes under the pressure of a quite different rationality, or different conceptions of time and space. Everything now depends on Hosea's own effort, and not on the security of his traditional status. Whatever certainty there is must be dredged up from within his subjective consciousness. It can no longer be derived from the external, socially shared world of meanings and values. Hosea is a representation of the breakdown of the modernist impulse. He has no rumblings about eternal truths.

In the postmodern world of *Montgomery's Children,* Hosea moves toward a quiet desert of moderation where he forgets the passion of moral and spiritual restlessness. He only has surface meaning. His desiring machines have been liberated from any external narrative. Therefore, he has no unconscious, which results because an imposed moral narrative has repressed certain impulses and desires that do not complement its construct. In his fictional situation, the aura of the human is replaced by the nihilism of satiety. The questions confronting him are not ,What are the conditions of existence? Who am I? What is there to know in the world? How do I know it? The questions confronting him are, What world is this? What is to be done in it? Which of my selves is to do it? Hosea has no ultimate concerns, only present ones. The world is perceived as an arena for the achievement of his own success and satisfaction.

Hosea's desiring machines are liberated. He becomes a conflicting and contradictory network that has many desires and subjective positions that coexist in the same person. He moves between two worlds in Montgomery. With Alice, Hosea "daily [breaks] the law ... , [sells] substances that shipwrecked human life," buys off the legal authorities, and developes an illegal drug trade. He moves from this world to the world of being a responsible father who builds a prosperous laundry business and sends his younger daughters Susan Ann and Joyce to community college to take secretarial and business courses. He wants them "to run the laundry when they [have] the skills." The two worlds are superimposed upon each other, and Hosea moves between them, unsure and not caring which is the true reality or the superior desire.

At the end of the novel, Montgomery has changed; it has become a postmodern city. The postmodern Hosea has changed with Montgomery. He is as much a part of Montgomery at the end when it becomes postmodern as he was in the beginning when the church dominated and he was a husband and a deacon. At the end, he is in power. He is one of the town's major legal and illegal entrepreneurs. Economically and personally, in *Montgomery's Children,* it is the two postmodern characters who truly prosper: Hosea, with his desiring machines fully liberated, lives in a white mansion on a hill and has the town's politicians on his payroll, and Josephine has inherited a large sum of money that will allow her to live as she desires. The modern narratives of Meredith, Pastor Mclain, and the NAACP are missing or have become repressed or ineffective. The pre-modern, black magical narrative is "killed off" with Norman. *Montgomery's Children* does not chronicle the downfall of a city, but that of an ancient narrative and the subordination of modern narratives.

But *Montgomery's Children* as a novel at the end exposes itself as a construct. It refuses to give the illusion that it stands in for the real. The novel ends with the narrator informing the reader that "what you see is what you get (282)." The statement means that reality and perception are relative, that they are provisional rather than essential, that there is no one-to-one correspondence between the social real and the textual real. What the narrator forces the reader to acknowledge at the end is that *Montgomery's Children* is an artifice and, therefore, is suspect. How we view the events of the past or the present is contingent upon our own (or the writer's, or the narrator's) subjective experiences, our own point of view. *Montgomery's Children* gives the reader Montgomery after it has become a postmodern society, and it gives it to him from a postmodern perspective or a postmodern point of view. Someone with another point of view or perspective will interpret or construct the events or the same materials differently. Some other interpreter might use just the "ordinary vision" in textualizing the same materials. In constructing the text we hold in our hands, the narrator chooses from the "vast range of experience [that] lies just beyond ordinary vision ... . Some facts are mystery ... . One man's sleight of hand is another's magic (282)." Either way, the reader becomes aware that the text, *Montgomery's Children,* is a production, is a product of language.

Kingston's *Tripmaster Monkey,* which imposes a structure on her protagonist's desires and impulses, and Perry's *Montgomery's Children,* which does not, are received differently by mainstream and minority reviewers and critics. Mainstream reviewers give *Tripmaster Monkey* mixed reviews, praising its innovation in craft but castigating its main protagonist and Kingston's move to repress the main protagonist's desires. Writing in *Ms.* magazine, Pamela Longfellow argues that *Tripmaster Monkey* "is wonderful and awful—the violent vision of Wittman, the fastest word-slinger in the west. ... But the play, and the book itself, end with a bad-tempered rush of explanation. Betraying the storyteller, betraying the artist in the monkey, the pure creator in Maxine Hong Kingston."[24] Ann Tyler, in *The New Republic,* reaffirms the novel's mixed reception with: "*Tripmaster Monkey* is a novel of excesses—both the hero's and the author's."[25] Kitty Chen Dean, in *Library Journal,* writes: " ... the book's great weakness is Wittman Ah Sing himself—a hippie stereotype difficult to feel for because does not seem real. ... This first novel ... is thus not entirely successful."[26] And Le Anne Schreiber, in *The New York Times Book Review,* reiterates the common criticism that Kingston aborts Wittman's desires: "In *Tripmaster Monkey* the ventriloquism is too complete. Except in occasional descriptive passages, I cannot hear the precise, sinewy, and ... beautiful voice of the author above the racket of her creation, the creation who speaks but never listens."[27]

But in the sole critical essay by an Asian American critic, Elaine Kim appropriates *Tripmaster Monkey* into the institutionalized and pre-modern literary values of community, historical continuity, and social responsibility, which seem to dominate minority critical practices. "The narrator [of *Tripmaster Monkey*] gives him [Wittman Ah Sing]," writes Kim, "opportunities, challenging him to make the world better, and he meets the challenge by becoming a social artist who gives voice to a community of actors with the gift of his play, in which everyone can be a star."[28]

Unlike *Tripmaster Monkey, Montgomery's Children* was reviewed favorably by mainstream critics. Writing in *The New York Times Book Review,* Mel Watkins argues that *"Montgomery's Children* is an impressive novel about the evils of modernism and the redemptive powers of the spirit, and Richard Perry is an extremely talented writer whose work bears watching."[29] John Kissell praises *Montgomery's Children* for its craft in *The Los Angeles Times Book Review* with: *"Montgomery's Children* is a beautiful novel, elegantly written and well thought out."[30] In *The New Yorker,* Whitney Balliett lauds Perry's craft: *"[Montgomery's Children]* has many voices, all of them original and patient and unflinching: it is a comic novel, a realistic novel, a light-handed fantasy. ... Perry is well equipped. He has a good and a nice oral prose sense. His humor and irony are cool and just. He mixes his voices with consumate ease."[31] *Publishers Weekly* found that "Perry's wit and the satisfying complexity of his plot and characterization prove him an original from whom more books will be eagerly awaited."[32] Finally, Geoffrey Stokes, writing in *The Village Voice,* calls *Montgomery's Children* a "first-rate effort."[33] Interestingly, these mainstream critics and reviewers focus on Perry's craft and ignore totally the postmodern life and vision he presents in the text. They repress completely his critique or exposure of pre-modern and modern social models and guideposts.

But *Montgomery's Children* has been repressed and ignored

completely by African American critics. It is currently out of print. In the current Modern Language Association Bibliography, which lists all the articles published on a particular author or book between 1984 and 1994, Toni Morrison's *Song of Solomon* (1977) has more than one hundred citations or entries, N. Scott Momaday's *House Made of Dawn* (1986) has more than fifty, Maxine Hong Kingston's *The Woman Warrior* (1976) has more than fifty, David Bradley's *The Chaneysville Incident* (1981) has five, Andrea Lee's *Sarah Phillips* (1984) has one, and Richard Perry's *Montgomery's Children* (1984) has none. Why the unevenness of entries between *Song of Solomon* and *Montgomery's Children* in the MLA Bibliography? Is it because Morrison, who had published two novels before *Song of Solomon*, has a track record? Ishmael Reed has published more than eight novels, yet most of his books have very few entries in the MLA Bibliography and are constantly out of print. What about his track record? Is *Song of Solomon* simply a better book? Or does *Montgomery's Children* not meet those literary assumptions and ideological values that American and African Americans critics use to determine the worth and value of literary texts? An earlier discussion of *Song of Solomon's* reception by African American critics showed how most of these critics appropriated *Song of Solomon* into their own ideologically constructed racial traditions which define the African American experience. The examination of these critics's reviews and articles shows how they privileged themes and motifs in *Song of Solomon* that generate or affirm their particular belief systems and their view of nature. They assumed racial essentialism; they focused on social identification, historical continuity, wholeness, and African and African American traditions in the text. (Interestingly, these themes and motifs accented by African American critics are very similar to those of other Western writers and critics such as Hemingway, Faulkner, R. B. W. Lewis, Malcolm Cowley, etc.) Could they not find a way to use *Montgomery's Children* within their social and institutional life?

When American, African American, and minority critics and scholars are unable to select, process, correct, and rewrite minority texts into their institutionalized and essentialized norms of the literary (and here, we are talking about ideologically and racially constructed traditions that are represented by certain qualities as collective community, historical continuity, and wholeness), and when they cannot appropriate certain literary texts to serve their political and ideological needs, they simply ignore them. Richard Perry's *Montgomery's Children,* like Don Belton's *Almost Midnight,* Gerald Vizenor's *The Heirs of Columbus,* Ana Castillo's *The Mixquiahuala,* Gloria Anzaldua's *Borderlands/La Frontera,* and Louise Erdrich's *Love Medicine,* does not reproduce normative minority literary experiences, the literary themes of wholeness, community, and historical continuity. These texts do not present an essentialized, pre-modern, pure notion of minority culture that will allow minority critics, who operate from the same supposition, to sanction. These texts critique and expose racial essentialism and deconstruct notions of racial wholeness and historical continuity. They show the ineffectiveness of the pure notion of culture in a postmodern world. Since they cannot be appropriated to generate or affirm the political beliefs and ideological values that most American and minority critics have about minority life, "the interpretations of the past," and "versions of the present and hopes for the future," they are repressed, ignored, and excluded. The fact that *Montgomery's Children* brings the repressed discourse of postmodernity—with its emphasis on rejecting any postulates that are considered totalizing, metaphysical, and/or essentialist—to the center places it in an antagonistic relationship with most African American and other minority hegemonic critical practices. And this explains why Morrison's *Song of Solomon* and Momaday's *House Made of Dawn,* which can be read to generate sanctioned pre-modern values and political beliefs and which can be appropriated to reinforce certain established assumptions about life, human nature, and society, have more than one hundred entries in the MLA Bibliography, while *Montgomery's Children,* which generates no sanctioned pre-modern values, has none. Thus, we see how literary texts comprise a social institution that functions culturally and politically. Those literary texts that speak the hegemonic minority political discourse better, that conform to the established literary standards, are certified. Those texts that do not conform in subject and perspective are excluded.

In repressing, ignoring, and rejecting the modern and postmodern experiences presented in novels and texts such as Lee's *Sarah Phillips,* Rodriguez's *Hunger of Memory,* Bradley's *The Chaneysville Incident,* Perry's *Montgomery's Children,* Don Belton's *Almost Midnight,* Gloria Anzaldua's *Borderlands/La*

Frontera, Islas's *Migrant Souls,* Gerald Vizenor's *The Heirs of Columbus,* Charles Wright's *The Messenger,* Nathan Heard's *Howard Street,* and Perry's *Montgomery's Children,* hegemonic minority critical practices join with broader cultural and ideological values and political beliefs, which have at bottom an essentialist, pre-modern origin, in repressing the modern and postmodern racial experiences that have become so much a part of the lives of people of color since the 1960s. This means that those racial individuals who have modern and postmodern lived experiences, inevitable in today's world, are told by hegemonic minority critical practices, opponents of racial traditions and cultural nationalist leaders that those lived experiences are abnormal.

The rationale for perpetuating codified racial and sexual narratives is that they are necessary for the political, social, and psychological survival of racial and sexual groups. The argument is that racial minorities and women need the racial and sexual collective to mount attacks on racism and sexism in the United States. Of course, we can see the logic of this argument. But we can also see, we must also see, how these codified racial and sexual narratives are totally devastating in repressing racial individuals who choose to live by other rules, or who have desires and wants and experiences that are not sanctioned by these codified racial and sexual narratives. If racial and sexual groups need narratives to survive politically and socially, they should have them. But they should be provisional. We must always know that they are constructs, which are the product of a selective process, and we must always recognize that racial and sexual narratives should not exist at the expense of the growth of, and repression of, racial and sexual individuals. In a postmodern America where racial and sexual individuals live lives that bridge on many traditions and narratives, naturalized racial narratives and racial traditions become *just* a few of the many language games or mini-narratives that modern and postmodern racial and sexual individuals choose. We also need the guideposts and models produced by modernity and postmodernity, even if they counter essentialized pre-modern values that are held in high esteem, to help articulate and explain the modern and postmodern lived experiences of racial individuals. The modernization process has an equal, if not greater, influence on the modern lives of racial individuals. Thus, essentialized racial and sexual narratives can explain only partially the subjective lived experiences of modern and postmodern racial and sexual individuals. People of color in the United States are an integral part culturally, socially, and economically of a modern and postmodern American society. The advocates of the grand narratives such as codified racial narratives that are based in communal existence might not like to admit this, but I believe this is how we live, now.

NOTES

1. Andreas Huyssen, *After the Great Divide: Modernism, Mass Culture, Postmodernism* (Bloomington: Indiana University Press, 1986), p. 184.

2. *Ibid.,* p. 184.

3. Andreas Huyssen, *After the Great Divide,* p. 185.

4. Ralph Ellison, *Invisible Man* (New York: Vintage Books, 1972), pp. 486–487.

5. Guy Garcia, *Skin Deep* (New York: Farrar, Straus and Giroux, 1988), p. 149.

6. Marita Golden, *Long Distance Life* (New York: Doubleday, 1989), p. 277.

7. Maxine Hong Kingston, *Tripmaster Monkey: A Fake Book* (New York: Alfred A. Knopf, 1989), p. 204. All further references will be to this edition and will be given in the text.

8. Anthony C. Yu, editor and translator, *The Journey to the West* Vol. I (Chicago: University of Chicago Press, 1977), p. 108.

9. Gilles Deleuze and Felix Guattari, *Anti-Oedipus: Capitalism and Schizophrenia* (Minneapolis: University of Minnesota Press, 1983), p. 5.

10. *Ibid.,* p. xx.

11. Manfred Frank, *What Is Neostructuralism?,* translated by Sabine Wilke and Richard Gray (Minneapolis: University of Minnesota Press, 1989), p. 322.

12. Manfred Frank, *What is Neostructuralism?,* p. 330.

13. Elaine Kim, "'Such Opposite Creatures': Men and Women in Asian American Literature," *Michigan Quarterly Review* 29 (Winter 1990), p. 88.

14. Lawrence Grossberg, "MTV: Swinging on the (Postmodern) Star," in *Cultural Politics in Contemporary America*, edited by Ian Angus and Sut Jhally (New York: Routledge, 1989), p. 63.

15. Robert Alter, *Partial Magic: The Novel as a Self-Conscious Genre* (Berkeley and Los Angeles: University of California Press, 1978), p. 138.

16. Marilyn Chin, "Writing the Other: A Conversation with Maxine Hong Kingston," *Poetry Flash*, no. 198 (September 1989): p. 4.

17. Walter H. Sokel, "The Revolution of the Self in *The Notebooks of Malte Laurids Brigge*," in *Rilke: The Alchemy of Alienation*, edited by Frank Baron, Ernst S. Dick, and Warren R. Maurer (Lawrence: The Regents' Press of Kansas, 1980), p. 173.

18. Marilyn Chin, "Writing the Other," p. 4.

19. Terry Eagleton, "Capitalism, Modernism, Postmodernism," in *Against the Grain: Selected Essays* (London: Verso, 1986), p. 143.

20. Richard Perry, *Montgomery's Children* (New York: New American Library, 1985), p. 13. All further references will be to this edition and will be given in the text.

21. Berger, Berger, and Kellner, *The Homeless Mind*, p. 18.

22. Linda Hutcheon, *A Poetics of Postmodernism: History, Theory, Fiction* (New York: Routledge, 1988), p. 12.

23. Terry Eagleton, "Capitalism, Modernism, Postmodernism," in *Against the Grain*, p. 143.

24. Pamela Longfellow, "Monkey Wrenched: Ranting and raving, Maxine Hong Kingston puts the reader through the wringer," *Ms.* XVII (June 1989): p. 66.

25. Anne Tyler, "Manic Monologue," *The New Republic* 200 (April 17, 1989): p. 44.

26. Kitty Chen Dean, "Fiction," *Library Journal* 114 (April 1, 1989): p. 112.

27. Le Anne Schreiber, "The Big, Big Show of Wittman Ah Sing," *The New York Times Book Review*, April 23, 1989: p. 9.

28. Elaine H. Kim, "'Such Opposite Creatures': Men and Women in Asian American Literature," *Michigan Quarterly Review* 29 (Winter 1990): p. 89.

29. Mel Watkins, "*Montgomery's Children* by Richard Perry," *The New York Times Book Review* 89 (August 5, 1984): p. 19.

30. John Kissell, "*Montgomery's Children* by Richard Perry," *The Los Angeles Times Book Review,* February 19, 1984: p. 7.

31. Whitney Balliett, "Books" *The New Yorker* 59 (February 6, 1984) p. 124.

32. *Publishers Weekly,* 227 (March 1, 1985): p. 79.

33. Geoffrey Stokes, "Remainderama," *The Village Voice* 29 (April 17, 1984): p. 44.

Bibliography

The following is a list of books that I found useful for this study.

Aguilar-San Juan, Karin, ed. *The State of Asian America: Activism and Resistance in the 1990s*. Boston: South End Press, 1994.

Alter, Robert. *Partial Magic: The Novel as a Self-Conscious Genre*. Berkeley and Los Angeles: University of California Press, 1978.

Anaya, Rudolfo A. *Bless Me, Ultima*. Berkeley: Tonatiuh International Inc., 1972.

Angus, Ian, and Sut Jhally, eds. *Cultural Politics in Contemporary America*. New York and London: Routledge, 1989.

Anzaldúa, Gloria. *Borderlands/La Frontera: The New Mestiza* San Francisco: Spinsters/Aunt Lute, 1987.

Baldwin, James. *Another Country*. New York: Dial, 1962.

Bambara, Toni Cade. *The Salt Eaters*. New York: Random House, 1980.

Barbour, James, and Thomas Quirk, eds. *Romanticism: Critical Essays in American Literature*. New York: Garland Publishing Inc., 1986.

Baron, Frank, Ernst S. Dick, and Warren R. Maurer, eds. *Rilke: The Alchemy of Alienation*. Lawrence, Kansas: The Regents' Press of Kansas, 1980.

Barthold, Bonnie J. *Black Time: Fiction of Africa, the Caribbean, and the United States*. New Haven: Yale University Press, 1981.

200 · Race, Modernity, Postmodernity

Belton, Don. *Almost Midnight*. New York: William Morrow, 1986.

Berger, Peter L. *Modern Society and the Rediscovery of the Supernatural*. Garden City, N.Y.: Doubleday, 1969.

Berger, Peter L., Brigitte Berger and Hansfried Kellner. *The Homeless Mind: Modernization and Consciousness*. New York: Vintage Books, 1974.

Berman, Marshall. *All That Is Solid Melts into Air: The Experience of Modernity*. New York: Penguin Books, 1982.

_____. *The Politics of Authenticity: Radical Individualism and the Emergence of Modern Society*. New York: Atheneum, 1970.

Black, Cyril. *The Dynamics of Modernization*. New York: Harper & Row Publishers, 1966.

Bradley, David. *The Chaneysville Incident*. New York: Avon Books, 1982.

Calinescu, Matei. *Five Faces of Modernity: Modernism, Avant-Garde, Decadence, Kitsch, Postmodernism*. Durham, N.C.: Duke University Press, 1987.

Castillo, Ana. *The Mixquiahuala Letters*. Tempe: Bilingual Press, 1986.

Chan, Jeffrey Paul, Frank Chin, Lawson Fusado Inada, and Shawn Wong, eds. *The Big Aiiieeeee!: An Anthology of Chinese American and Japanese American Literature*. New York: A Meridian Book, 1991.

Chavez, Denise. *The Last of the Menu Girls*. Houston: Art Publico Press, 1987.

Chin, Frank. *Donald Duk*. Minneapolis: Coffee House Press, 1991.

Chu, Louis. *Eat A Bowl of Tea*. Secaucus, New Jersey: Lyle Stuart, 1961.

Cisneros, Sandra. *House on Mango Street*. New York: Vintage Books, 1989.

_____. *Women Hollering Creek and Other Stories*. New York: Random House, 1991.

Deleuze, Gilles, and Felix Guattari. *Anti-Oedipus: Capitalism and Schizophrenia*. Minneapolis: University of Minnesota Press, 1983.

de Man, Paul. *Blindness and Insight*. Minneapolis: University of Minnesota Press, 1983.

Derrida, Jacques. *Of Grammatology*. Translated by Gayatri Chakrovorty Spivak. Baltimore: John Hopkins University Press, 1967.

_____. *Margins of Philosophy*. Translated by Alan Bass. Chicago: University of Chicago Press, 1982.

_____. *Positions*. Translated by Alan Bass. Chicago: University of Chicago Press, 1981.

Dinnerstein, Leonard, et al., eds. *Natives and Strangers: Ethnic Groups and the Building of America.* New York and London: Oxford University Press, 1979.

Dulcep, Harreit Orcutt. *The Economic Status of Americans of Asian Descent: An Exploratory Investigation.* Washington, D. C.: U.S. Commission on Civil Rights, 1988.

Eagleton, Terry. *Literary Theory: An Introduction.* Minneapolis: University of Minnesota Press, 1983.

———. *Against the Grain: Selected Essays.* London: Verso, 1986.

Ehrenreich, Barbara. *Fearing of Falling: The Inner Life of the Middle Class.* New York: Harper Perennial, 1990.

Ellison, Ralph. *Invisible Man.* New York: Vintage Books, 1952.

Erdrich, Louise. *Love Medicine.* New York: Harper Perennial, 1984.

Frank, Manfred. *What is Neostructuralism?* Translated by Sabine Wilke and Richard Gray. Minneapolis: University of Minnesota Press, 1989.

Foster, Hal, ed. *The Anti-Aesthetic: Essays on Postmodern Culture.* Port Townsend, Wash.: Bay Press, 1983.

Foucault, Michel. *The Archaeology of Knowledge and the Discourse on Language.* Translated by Sheridan Smith. New York: Harper Colophon Books, 1972.

Gablik, Suzi. *Has Modernism Failed?* New York: Thames and Hudson, Inc., 1984.

Garcia, Guy. *Skin Deep.* New York: Farrar, Straus and Giroux, 1988.

Gates, Henry Louis, ed. *Black Literature and Literary Theory.* New York: Methuen, 1984.

Geertz, Clifford. *The Interpretation of Cultures.* New York: Basic Books, Inc., 1973.

Golden, Marita. *Long Distance Life.* New York: Doubleday, 1989.

Hagedorn, Jessica. *Dogeaters.* New York: Penguin Books, 1990.

Harris, Trudier. *Exorcising Blackness: Historical and Literary Lynching and Burning Rituals.* Bloomington: Indiana University Press, 1984.

Harvey, David. *The Condition of Postmodernity: An Enquiry into the Origins of Cultural Change.* Cambridge: Basil Blackwell, 1989.

Heard, Nathan. *Howard Street.* Los Angeles: Amok, 1968.

Highwater, Jamake. *The Primal Mind: Vision and Reality in Indian America.* New York: A Meridian Book, 1982.

———. *Kill Hole.* New York: Grove Press, 1992.

Howe, Irving, ed. *Literary Modernism.* Greenwich, Conn.: Fawcett Publications, 1967.

Hutcheon, Linda. *A Poetics of Postmodernism: History, Theory, Fiction.* New York: Routledge, 1988.

Huyssen, Andreas. *After the Great Divide: Modernism, Mass Culture, Postmodernism.* Bloomington: Indiana University Press, 1986.

Hwang, David Henry. *F O B and Other Plays.* New York: A Plume Book, 1990.

Islas, Arturo. *Migrant Souls.* New York: William Morrow, 1990.

Jaimes, M. Annette, ed. *The State of Native America: Genocide, Colonization, and Resistance.* Boston: South End Press, 1992.

Jameson, Fredric. *Postmodernism, or The Cultural Logic of Late Capitalism.* Durham, N.C.: Duke University Press, 1991.

Jen, Gish. *Typical American.* Boston: Houghton Mifflin, 1991.

Johnson, Charles. *Faith and the Good Thing.* New York: The Viking Press, 1974.

Kim, Elaine H. *Asian American Literature: An Introduction to the Writings and Their Social Context.* Philadelphia: Temple University Press, 1982.

King, Thomas. *Medicine River.* New York: Penguin Books, 1989.

Kingston, Maxine Hong, *Tripmaster Monkey: A Fake Book.* New York: Alfred A. Knopf, 1989.

_____ . *The Woman Warrior: Memoirs of a Girlhood among Ghosts.* New York: Vintage Books, 1977.

Lee, Andrea. *Sarah Phillips.* New York: Penguin Books, 1985.

Levi-Strauss, Claude. *The Savage Mind.* Chicago: University of Chicago Press, 1966.

Lim, Shirley Geok-lin, and Amy Ling, eds. *Reading the Literatures of Asian America.* Philadelphia: Temple University Press, 1922.

Louie, David Wong. *Pangs of Love.* New York: A Plume Book, 1992.

Lyotard, Jean Francois. *The Postmodern Condition: A Report on Knowledge.* Minneapolis: University of Minnesota Press, 1984.

Macherey, Pierre. *A Theory of Literary Production.* London: Routledge, 1978.

McHale, Brian. *Postmodernist Fiction.* New York: Methuen, 1987.

Marcuse, Herbert. *One-Dimensional Man: Studies in the Ideology of Advanced Industrial Society.* Boston: Beacon Press, 1964.

Marshall, Paule. *Praisesong For the Widow.* New York: Dutton, 1983.

Momaday, N. Scott. *House Made of Dawn.* New York: Perennial Library, 1977.

Morrison, Toni. *Song of Solomon.* New York: Signet, 1979.

_____ . *Sula.* New York: Knopf, 1974.

Murray, Albert. *The Spyglass Tree.* New York: Pantheon Books, 1991.

Ng, Fae Myenne. *Bone.* New York: Hyperion, 1993.

Okada, John. *No-No Boy.* Seattle and London: University of Washington Press, 1979.

Otten, Terry. *The Crime of Innocence in the Fiction of Toni Morrison.* Columbia and London: University of Missouri Press, 1989.

Perry, Richard. *Montgomery's Children.* New York: New American Library, 1985.

Raus, Charles. *Conversations with American Writers.* New York: Knopf, 1985.

Reed, Ishmael. *Mumbo Jumbo.* New York: Atheneum, 1966.

Rilke, Rainer Maria. *The Notebooks of Malta Laurids Brigge.* Translated by Stephen Mitchell. New York: Vintage International, 1982.

Rodriguez, Richard. *Hunger of Memory: The Education of Richard Rodriguez.* New York: Bantam Books, 1983.

Ross, Andrew, ed. *Universal Abandon? The Politics of Postmodernism.* Minneapolis: University of Minnesota Press, 1988.

Samuels, Wilfred, and Clenora Hudson-Weems. *Toni Morrison.* Boston: Twayne Publishers, 1990.

Schubnell, Matthias. *N. Scott Momaday: The Cultural and Literary Background.* Norman: University of Oklahoma Press, 1986.

Silko, Leslie Marmon. *Ceremony.* New York: Viking Penguin, 1977.

Simone, Timothy M. *About Face: Race in Postmodern America.* New York: Autonomedia, 1989.

Takaki, Ronald. *Strangers from a Different Shore: A History of Asian Americans.* New York: Viking Penguin, 1989.

Tan, Amy. *The Joy Luck Club.* New York: Ivy Books, 1989.

Wall, Cheryl A., ed. *Changing Our Own Words: Essays on Criticism, Theory, and Writing by Black Women.* Brunswick: Rutgers University Press, 1989.

Welch, James. *Death of Jim Loney.* New York: Penguin Books, 1971.

———. *Winter in the Blood.* New York: Penguin Books, 1974

West, Cornel. *Race Matters.* Boston: Beacon Press, 1993.

Weyr, Thomas. *Hispanics. U. S. A.: Breaking The Melting Pot.* New York: Harper & Row, 1988.

White, Hayden. *The Content of the Form: Narrative Discourse and Historical Representation.* Baltimore: John Hopkins University Press, 1987.

Wideman, John Edgar. *Philadelphia Fire.* New York: Henry Holt, 1990.

Williams, Raymond. *Marxism and Literature.* Oxford: Oxford University Press, 1977.

Wilson, Robert A., and Bill Hosokawa. *East to America: A History of the Japanese in the United States.* New York: William Morrow, 1980.

Wilson, William Julius. *The Truly Disadvantaged: The Inner City, the Underclass and Public Policy.* Chicago: University of Chicago Press, 1987.

Wong, Sau-ling Cynthia. *Reading Asian American Literature: From Necessity to Extravagance.* Princeton: Princeton University Press, 1993.

Wright, Charles. *The Messenger.* New York: Farrar, Straus and Company, 1963.

Wright, Richard. *Native Son.* New York: Harper Perennial, 1940.

Young, Al. *Who Is Angelina?* New York: Holt, Rinehart and Winston, 1975.

Yu, Anthony C., editor and translator. *The Journey to the West.* Vol. I. Chicago: University of Chicago Press, 1977.

Index

Affirmation Action Programs, 18, 105
After the Great Divide, 86. *See also* Andreas Huyssen
African Americans, 1, 6, 7–8, 10, 11, 13, 21
Allen, Bruce, 146
Almost Midnight, 154, 193
Alter, Robert, 163
angry white men, 18
Another Country, 30
anti-miscegenation laws, 12
Anti-Oedipus, 156
Anzaldúa, Gloria, *Borderlands/La Frontera*, 154, 193
Archaeology of Knowledge, The, 143
Aronowitz, Stanley, 18
Asian Americans, 1, 6, 7–8, 10, 11, 13, 21

Baldwin, James, 30, 31; *Another Country*, 30
Balliett, Whitney, 191
Bambara, Toni Cade: *The Salt Eaters*, 29
Barker-Nunn, Jeanne, 146
Barthold, Bonnie J., 40
Bayles, Martha, 69

Belton, Don: *Almost Midnight*, 154, 193
Berger, Berger, and Kellner: *The Homeless Mind*, 33, 56, 62, 176
Berger, Peter L., 48–49
Berman, Marshall, 32, 99–100
bildungsromans, 68
"The Bill Cosby Show," 14
bilingual education, 77, 105
Black, Cyril: *The Dynamics of Modernization*, 41–42
Blackburn, Sara, 145
"Black Feminist Theory and the Representation of the 'Other,'" 106
Bloom, Allen: *The Closing of the American Mind*, 18
Bourjaily, Vance, 146
Bradley, David, 111, 112, 192, 193
Brown, Orlando, 10

California Supreme Court, 12
Calinescu, Matei, 104
Castillo, Ana, 154, 193
Ceremony, 29
Cha, Theresa Hak Kyung, 154

Chan, Jeffy Paul, 143–144
Chaney, Lynne, 18
Chaneysville Incident, The, 111, 112, 192, 193; critical analysis of, 128–142; critical reception of, 142–143, 146-148. *See also* David Bradley
Chang, Hui-Chuan, 144
Chin, Frank, 143–144; *Donald Duk,* 29
Chinese Monkey, 155
Christian, Barbara, 71
Cisneros, Sandra, 76
Civil Rights laws, 12–13
Civil Rights Movement, 22
"The Civil War," 14
Clark, Norris, 71
"cognitive minority," 48-49. *See also* Peter L. Berger
Condition of Postmodernity, The, 39
continuity, 3
cultural diversity, 105
cultural nationalism, 29
culture, 6

Dean, Kitty Chan, 190
Death of Jim Loney, The, 67, 76
Dedalus, Stephen, 70
Deleuze, Gilles, 156
de Man, Paul, 32, 76–77
Derrida, Jacques, 7
Dict ee, 154
Donaldson, Mara E., 146
Dynamics of Modernization, The, 41–42

Eagleton, Terry, 24–25, 62
Economic Status of Americans of Asian Descent, The, 13
Erdrich, Louise, 15, 67, 193
Ehrenreich, Barbara, 92
Ellison, Ralph, 31; *Invisible Man,* 30, 152
Emerson, Ralph Waldo, 68
Enlightenment, 5, 14, 23

Ensslen, Klaus, 147, 148

Faith and the Good Thing, 153
Family Devotion, 76
Fa Mu Lan legend, 122–123, 125–126
Faulkner, William, 68, 70
Fauset, Jessie, 107
federal set-aside programs, 13, 18
FOB, 76
Foucault, Michel, 143
Frye, Joanne, S., 146

Gablik, Suzi: *Has Modernism Failed?,* 30, 33
Garcia, Guy: *Skin Deep,* 29, 153
Geertz, Clifford, 3
Golden, Marita: *Long Distance Life,* 153, 154
Goong, Gwan, 154–155
Gray, Paul, 145
Guattari, Félix, 156

Habermas, Jurgen, "Modernity— An Incomplete Project," 29
Harlem Renaissance, 107
Harris, Trudier, 147, 148
Harvey, David, 39
Hassan, Ihab, 151
Heard, Nathan: *Howard Street,* 194
Heirs of Columbus, The, 67, 154, 194
Hemingway, Ernest, 68
heterogenous society, 15, 18–19
Highwater, Jamake: *Kill Hole,* 67
Hispanics, 1, 6, 7, 8–9, 10, 14, 21
Hoggart, Richard, the scholarship boy, 77–78, 81
House Made of Dawn, 29, 30, 69, 70, 71, 76, 111, 121, 153, 168, 192, 193; critical analysis of, 50–68; critical reception of, 70–71. *See also* N. Scott Momaday
House on Mango Street, The, 76
Houston, Whitney, 15

Howe, Irving, 75, 151; "The Idea of the Modern," 102
Hudson-Weems, Clenora, 36
Hunger of Memory, 76, 77, 104, 111, 112, 113, 115, 116, 121, 193; critical analysis of, 77–89; critical reception of, 105, 107–108. *See also* Richard Rodriguez
Hunt, Linda, 144
Hurston, Zora Neale, 106
Hutcheon, Linda, 20, 142; *A Poetics of Postmodernism,* 112, 181; "historiographic metafiction," 112; "the performativity of the text," 128
Huyssen, Andreas, 6, 20, 86, 151
Hwang, Henry David, 76

"The Idea of the Modern," 102
"Ideologies of the Self," 108
industrial culture, 13–14
Invisible Man, 30, 152
Islas, Arturo: *Migrant Souls,* 76, 154, 194

Jameson, Fredric, 1, 20, 64
Japanese American Research Project, 13
"The Jefferson," 14
Jen, Gish: *Typical American,* 76
Jim Crow, 7
Johnson, Charles, 153
Journey to the West, The, 155
Joy Luck Club, The, 76
Joyce, James, 70

Kill Hole, 67
Kim, Elaine, 145–146, 159–160, 191
Kingston, Maxine Hong, 15, 163, 165; *Tripmaster Monkey,* 154–167, 190–191; *The Woman Warrior,* 111, 112, 113–128, 140, 142–146, 192
Kissell, John, 191
Kramer, Jane, 145

Larsen, Nella, 107
Lee, Andrea, 105; *Sarah Phillips,* 76, 77, 89–105, 105–107, 111, 112, 113, 121, 153, 168, 192
Leonard, John, 144
Li, David, 144
Lim, Geok-lin, 146
Ling, Amy, 145
literary modernism, 75–76, 103–104, 105
Literary Theory: An Introduction, 24–25, 62
Long Distance Life, 153, 154
Longfellow, Pamela, 190
Love Medicine, 67, 193
Lyotard, Jean-Francois, 2, 46, 141

Madrid, Arturo, 108
Macherey, Pierre: *A Theory of Literary Production,* 36–37
Marcuse, Herbert: *One-Dimensional Man,* 47
Marshall, Paule: *Praisesong For the Widow,* 29, 33
mass culture, 20
McHale, Brian: *Postmodernist Fiction,* 142
Messenger, The, 30, 77
Migrant Souls, 76, 154, 194
Miller, Lucien, 144
Mixquiahuala Letters, The, 154, 193
modernity, 5, 100
"Modernity—An Incomplete Project," 29
modern subject, 120, 152
modernization process, 4, 14, 20, 39
Momaday, N. Scott, 15; *House Made of Dawn,* 29, 30, 50–68, 69, 70–71, 76, 111, 121, 153, 168, 192, 193
Montgomery's Children, 154, 193; critical analysis of, 167–190; critical reception of, 191–192. *See also* Richard Perry
Morales, Alejandro, 154

Morrison, Toni, 15, 30, 68; *Song of Solomon,* 29, 30, 31–50, 69, 70–71, 76, 103, 111, 121, 168, 192, 193; *Sula,* 30
Mouffe, Chantel, 2
multiculturalism, 18
Mumbo Jumbo, 154

Native Americans, 1, 6, 8, 9–10, 11, 21; Treaties, 10
Native Son, 30
Notebooks of Malte Laurids Brigge, The, 155–156, 157, 162, 165

Oedipus, 68
Omi, Michael, 22
One-Dimensional Man, 47
Other, 45
otherness, 6, 17–18

people of color, 6–7, 10, 11; integration into America's classical modernity, 14–17, 22–24; in education, 12–13; in industrial culture, 13–14
Perry, Richard: *Montgomery's Children,* 154, 167–190, 191–192, 193
Philadelphia Fire, 154
Poetics of Postmodernism, A, 112, 181
Postmodern Condition, The, 2, 46
postmodern literature, 151, 152
postmodernism, 1–2, 151–152
Postmodernist Fiction, 142
postmodernity, 1, 2, 5–6, 20–21, 151
postmodern subject, 64–65, 152–154
poststructuralism, 152
Praisesong For the Widow, 29, 33
Prometheus, 68
Public Enemy, 21

Pueblo Culture, 69

Rabine, Leslie W., 146
racial attitudes in United States, 12
racial communities, 4, 7, 10, 20
racial tradition, 2–3, 4–5, 14
Reed, Harry, 71
Reed, Ishmael, 192; *Mumbo Jumbo,* 154
Richie, Lionel, 15
Rilke, Rainer Marie, 155–156, 157, 162, 165
Rivera, Tomás, 107–108
Rodriguez, Richard: *Hunger of Memory,* 76, 77-89, 104, 105, 107–108, 111, 112, 113, 115, 116, 121
"Roots," 14
Ross, Diana, 15

Saldivar, Ramon, 108
Salt Eaters, The, 29
Samuels, Wilfred, 36
Sarah Phillips, 76, 77, 111, 112, 113, 121, 153, 168, 192; critical analysis of, 89–105; critical reception of, 105–107. *See also* Andrea Lee
schizophrenia, 64
Schreiber, Le Anne, 191
Schubnell, Matthias, 53
Simone, Timothy, 21
Silko, Leslie Marmon: *Ceremony,* 29
Skin Deep, 29, 153
Smith, Valeria, "Black Feminist Theory and the Representation of the 'Other,'" 106
Song of Solomon, 29, 30, 69, 70, 71, 76, 103, 111, 121, 168, 192, 193; critical analysis of, 31–50; critical reception of, 70–71. *See also* Toni Morrison

Sontag, Susan, 151
Stokes, Geoffrey, 191
Sula, 30
supplement, 7. *See also* Jacques
 Derrida

Tan, Amy, 15
*Theory of Literary Production,
 The,* 36–37
Theseus, 68
Thoreau, Henry David, 68
Toni Morrison, 36
Treaty of Guadalupe Hidalgo, 8
Tripmaster Monkey, 154; critical
 analysis of, 154–167; critical
 reception of, 190–191. *See also*
 Maxine Hong Kingston
Tyler, Ann, 190
Typical American, 76

Villasenor, Victor, 15
Vizenor, Gerald: *The Heirs of
 Columbus,* 67, 154, 194

Walker, Alice, 15

Wang, Alfred S., 144
Watkins, Mel, 191
Welch, James, 67, 76
West, Cornel, 15, 92
Whitman, Walt, 68, 157, 165
Who Is Angelina?, 154
Wideman, John Edgar:
 Philadelphia Fire, 154
Williams, Raymond, 127
Williams, Sherley Ann, 106–107
Willis, Susan, 49
Winant, Howard, 20
Winter in The Blood, 67, 76
*Woman Hollering Creek and
 Other Stories,* 76
Woman Warrior, The, 111, 112,
 113, 140, 192; critical analysis
 of, 113–128; critical reception
 of, 142–146. *See also* Maxine
 Hong Kingston
Wong, Sau-ling Cynthia, 144–145

Young, Al, 154
Yu, Anthony C.: *The Journey to
 the West,* 155